ONLY ONE POLACK

BY ADRIAN ALPHONSE ZAIONTZ

Copyright © 2018

All rights reserved, including the right to reproduce this book or portions thereof in any form, store in a retrieval system, or transmit in any form or by any means, electronic, mechanical, photocopy, recording, or otherwise without permission in writing from the author, except by a reviewer who may quote brief passages in a review.

ISBN: 978-0-692-11536-7

Only One Pollack

Adrian Alphonse Zaiontz

This book is dedicated to my dear wife and life-long soul mate,
Mary Catherine Lukawitz Zaiontz.
At the time of this writing,
we have been married sixty-eight years.

ACKNOWLEDGMENTS

First, I want to acknowledge my wife, Mary, the mother of all my children. She has been there for all the little things but more importantly, for all the big things. She has been my nurse for all my sicknesses—both real and imaginary—and all my surgeries, and the nurse to all our children through their childhood diseases. She has been my babysitter, my cook and nutritionist, and a second driver when my children had to be at a certain place at a certain time.

Mary is my listening post every moment, every hour, and every day. At times I recalled my early youth experiences to Mary and she would say "you ought to write a book." I thought about this but I felt that I had neither the skill nor the courage.

As it came to pass, the family tree came into my hands. I found out who my ancestors were, but very little other information, like how they lived, what occupations they had, their accomplishments and failures. I decided to record my life so that my grandchildren and great- grandchildren would know something more of their roots.

I want to thank my daughter Barbara Lucille and her husband Raymond Turner for all their help. I wrote the first chapter *The Pencil Box and the Violin* in June of 2009. On September 1, 2009, at our sixtieth wedding anniversary celebration, which was held at Snoga's Catering (owned by my first cousin Alvin Snoga), I asked Barbara and Ray if they would help me with the book. Both of them had experience in writing and publishing college text books. They agreed to help and did research, computerized my hand-written manuscripts, and edited all my copies. Without their invaluable help, my book would never have achieved fruition.

Last, but not least, I want to thank the people who read the chapters as soon as copies were available and gave me valuable feedback and encouragement to continue and not to lose heart. These include Raymond and Frances Sultenfuss, Joe Guerrero, Bill Schutte, Jerry Vogel, and Colonel Joseph Ortega from my PTSD therapy group at Audie L. Murphy VA Hospital.

PREFACE

I am writing *The Pencil Box and the Violin* because I owe my children an explanation. Likely they were puzzled all the years they knew I had a violin yet never played it nor talked about it. Also, if my family can find them, I want the children of Sally Swiger Frantsen to hear my story about a wonderful and compassionate young girl who became their mother.

I never tried to contact Sally when we were both living in San Antonio. I did not know she had ever lived in San Antonio until I read her obituary. Now, for my children and hers, these are my memories. This story happened long ago and may have an error or two, but this is how I recall it happening.

I write this so our great-grandchildren will remember that all the technology they use daily was not always there and that even without these, life was just as good, and arguably better. When I was a boy, the only technologies we had were automobiles, radios, and an occasional traveling, silent, black and white movie. All of the gadgets we experience today Mary and I tolerate, but we do not accept them willingly. I suppose our attitude stems from our desire to have things as they were in bygone times and not as they are in today's complicated, fast-paced world. We limit ourselves to TV, radios, an automobile, telephone (land line) and a microwave oven—no computers at all except those built into our car and appliances. When our great-grandchildren grow up to be young adults, the technology of 2010 will have been eclipsed many times over. We hope and pray that the fulfilling and loving life that we knew will be available to our children, grandchildren, and great-grandchildren in their future.

Most dictionaries have the same definition of a Polack—a person of Polish descent or birth; an offensive term used derogatorily. It was used this way until the election of John Paul II as the Polish Pope in 1978. Then it became a source of pride among the Polish people. There are many Polish jokes:

- How many Polacks does it take to make popcorn? Five: one to hold the pan and four to shake the stove.
- How many Polacks does it take to change a light bulb? Forty-one: one to change the bulb and forty to raise the floor.

I have heard them all. In Texas the word Polack is interchangeable with Aggie or Longhorn or Square-Heads or Dagos or Coons as long as the word is used in a good-natured way and not derogatorily.

There is one derogatory word I have used in this book, "Jap." The abbreviation for Japanese, widely used during World War II, was intended to be derogatory. While Japanese Americans find the term offensive, the abbreviation did reflect the mind set of war-time America. I use the term in order to add weight to my personal experiences while under fire.

The book by the Reverend Edward J. Dworaczyk, *The First Polish Colonies of America in Texas*, published in 1936 is referenced liberally in Chapter 2.

This is not a work of fiction. Names, characters, places, and incidents are the product of the author's intentions. Any resemblance to actual persons, living or dead, business establishments, events or locals is entirely intentional.

– **Adrian A. Zaiontz**

TABLE OF CONTENTS

Acknowledgments v

Preface vii

Chapter 1: The Pencil Box and the Violin 1

Chapter 2: The Early Years 5

Chapter 3: My Father, My Mother, and My Ancestry 21

Chapter 4: Alphonse in the Middle 33

Chapter 5: School Years in Cuero and Summers on the Farm 43

Chapter 6: The Home Front 55

Chapter 7: Citizen Soldier or PFC 65

Chapter 8: Transition from the 38th Infantry Division to the 86th Infantry Division 89

Chapter 9: Transition from Citizen Soldier to Regular Army 101

Chapter 10: Return to Civilian Life 115

Chapter 11: Our First Years of Married Life 127

Chapter 12: Making a Living and Family Living 131

Chapter 13: Family Obligations 143

Chapter 14: At Last, Retirement! 147

A Note from Adrian's Family 151

Chapter 1
THE PENCIL BOX AND THE VIOLIN

I was born and lived my early years in Panna Maria, Texas. Like all of the citizens of Panna Maria in those years, my family mostly spoke Polish. We spoke Polish at home. We spoke Polish in school. The nuns at school taught their classes in Polish.

My father lost his grocery business in 1931 due to the crash of 1929. He found a job as a turkey buyer for the Cudahy Packing Company in Kenedy, Texas. He bought turkeys from the same people who were his customers when he owned the Country Store Grocery in Panna Maria. We moved to Kenedy, Texas, when Dad took the job with Cudahy Packing Company. The move occurred two months before the end of the school year. I was in the first grade and transferred from an all-Polish-speaking Catholic school to an all-English-speaking public school in Kenedy. I do not remember very much about these last two months of the first grade as I understood very little English. Neither did I accomplish much academically during these two months. My memory of them is quite hazy.

Next, my father was transferred to Beeville, Texas, with a raise to $22 per week to become a truck driver. We rented a small two-bedroom house for $8 a month and were all settled in before I started second grade.

I remember the first day I went to the parochial school in Beeville. There were three grades taught in each classroom. A nun taught all of the students in each of the three grades in that one room. With twelve to fifteen students per grade, there was a lot going on. Back then there were no restrictions on the number of students in a classroom. This was traumatic! I was scared, I did not fit in, and I was laughed at because I knew so little English.

There was a little girl in the same class and about the same age. Her name was Sally Suzanne Swiger.[1] Sally did not laugh at me. In fact, she adopted me. She and I studied and played together all the time. Many times we did not go out at recess but stayed in

---

[1] She pronounced her middle name as "Susanne." This may be a way to confirm her identification as nowhere in the obituary is her middle name mentioned.

the classroom and studied.

Because we were always together—and as children in the second grade often did—we began to notice signs of teasing all around us. These signs were everywhere and occasionally even on the blackboard. This never embarrassed Sally or me as it was true. We were the fondest of friends and proud of our closeness.

Our relationship blossomed and continued through the second grade, the third grade, and half of the fourth grade. Sally was an "A" student and she finally made me an "A" student as well. Sometimes we went to her house and studied after school or on Saturdays. She lived close to the school in a big house. We never went to my house because it was across town. The Zaiontz family had only a small, two-bedroom house and I was ashamed to have her see it.

Together, Sally and I studied the alphabet, English, reading, spelling, and arithmetic. There were games in class, usually on Fridays. We had multiplication races, subtraction races, and spelling sit-downs. (Everyone stood up and spelled in turn. When you misspelled a word that the teacher gave you, you sat down.) Sally usually came in first. Sometimes I came in second.

I remember and still use the times tables that we studied over and over. Sally also taught me a trick for fast multiplication. For example, how much is:

13x22?	22x30?	28x30
10x22=220	20x30=600	30x30=900
3x22= 66	2x30= 60	-2x30= 60
13x22=286	22x30=660	28x30=840

I learned to do this in my head. My quickness with multiplication amazed my friends.

I realized much later that the teacher had a reason for our Friday games. She was better able to gauge the effectiveness of her teaching methods and to determine who needed extra help and attention. The larger multiple-grade classrooms even became an advantage to me. When the teacher directed her attentions to the other grades, even though I was working on my own assignments, I still heard and absorbed some of the other lessons.

My father and mother loved good music. When my mother was young, she played the organ in church. I remember seeing an organ in the house in Panna Maria. My father loved violin music. He never played an instrument himself, but his younger brother, my Uncle Hilly (Heliodor), played violin in a country music band.

While I was seven and in the second grade in Beeville, my father learned that some of the nuns in our school also gave music lessons. I was enrolled in violin lessons with Sister Monica (not my classroom teacher) two days a week. The sessions were one hour each and cost a dollar per session. I studied the violin for more than two years. I liked the violin and, to my delight, Sally enjoyed listening to me play. I played the violin at Christmas and for programs during the school year. Other students played other instruments or acted on stage in school plays. My mother and father were so proud of me.

I learned later that Sally's father was a petroleum geologist and, like my father, had to go where the jobs were. In the fourth grade, in January, my father was transferred back to Kenedy, Texas. When I told Sally that we were leaving Beeville to move back to Kenedy, she cried real tears as if her heart was breaking. I did not know what to make of this as no one had ever cried over me before.

When Sally knew for sure that I was leaving, she gave me her pencil box. In the early 1930s if a student had a pencil box, it was a real status symbol. The students whose families were well-off had pencil boxes. The poorer students did not. The pencil box was half the size of a loaf of bread and half as

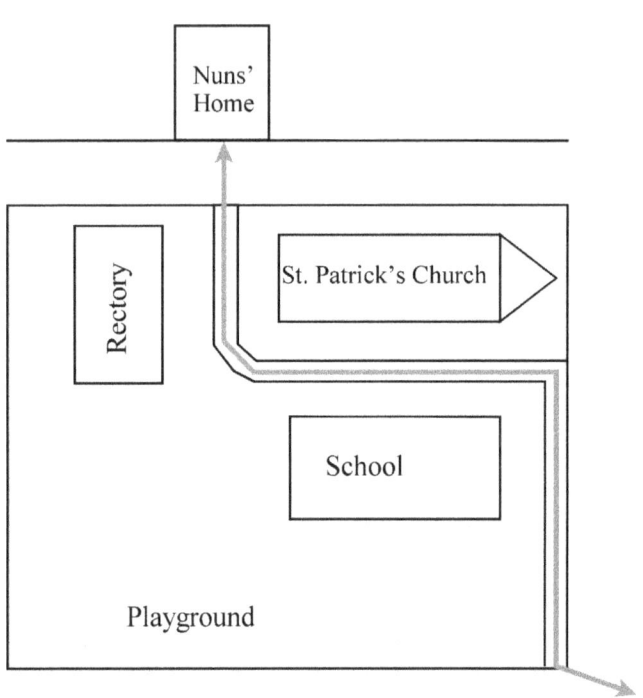

My route from bus station to nuns' home for violin lessons in Beeville.

high. It had compartments for pencils, crayons, scissors, erasers, etc. That pencil box was a marvelous thing. Sally had a pencil box. I did not. And this wonderful young girl, my best friend, gave her pencil box to me. I guess she wanted me to remember her always. Sadly, I did not appreciate this loving gesture at the time.

On my last day in class, I left the pencil box in my desk with a note asking to please give it back to Sally "because it was too expensive for me." Yes, I could now use long English words such as "expensive." I could even write letters, thanks to Sally and her ever persistent tutoring. Finally, I wanted to give the pencil box back to Sally, because my mother and father would want to know where I got it. As a fourth grader, I was not prepared to discuss these very personal events with them.

When I resumed the fourth grade back in the Kenedy public schools, I had no problem keeping up with the other students. In fact, I was way ahead of them. Sally had mentored me well. I never again felt inferior in any class—not ever.

When we left Beeville, my father made arrangements with my violin teacher to continue the lessons. This involved riding thirty-two miles on the Greyhound bus every Saturday. The bus driver picked me up about a block from our rented house. His route was from the downtown bus station to the main highway to Beeville. Upon arriving at the Beeville bus station, I walked about three blocks to the nuns' home for my violin lesson. I do not know where else the bus went, but it was ready to return to Kenedy in about two hours. The cost of the bus ride must have been reasonable; otherwise, we could not have afforded it. Now a nine-year-old boy traveling by himself and carrying a violin case might seem strange today, but that was a different time and place back in the 1930s, not a big deal. I continued with this travel and with the violin lessons for about three months. But I never saw Sally during this time.

One Saturday, my former classroom teacher in Beeville, saw me in the nuns' home during my violin lesson. This teacher, whom I choose not to name, dismissed my violin instructor, then berated me at the top of her lungs. This went on for what seemed an eternity but was more likely just minutes, certainly less than ten. She told me in no uncertain terms that I really broke Sally's heart by not accepting the pencil box. I sobbed and cried all the way to the bus station for my return trip to Kenedy. I was nine years old. This episode should not detract from this nun as a teacher. She was a truly excellent classroom teacher. Never, ever had I witnessed a cross word to me or any other student in the classroom. She just lost it when she saw me again.

I returned home that Saturday, more sad than I had been at any time since leaving Sally. When I saw my father, I announced that I no longer wanted to take violin lessons. He was agreeable as they put a strain on our finances. I never again played the violin.

I know my wife, Mary, and our five children wondered why I kept a violin but never played it nor even talked about it. With no understanding of why, Mary knew the violin was a tender subject for me and no doubt cautioned my children to leave it be, just not to mention it. It was a mystery best left unsolved.

When I told Mary this whole story in early 2009, she asked if I ever contacted Sally, had I tried to find her? I said "No." She asked "Why not?" and I said it was because "I was too ashamed!"

Do I regret not looking up Sally? You bet! I always intended to find Sally, to see her once more, and to apologize. I never had the means until I got out of the army, and then other things always came up. The years went by. I was married in 1949, started working in the post office, then graduated from St. Mary's University. Mary and I had a home and five children to raise. Time passed. I never heard from or saw Sally again. Then in January of 2003, the following obituary appeared in the *San Antonio Express*:

SALLY SWIGER FRANTSEN
DECEMBER 26, 1926-JANUARY 11, 2003

Sally Swiger Frantsen, 76, of Grand Junction, CO, died January 11, 2003, of congestive heart failure at the home she shared with her daughter, Marsha, and son-in-law, Jim Kearns. She was born in Abilene, TX to Rual B. and Virginia Swiger. Her father, a petroleum geologist, moved the family around Texas, eventually settling in San Antonio, where Sally attended Trinity University before transferring to the University of Texas at Austin. She married Dave Frantsen on September 2, 1948, in San Antonio. He died in 1997 in Austin, TX. They raised a family of four in Lee's Summit, MO. She is survived by their children, Marsha and husband Jim Kearns and Polly Frantsen of Grand Junction, Scott and wife Cindy Frantsen of Payson, AZ, Dan Fransten of Pleasant Hill, MO; five grandchildren, and many dear and caring friends. Mrs. Frantsen was a long-time substitute teacher at Lee's Summit High School, where she was a favorite of her "little kumquats" and became known as the Kumquat Queen. She also enjoyed gardening, reading murder mysteries, and cooking for family and friends. Most of all, she loved to laugh. She was cremated and taken home to Texas, as close to heaven as she ever wanted to be.

So Sally and I never met again after that last day in the fourth grade in Beeville. There are a lot of the things I did not know before I read them in her obituary. For instance, Sally probably thought that she had found some stability in her life—not having to move any more. Then she found out I was moving and this no doubt unsettled her again.

Unknown to each of us our separate lives had many parallels. I note these verisimilitudes:

SALLY	ADRIAN
Married Sept. 2, 1948, to Dave Frantzen	Married Sept. 1, 1949 to Mary C. Lukawitz
4 children 5 grandchildren	5 children 5 grandchildren, 2 great-grandsons born in 2006
Settled in San Antonio	Settled in San Antonio
Attended Trinity University, transferred to University of Texas at Austin	Attended St. Mary's University starting in summer, 1947, after discharge in Jan. 1947. Graduated in 1954, finishing part time.
Substitute teacher for many years	Substitute teacher in 1950s for extra income
Enjoyed gardening	Enjoys gardening
Enjoyed reading mysteries	Enjoys reading mysteries
	All five of my children graduated from the University of Texas at Austin.

Thank you Sally.

Chapter 2
THE EARLY YEARS

PANNA MARIA, TEXAS
The first Polish Catholic community in the United States of America
My hometown

In 1772 Poland was partitioned between Prussia (old Germany), Russia, and Austria. A second partitioning occurred in 1793 and a third in 1795. Although the Polish people had their own language, traditions, and Roman Catholic faith, they had no country for almost 150 years. They were ruled by one of the three annexing countries, depending on where in Poland they lived.

The prominent Polish Generals Kazimierz Pulaski and Thaddeus Kósciuszko—Polish Patriots who fought for Polish independence from Russia—also served as Generals under George Washington during the American Revolution. General Pulaski was known as the "Father of the American Cavalry" and once saved George Washington's life. He was mortally wounded in the American siege of Savannah on October 9, 1779, and died two days later. General Kósciuszko returned to Poland after the American war for independence to continue the fight for Polish independence. The Last Will and Testament of General Kósciuszko is shown here to illustrate the beautiful mindset of no discrimination by the Polish people. General Kósciuszko died in 1817.

In the mid-1800s Polish priest Leopold Moczygemba was in San Antonio, Texas. He had been sent there by the diocese of Galveston to minister to newly arrived German Catholic immigrants in Fredricksburg, New Braunfels, and Castroville. Father Leopold observed how well these German immigrants were received and treated and how much they enjoyed their newfound freedoms in Texas. He longed for his fellow Poles to experience these same benefits.

In September of 1854, after repeated letters from Father Leopold to the people of Płużnica, Silesia, Poland (Prussia), more than a hundred families boarded the ship *Weser* and departed the German port of Bremen on the Baltic Sea bound for a new life in America. In the group were Father Leopold's four brothers, Joseph, Anton, August, and John, and their families. Everyone in south central Texas whose last name is Moczygemba is a descendant of one of these brothers, and there are a lot of Moczygembas in south central Texas. More than a hundred listings are in the San Antonio telephone directory and Zeke (Ezekiel) Moczygemba is a deacon in our church, St. Margaret Mary.

Needing all of their financial resources and knowing that they would never be returning to their Polish homeland, these people sold all their possessions, converting everything to gold or easy-to-carry items. Probably the hardest thing for them to endure was leaving the remainder of their families and all of their friends. Just imagine yourself today, leaving everything you have, everything you own, and everyone you know, and starting over in a new country and with a new way of life.

The decision to uproot their lives and try a new

A LAST WILL

I, Thaddeus Kósciuszko, leaving America, hereby dispose and declare, on my failure to return, my friend Thomas Jefferson authorized to use all my possessions in the States of America to buy any of his slaves and the slaves of others and in my name give them freedom and opportunity in education: prepare them for their new life by training them in their moral obligations that they might become good neighbors, good fathers and mothers, husbands and wives; that by training in their civic duties, they might become defenders of their own freedom and their country; and, in general, teach them everything that might make them happier and useful. I name the above mentioned Thomas Jefferson as the executor of my Will.

Thaddeus Kósciuszko
May 5, 1798
(Translation from M. Haiman)

The first Polish Church in America, built in 1855.

beginning in America was not so much driven by their sense of adventure and opportunity as it was an escape from Prussian oppression. These people, my ancestors among them, were all virtually slaves under the Prussian government. They paid high taxes to a German-dominated society that discriminated against the common Polish people. Conscription of their sons into the Prussian Army, epidemics, natural disasters, and a major economic downturn drove them to the decision to leave their old world, the world of their ancestors for a thousand years.

After two months at sea, the *Weser* docked in Galveston, Texas, in early December 1854. The Polish immigrants immediately booked passage for Indianola, some 120 miles farther down the Texas coast. They then set out, mostly on foot, for San Antonio 150 miles northwest of Indianola, where they were to meet Father Leopold. It was a long, hard walk, and a few of them died along the way.

Nearly all the new land that the Polish people were to settle was owned by Mr. John Twohig. Twohig was an Irish immigrant who had become a successful merchant and banker in San Antonio gaining large land holdings south and southeast of the city. Father Leopold negotiated with Mr. Twohig for land from the Hernandez Grant at the confluence of Cibolo (Onion) Creek and the San Antonio River. Twohig grossly overcharged the Poles for this land. While the going rate was less than $2 per acre, the Silesian people were charged from $5 to $10.80 per acre. A total of 728 acres was purchased, 238 acres of which were bought by Father Leopold with money from the Catholic Church. Father Leopold reserved twenty-five acres on which to build a church and divided the remainder among the less affluent of the Polish people. The division was made so as to give each parcel access to the river. Some of the strips were 100 to 200 yards wide by a mile long.

From San Antonio Father Leopold led the people about fifty miles southeast of San Antonio to the chosen spot. They arrived on Christmas Eve, 1854. On the tallest hill north of the San Antonio River, under a great oak tree, they celebrated their safe arrival in this new land with a Mass. Three months after leaving Poland, my people finally had a new homeland. Now, 156 years later, and with the help of some concrete supports, this oak tree still stands next to St. Mary's Church in Panna Maria, Texas. And from this hill you can still plainly see the long, skinny strips of land stretching southward to the river.

As anyone who has lived in central Texas in the winter can attest, the cold, the rain, and the humid wind can be brutal. So the next order of business was providing shelter for all the families. The men started building dugouts,[2] brush arbors, and lean-tos. Mesquite trees, brush and tall grasses were plentiful for construction and thatching. Thus, Panna Maria was born during the Christmas season of 1854.

The next order of business was erecting a proper church building. The Immaculate Conception of the Blessed Virgin Mary Church was built in Panna Maria in 1855. Funding was provided by Bavarian Franciscans in the amount of $3,000. This church was destroyed by lightning and fire in 1877. The walls left

---

[2] A dugout, also known as a pithouse, earth lodge, or mud hut, is a shelter for humans or domesticated animals and livestock based on a hole or depression dug into the ground. These structures are one of the most ancient types of human housing known to archeologists. Dugouts can be fully recessed into the earth, with a flat roof covered by ground, or dug into a hillside. They can also be semi-recessed, with a constructed wood or sod roof standing above the ground. The same methods have evolved into modern "earth shelter" technology. Source: wikipedia.org

Left: Church of the Immaculate Conception of the Blessed Virgin Mary

Below: St. Joseph's School

standing were deemed too hazardous and were razed by residents of Panna Maria. A new church was built in its place in February of 1878 and still stands today beside the grand old oak tree which sheltered that first Mass on Christmas Eve, 1854.

A mere six years later Confederate forces fired on the US military installation at Fort Sumner, South Carolina, and the American Civil war began. The sympathies of the new Polish Texans could not be reconciled with the Confederacy's absolute subjugation of the colored race. While twenty, thirty, or even more young Polish men were conscripted for Confederate service, a like number served the Union, some after being captured by Union troops.

When I was young, an older colored woman of about eighty lived in Panna Maria. Her name was Martha Pocket. I think she had been a slave as a young girl. Oh, what stories she could have told if only someone could have interviewed her that was interested in her experiences. I do not know when she died but it was after we moved from Panna Maria in the early 1930s. Martha is buried in the Panna Maria cemetery. Her grave in the middle northeast corner of the cemetery was still recognizable in the 1970s but is now lost as are many of the graves of the early settlers.

Occasionally the citizens of Panna Maria were harassed by other inhabitants of the area, especially the cowboys. But many other neighbors were sympathetic and provided different grains and cattle that kept the Polish immigrants from starving. As time passed and adversities such as yellow fever, poor crops, and drought were faced, some families moved elsewhere, founding the other Polish settlements of Cestohowa, Kosciusko, St. Hedwig, and Bandera. Some also settled in San Antonio and as far north as White Deer, which is near Amarillo in the Texas panhandle.

Discrimination was virtually nonexistent in Polish culture and this was certainly true in Panna Maria. Perhaps this was a reaction to their oppression by the Prussians. In the church and in the school I attended there were a few Hispanic students. I particularly remember the Hernandez and Colunga families and Pedro Hernandez was a good friend of mine, with whom I played during recess and after school. We ran and we wrestled quite a bit. The Hispanic students learned Polish and some English just as the Polish students learned some English.

The Catholic School of St. Joseph's was built in 1868 and was the first Polish school in the United States. The school building is now a museum. I was a first grade student in St. Joseph's School in 1931. A few years later the Karnes City Independent School District took over the school.

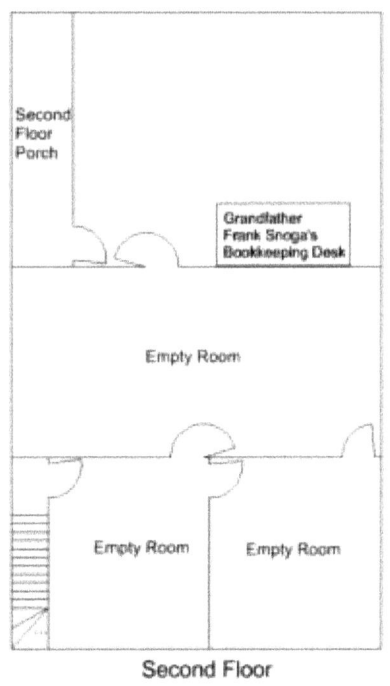
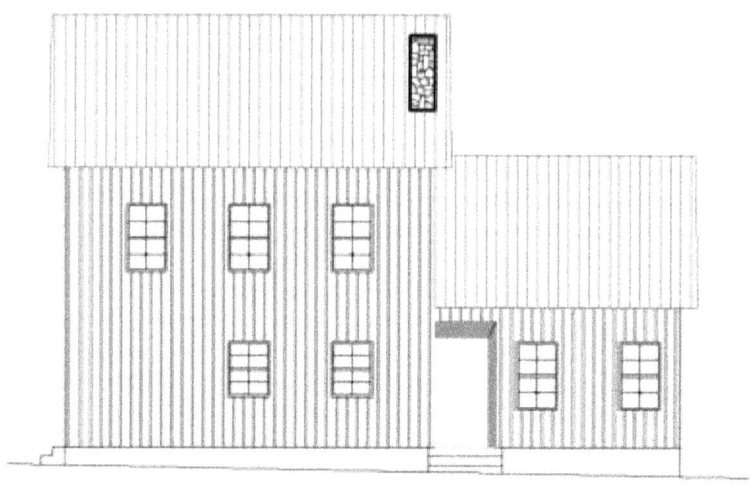

Floor plan and exterior of our house

8 ONLY ONE POLLACK

The school and Mr. Twohig's storehouse, now Snoga's grocery building owned by the Panna Maria Historical Society, were built from limestone blocks two feet thick, which were quarried nearby. As a result of this massive, durable construction, the church, school, and Snoga's store still stand to this day. Sometime later, the Pilarczyk[3] grocery building was probably built of the same type of stones.

A BOY IN PANNA MARIA

My parents owned the only two-story residence in Panna Maria. A drawing of the floor plan and exterior is shown here. This style of a house was known as a dog trot house because it had a breezeway separating the main part of the house from some of the other rooms. The breezeway was where dogs would always lie to get out of the sun on a hot day, thus giving this style of a house its name. Originally built by the Schulzes in 1885, the house included a huge fireplace made from limestone blocks about one foot thick. The stones of the fireplace that were exposed in the breezeway were used for sharpening knives and tools. Some of these stones were worn off five or six inches from all this sharpening.

When its sixty-three-year-old tin roof started leaking in 1948, my father rebuilt the house. The fireplace was saved in place and incorporated into the new house. Otherwise, the two-story house was completely torn down and the new house built entirely using only the old lumber from the house and from the barn. This house is now owned by Glen Bednarz, who still uses that old fireplace.

Everyone slept in the large bedroom at the back of the house. My brothers and I slept in the right corner near the living room and my parents slept in the right corner on the back wall. We had chests of drawers in the bedroom instead of closets. The windows in our bedroom were at least eight feet high. During storms I remember hiding under the covers because I could see the lightning over the river.

A hand pump, wash tub and wash board.

The kitchen had a table in one corner where we ate our meals. The only running water was from one hand pump in the kitchen. It was the only source of water in the entire house. We did not have washing machines. Clothes washing was done in ten-gallon wash tubs with wash boards. Back then water was heated in pots on the wood-burning cook stove. There was no electricity—no electric lights, no air conditioning, nothing that is powered by electricity today. The Rural Electrification Administration (REA) Program came to Panna Maria in the 1930s.[4] The only refrigeration was an icebox using real ice, which was delivered twice a week for those who could afford it.

Likewise, there were no bathing facilities except for the wash tubs. Again, we heated water on the stove for bathing and used the same wash tubs for bathing that we used for laundry. However, I re-

---

[3] Victor and Mary Pilarczyk were my mother's aunt and uncle. Victor bought the store in 1913. It is now used as the Visitors Center for the Panna Maria Historical Society. Victor lost his right arm in a hunting accident. It was amputated just below the shoulder. The first time I saw Victor, I kept staring at where his arm should have been because I had never before seen a man without an arm.

[4] The REA was created on May 11, 1935, with the primary goal of promoting rural electrification. In the 1930s, the US lagged significantly behind Europe in providing electricity to rural areas due to the unwillingness of power companies to serve sparsely populated farmsteads. By 1939, the REA served 288,000 households, prompting private business to extend service into the countryside and to lower rates. Source: wikipedia.org

member the employees at the gin having showers. This seemed very strange to me. Although they were completely out of sight, the showers were on the outside of the gin, on the back side of the building, near the huge steam engines. I remember my dad, older brother Joe, and me sneaking over there in the dead of night to take a quick shower on Saturday or Sunday. That water was very cold, even in the middle of summer. There were no deodorants or sweet-smelling soaps or perfumes. We did not have toothbrushes or toothpastes. I do not remember ever brushing my teeth before I went into the army.

There were no indoor toilet facilities. The outhouse was about twenty to thirty yards on the south side of the house. Since we had no toilet tissue, we used old paper catalogs and corn cobs. (Ouch!)

The two-story house had a cedar post foundation and was built on a grade. The southeast corner of the house was one or two feet off the ground while the southwest corner was three to four feet above ground level. The ceilings were twelve feet high. Because of this, there were about fifteen to eighteen steps on the stairway between the floors. A very large closet occupied the space under the stairs. The house was sided with vertical one-by-twelves with a smaller board overlapping the joints in a style called board and batten. The house was painted yellow and had a steep metal roof.

On the west side of the house there was a carbide station.[5] This device used carbide and water to create a gas that could be ignited to provide light in the house. (Miners wore small carbide lamps on their hats to illuminate their work areas.) We never used this system but the original owners, the Schulzes, installed and used it. Pipes from the carbide station were in every room. No doubt this was the latest in technology in its day. One winter it snowed six to eight inches and built up quite an accumulation on top of the station. Innocent young lad that I was, I ate some of the snow. I remember that snow did not taste very good.

We had perhaps a dozen or more pomegranate bushes around the two-story house on the front and east side. Pomegranates are useless as fruit as they are just peeling and seeds; however, their use as missiles was not overlooked by the young Zaiontz brothers in Panna Maria. (Today wine and juice are made from the pomegranate. Have you checked the prices of these items lately?)

That is I in Mother's tummy. A few weeks after this photo was taken, in early August, 1926, Mom gave birth to me. I assume that I was born at home

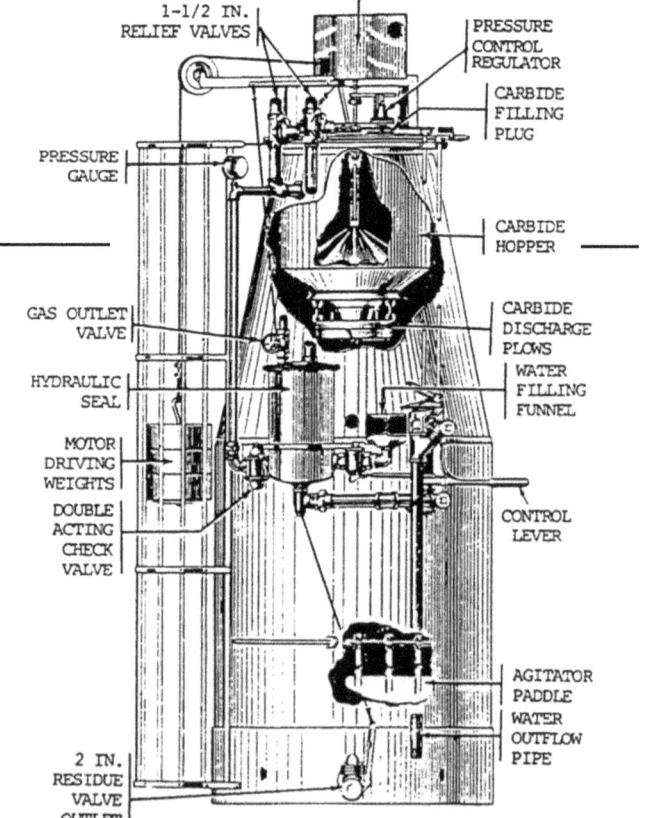

---

[5] In 1862, it was discovered that calcium carbide decomposes in water to produce a flammable gas called acetylene. In the early 1890s, calcium carbide was being commercially produced in electric furnaces where coke and limestone were heated to create calcium carbide (CaC_2).

Late in the 19th century there were many inventors filing patents for "acetylene generators." These were self-contained devices that generated and stored acetylene by either dropping pellets of calcium carbide into water, or dripping water onto the calcium carbide. The gas was then captured in a "bell" that would rise and fall with the volume of gas, thus slightly pressurizing it for piping into the building.

Sure, there was the danger of an explosion and it was probably not a good idea to refill the generator at night while holding a candle or an open flame lantern. Leaks could be an issue, but you would likely smell it. Acetylene has a nauseating odor, similar to rotting garlic.

One pound of calcium carbide could produce about 4.5 cubic feet of acetylene, making it a cheaper fuel for lighting than oil, kerosene, or "city gas." It also creates a brilliant white light, much brighter than with the other fuels. Source: www.oldhouseweb.com/blog/gas-lighting-beyond-the-city/

Left: Early photo of Lucy, Joe and Walter Zaiontz in front of pomegranate bushes.

Below: Alphonse at six months

as there were no hospitals nearby. Santa Rosa Hospital in San Antonio was some fifty miles away—no small journey in 1926.

Frank Snoga, whose store was northeast of our house and who owned property between our house and the river, was my grandfather. His son, Felix, was my mother Lucy's brother. Please note that the map of Panna Maria is as it was about 1930 and not as it is today. The gin lot, with its current house, is now owned by the Felix Moczygemba family. Dugi's Blacksmith Shop was replaced by a brick house built by Lucy Pawelek. She has since died and the house has been sold again. Elaine D. Moczygemba, historian for the Panna Maria Historical Society, now owns the former Felix Mika Mercantile. Father Leopold Moczygemba's tomb was not there in the 1930s.

Most of the families around Panna Maria farmed or worked in farming-related activities. Everybody worked hard all week with children expected to carry their weight with chores and help with the farming. On Sunday—a true day of rest and social engagement—all attended church for the 9 A.M. Mass. Afterwards the women congregated on the church grounds or at Pilarczyk's grocery store while the children played games on the church grounds. Snoga's store found a crowd of men drinking beer and discussing their week's activities. The din of dozens of simultaneous conversations raised one hu-

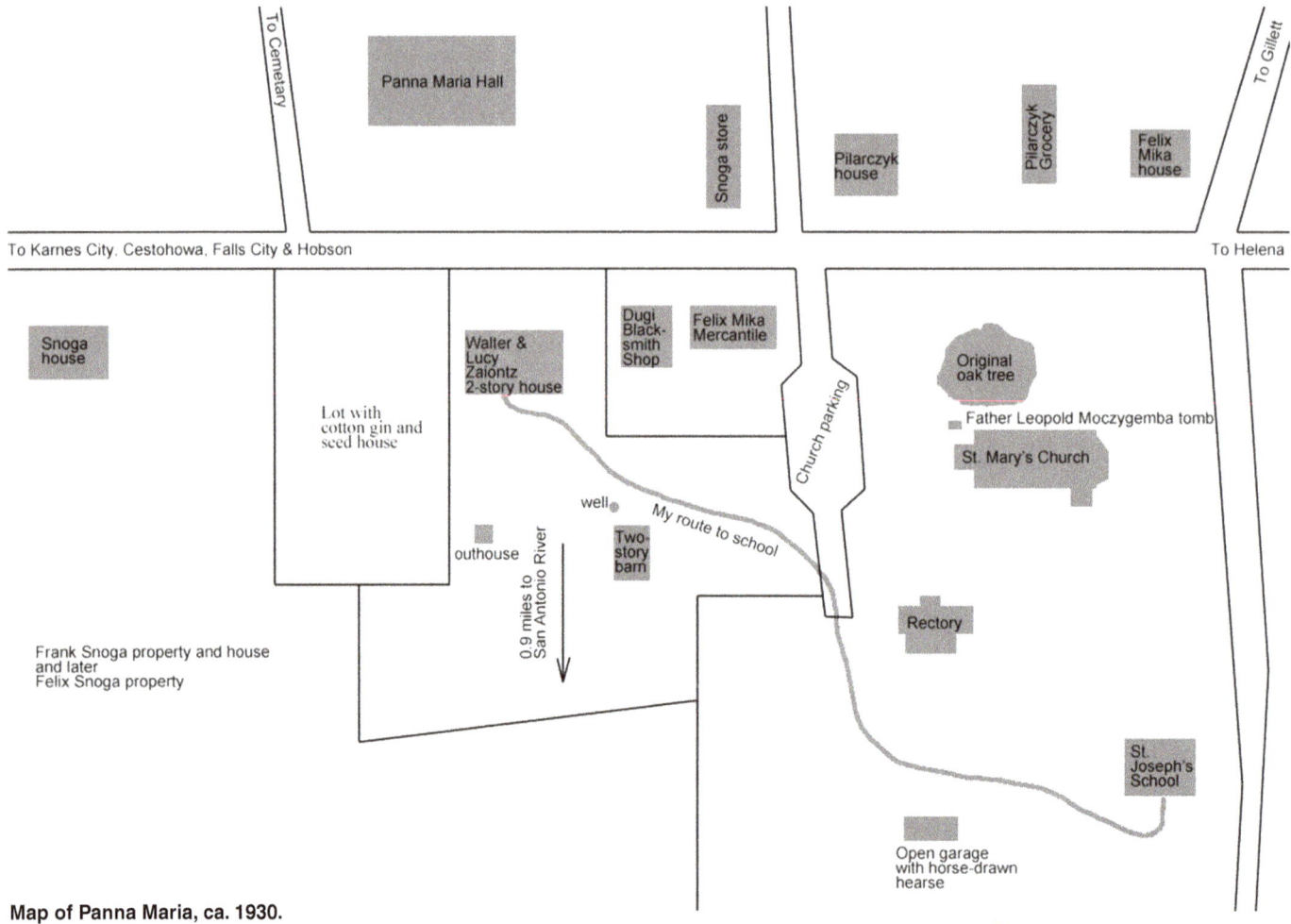

Map of Panna Maria, ca. 1930.

mongous roar. About 11 or 11:30 the weekly community gathering dissipated with the wives and daughters returning home to fix the traditional Sunday family meal.

Sunday afternoon was baseball time. Indeed, baseball was the men's principal form of entertainment. Each community had its own team and quite a rivalry developed between Panna Maria, Cestohowa, Falls City, Hobson, Kosciusko, and Karnes City. (That's right, our rival town of Kosciusko was named after that same general, Thaddeus Kósciuszko, who fought in the American Revolutionary War.) Some of the Panna Maria players in the 1930s were Robert (Rap) Kaczmarek, Ben Gavlik, and Joe Kyrish, with my brother, Joe Zaiontz, playing shortstop in the middle 1930s. Zaiontz, Kyrish, and Gavlik were known as "The Three Mesquiteers" because they were always together even though my brother Joe was considerably younger. Sadly, the games waned during the war years of the 1940s and the 1950s. Then during the 1970s a group of men including my uncle, Felix Snoga, tried to revive community baseball. Felix's son, my first cousin, Ivan Raymond Snoga, was the manager of the team. My son, Edwin Joseph, played catcher for Panna Maria for a couple of years while he also played for the University of Texas Junior Varsity. This required that Eddie drive about 110 miles from Austin to the Panna Maria area then back home to Austin each Sunday afternoon to play baseball. Eddie's only compensation was a free fill-up with gasoline at Uncle Felix Snoga's store. The Panna Maria Wildcats, as the revived team was named, played well and even won the championship one year. Eddie's second cousin, Brendan Fluitt, was a pitcher. But once again community baseball failed to survive. This

Pilarczyk grocery store

Snoga's store

The Early Years

time the technology of television brought an explosive growth in Sunday afternoon sports with which the local clubs could not compete.

Sunday afternoon social entertainment for the women included parties and quilting sessions. My mother was an expert seamstress and quilter. Many of her heirloom quilts are still in the family. Her patchwork tops were stitched together using a foot-powered sewing machine—remember that we had no electricity—but all of the quilting was done by hand while visiting with friends and relatives.

Dances were held every Saturday night and whenever there was a wedding. Weddings were great celebrations and everyone was invited. Weddings always culminated with a dance in the evening.

Men occasionally gathered to play a game called washers. This was similar to horseshoes but used two holes twenty-five feet apart, which were dug with spoons. Rather than ringing pins with horseshoes, large washers or silver dollar coins were pitched at the holes.

Perhaps two or three times a year, a traveling medicine show came to Panna Maria. A tent would be erected next to Snoga's store, chairs set up, and a silent, black-and-white movie would be shown. As was the objective, this always drew a crowd who would then hear a sales pitch for bottles of liniment. Mother thought this liniment was the greatest because it took away all kinds of pain. The problem was finding an extra 25¢ or 50¢ to pay for it. But as a child I had no interest in the liniment, just the movies. Being small, I usually got to sit in the front row. I thought these movies were the greatest things I had ever seen. Now that was technology! I particularly enjoyed Charlie Chaplin, Keystone Kops, and Buster Keaton.

In the late 1920s transportation was primarily by horse or buggy. Horse-drawn wagons hauled loads and there were some Ford Model T automobiles! I recall that one student and his sister rode a donkey to school. The donkey was staked out so it could graze during the school day.

In the 1930s Model A Fords became more common and were more plentiful than other makes of automobiles. Whenever someone got a new auto, the whole town admired it and talked about it at length. Buying a new car was a major expenditure of $300 to $500. A gallon of gasoline was 9¢ and there was no tax on gas. A tall gravity pump dispensed the gasoline. The cylinder on top was filled with the desired number of gallons by a hand-operated pump, which was then fed into the gas tank of the automobile by gravity. I pumped many a gallon of gas by the hand pump for my father and grandfather. It was not easy for a young boy, but it was quite a feeling of responsibility.

On the lot beside our house, stood a cotton gin. A cotton gin is a machine that separates seeds, hulls, and other unwanted materials from cotton after it has been picked. The cleaned cotton would then be compressed into huge bales and stored for sale and shipping to the fabric mills. All of the machinery in the cotton gin was run by steam. The engine was huge. I remember the boiler by itself was as big as our entire living room and dining area.

Cotton was a cash crop[6] for most of the farmers. In late summer during the harvest season, the gin

Fuel filled the clear cylinder by manually pumping the side handle. Once filled, gravity fed the fuel from the cylinder to the gas tank. Original pumps stood as high as fifteen feet!

---

[6] A cash crop is a crop which is grown for profit, as opposed to being grown for domestic consumption. In earlier times cash crops were usually only a small (but vital) part of a farm's total yield. Source wikipedia.org

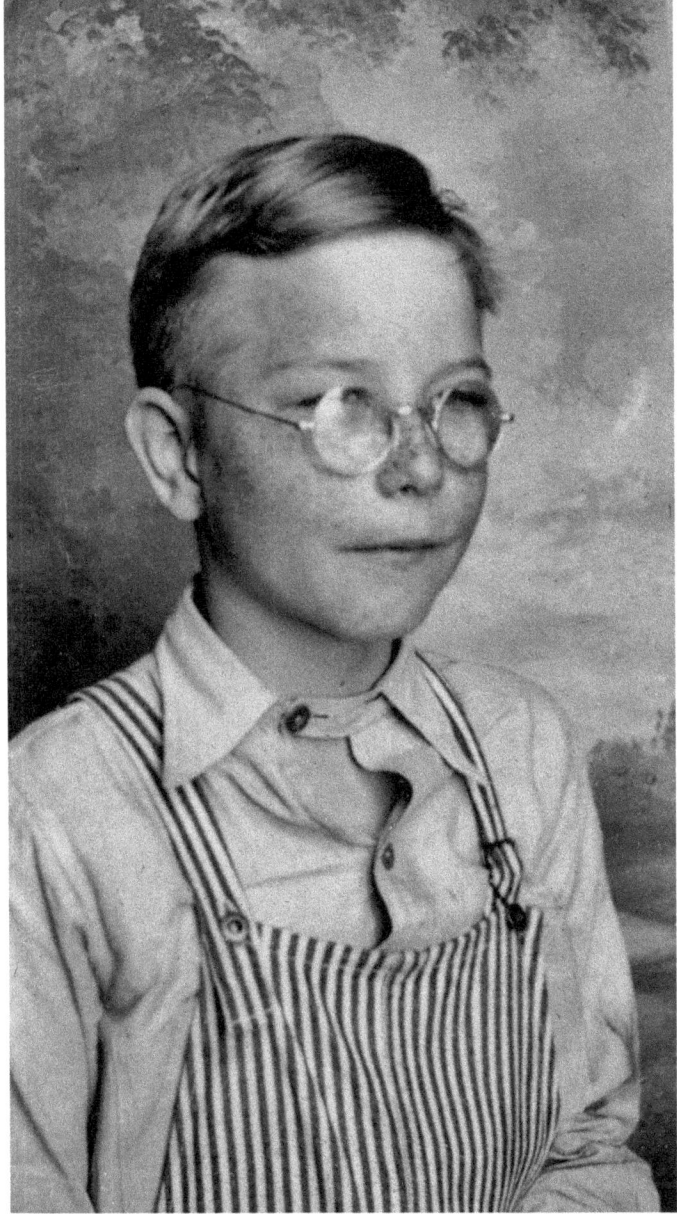

Alphonse with new glasses, 1931

ran from 6 A.M. until dark every day except Sunday. After school and on Saturdays, I often watched the men working at the gin. I particularly remember Lambert Johnson and Joe Kyrish working where the 500-pound bales were strapped and taken out of the compressor. The bales were then hauled onto the grounds of the gin by manual labor. Forklift technology had not yet reached Panna Maria.

The gentleman in charge of the gin was Mr. Billimek. He paid my mother to prepare dinner for him every day. I do not know how much he paid her but it was evident that he was crazy about Mother's cooking.

Sometimes there were as many as fifty huge bales on the gin grounds waiting to be inspected and sold. The bales would be all in a jumble—some sideways, others on end and some leaning against other bales. The Sunday afternoons of late summer found my friends and me climbing and jumping from bale to bale and sometimes trying to see how far we could go around the gin without touching the ground.

A few months after I started St. Joseph's school in Panna Maria, my teacher sent a note home to my father. In it she explained that she wished to discuss something with him. I remember thinking, "What have I done now?" After the conference Dad told Mom that I needed glasses. The teacher had explained that I could not see what she wrote on the blackboard, even after seating me in the front row. I found out years later that I was farsighted.

The first Saturday that Dad was free, he took me to San Antonio to see Dr. Doyle, whose office was on Commerce Street. I walked out with glasses that same day. I never knew how much, but the expense to the family must have been considerable. Dad was happy that I could see and eagerly told Mom how surprised I was at things I was now able to see. He told her how I looked with amazement at buildings, street cars, autos, and people.

While growing up, my older brother Joe and I had little supervision. Most of the time we did as we wished after chores were done. Some of my chores were feeding the chickens, gathering the eggs, and even chasing down the chickens if they got out of the pens. The eggs were traded for milk and other necessities. Dad worked and Mom was busy with cleaning, sewing, cooking, baking, and by now caring for my younger brother, Claude, who was three years younger than I.

Freedom begets exploration. Exploration begets escapade. And so another story: On the north side of the gin stood a separate building known as the seed house. Cotton seed traveled by conveyer belt for storage in the seed house after being removed

The Early Years

during ginning. Conveniently for the adventuresome boys of Panna Maria, there was just enough room above the locked door to allow passage of a gang of boys into the seed house. What a fabulous place! We built tunnels and caves in the compacted seeds. We threw seed balls at each other. We chose up sides and had battles. It was the greatest playground ever! However, if any of these tunnels or caves had collapsed, one of us could have suffocated.

Then one day I was so busy playing with the other boys that I lost my glasses in the immense mound of seed. And worse, I did not even realize that I had lost them! Back at home, my father was stricken when I told him that I had lost my glasses and did not even know where. When asked where was the last place I had been, I confessed "the seed house." So Dad found Mr. Billimek, got him to unlock the door, and several adults started looking through the tons and tons of cotton seeds. After a protracted search, Dad found my glasses, amazingly intact. He was overjoyed that he did not have to buy me a new pair of glasses. And you think he was happy! It was salvation for me. I was ecstatic at being extricated from this dark hole into which I had dug myself.

Another incident with a lasting impression happened when I was six and shortly after I started the first grade. It was customary for the Sisters to keep students after school if they lived nearby and if they had no or very few chores at home. These conscripts performed chores for the Sisters. Living virtually next door to St. Joseph's, I frequently stayed at school in the afternoons.

Now the nuns lived on the second floor above the school so we often carried books and other things upstairs for them. One day while I was dutifully hauling books up the stairs for my teacher, I looked up and with instantaneous horror saw another nun without her habit! She had short hair! She looked like the boys! I was in shock. I panicked, afraid that God would strike me dead! Bolts of lightning were mere seconds away! I had seen a bareheaded nun! ...

Then ... ever so slowly ... it settled in... From the terrifying chill came a slow and soothing warmth. ... Revelation: priests and nuns were human. They were people. They were just like me and Dad and Mom! Wow!

My best boyhood friend in Panna Maria was Lucian Mika. Lucian was two years older and lived across the road from the church, in a house next to Pilarczyk's grocery. I loved to hang out with him. We did everything together. I followed him like a puppy. I walked in his very footsteps. Lucian was really a good kid, full of life and a wonderful friend, but as young boys are prone to do, he led me astray on several occasions. The two most notable, I confess herein.

Uncle Felix, who lived on the other side of the gin from us, had a small wooden house on his property. It was called the "Mexican house." It was nothing fancy but it had four walls, two small bedrooms, a small kitchen and ... it had windows. Uncle Felix hired passing field hands to work on his farm. His fields included the land from this house all the way to the river, a distance of almost a mile. Uncle Felix always treated his workers fairly, even giving them free use of the house.

One day when Lucian and I were passing the house, which was unoccupied at the time, Lucian said "Let's bust out the windows." Even at a young age, I knew that this was wrong, but Lucian gathered some rocks and proceeded to break a window. In terror, I turned and ran home, which was about a half mile away. I could hear more windows breaking as I ran! I remember thinking, "What am I going to tell my dad or my uncle if I am asked?" I did not want to tell on my friend Lucian and I did not want to lie. Luckily for me no one ever asked about those windows. Maybe Uncle Felix assumed that the windows were knocked out by one of the frequent hail storms. Maybe he just thought some passing vagrants broke the glass. Maybe he just thought that they could never have been broken by any of Panna Maria's fine young Polish Catholic youths. Maybe God just protects scared little boys.

Another time Lucian said "Let's go to the river." I agreed. When we got there, a mile from home, we explored the river banks, which were very steep. We stayed there having fun for several hours exploring as we worked our way up the river. Then I noticed that the sun was going down. The shadows were growing long. Darkness was coming. Neither of us could swim and I did not want to get caught on the river in the dark. No one even knew where we were. If we had fallen in, we would have surely drowned.

I suggested to Lucian that we might better start for home. We were little boys and home was a long way away. Lucian allowed that he was not yet ready to leave so I left him on the banks of the river and started for home. I came up from the river at the wooden bridge on the old road to Karnes City. Running along the road toward Panna Maria and all alone in the near darkness, I began to cry. After about two miles, my father met me. Apparently Mom noticed that it was getting late and that I was nowhere to be found. Dad got home from work and they commenced searching. That day my father spanked me with his open hand, which made me cry all the more, then he drew me near, surrounding me with those big arms, and hugged me. Safe at last. This was the only time I remember my father ever spanking me. I do not know how or when Lucian got home. He was at home when I saw him the next day.

Another friend who lived close to Panna Maria was Louis Kroll. We played on Sunday afternoons because that was the only play time for Louie. He had assigned chores all week. We mostly played around the gin, jumping cotton bales. There were different bales in different places and positions every Sunday.

Walking to school from our house I passed a garage which was always open. In the garage was a horse-drawn hearse, which had been used at funerals since the 1850s. It was no longer in use, as an automotive hearse was now available. Lucian, Louie, Pedro, and I used to play in and on this hearse. I understand that it was donated to an early automotive museum at the World's Hemisfair in San Antonio in 1968. I do not know where it is now or if it even still exists.

Every adult male in Panna Maria smoked, including my father, but not a single woman smoked.

Horse-drawn hearse

Some smoked Bull Durham, which came in a cloth sack, or Prince Albert, which came in a tin can, or Bugler, which came in a paper pouch. A very few of the old timers chewed Spark Plug chewing tobacco. The boys, of course, wanted to imitate the men. (Here we go again!) So we saved the cigarette papers from "roll your own" cigarettes. One day some of my friends and I crawled under the southeast corner of our house. We peeled off some of the well-aged cedar bark from the foundation posts. Rubbing the strips together broke them up and we rolled this "tobacco" into the cigarette papers. These cedar posts were at least forty-five years old at that time, dry, dusty, and exposed to heaven knows what.

I do not remember who was with me. It could have been Lucian, it could have been Louie, or perhaps even my younger brother Claude. I suspect it was my older and much wiser mentor Lucian. Surely, I would not have thought of anything like this myself. Surely, with my keen analytical mind I would have thought this activity through and discounted any perceived value it might have had. Surely this was not my idea!

Alas, we got sick, so sick. Smoking this concoction was such a really bad idea. Fortunately, we did not set Mom and Dad's house afire or get bitten by a rattlesnake. Surely this was Lucian's scheme.

Once I found an old firecracker in a drawer of an old sewing machine. This firecracker was about two inches long and as round as a pencil. It had a very short fuse, perhaps a half inch long. I sneaked a match, picked up the firecracker and lit the fuse. I

The Early Years

lit that very same short little fuse. And behold, before I could throw it away, the world ended in a cataclysmic explosion! This piece of ordnance, which should never have been so carelessly left around in plain sight for an innocent youth to find, which in reality should have, with its very short fuse, been destroyed by the bomb squad, exploded in the fingers of my tiny right hand.

Stealing a look, and in fear that my whole arm had been vaporized, I could see that the skin on several of my little fingers was split. And they hurt! My mother put alcohol and the magic liniment from the silent-movie man on my fingers. Then she bandaged them. They hurt. I cried. They hurt for a long time, but my fingers never got infected. Everyone in school wanted to know what happened. I told them. To this day I do not like fireworks. Through all of the 4th of July celebrations since that day I have never had fireworks.

In one of the drawers of this same old sewing machine, I found a lead weight used to sink fishing lines. I put it in my mouth. The lead was quite soft. I chewed it and chewed it just like chewing gum.

In those days country folks did not know much about lead poisoning. I do not know if it was related to or because of this incident, but I started bleeding from my nose. I bled for several days while I was confined to bed. My mother put a pan under my nose so I would not soil the bedding. Time passed and I got so weak that I could not get up. My father called a doctor who was baffled as to why I was bleeding from my nose. The priest was also called and I assume it was Father Dworaczyk who came to see me. He asked me to pray with him and we said the Our Father and a Hail Mary in Polish. In a few more days, the bleeding stopped as fast as it started.

In the 1960s and 1970s we had the lead-paint scare where children were getting lead-paint poisoning. Then I remembered this incident with the lead fishing weight and wondered if my chewing the fishing-line lead and the protracted nose bleed could have been related.

In the early 1930s, my uncle Felix had a beautiful, thick, grass lawn. Uncle Felix's son Ivan, my brother Claude, and I loved to play cowboys on this lawn. Claude and Ivan were about age three. (Yes, this was the same Ivan Raymond Snoga who was the manager of the baseball team in the 1970s.) Since I was a six-year old, I became the horse. The game was that the younger boys took turns getting bucked off my back. Ivan was on my back and I bucked him off. He landed awkwardly and would not stop crying because his arm hurt. Someone ran to get Uncle Felix who ended up taking Ivan to a doctor. It must have been a sprain because I do not remember Ivan wearing a cast. Uncle Felix never got angry with me as I guess he realized that it was only an accident.

Some of my fondest memories were

■ Coming home from school and having a slice of fresh-baked bread with homemade preserves.

■ Sitting in front of our huge fireplace in the winter, when the coals were hot and glowing.

■ Mom giving me a bath on a Saturday night in a ten-gallon wash tub with water heated on the wood-fired cook stove.

■ Walking barefoot to the store for something Mother needed. (I don't remember ever wearing shoes before I started school.) All the roads were made of caliche[7] and in dry weather the caliche turned to the consistency of wheat bread flour. The soles of my feet were so calloused that even though the road was very hot the caliche actually felt good. I used to run across the back of the gin lot to Uncle Felix's house from our property. This area was full of cactus and grass burrs. I dodged the cactus and ignored the grass burrs. Tough feet!

---

[7] Caliche is a sedimentary rock, a hardened deposit of calcium carbonate. This calcium carbonate cements together other materials, including gravel, sand, clay, and silt. Source: wikipedia.org

- Helping my mother make soap in a kettle. I do not remember all of the ingredients but this homemade soap contained animal fats and lye, among other things. This mixture was cooked over a wood fire in the back yard. Once it had cooled and congealed, I helped Mother cut it into big blocks. Mom's soap was our only soap. We washed our hands and faces with it, bathed with it, and Mother did the laundry with it. The water for the laundry was also heated over a wood fire in the back yard.

- Drinking soft drinks from Snoga's store or Pilarczyk's grocery. After we moved from Panna Maria to Kenedy, eleven miles away, we continued to attend church in Panna Maria. Sometimes after church we had refreshments before returning home for dinner. Both stores had several brands and flavors of soft drinks. There was Hippo Size (the largest) and Nehi. (They really were knee high.) My brother Claude and I took turns drinking from one bottle. My favorite was Royal Crown Cola, which was carbonated. In 1936 or 1937 soft drinks cost a nickel. I remember my mother teaching Claude and me to put our upper lips below the rim of the bottle and not our whole mouths over the end. This allowed air into the bottle.

There were good times and there were serious times but through them all boyhood in Panna Maria was the happiest of times. By today's standards, we were poor and lived a simple life. Work was hard, without so many machines to do things for us. But life was good and honest and my memories are rich.

Chapter 3
MY FATHER, MY MOTHER, AND MY ANCESTRY

THE ZAIONTZ BRANCH

My great-grandfather was Ludwig Zając, who emigrated from Poland in 1855. That is as far back as this branch of my ancestry has been traced. The surname Zając is derived from the Polish word *zając,* literally translated as hare. Long ago, names were associated with the type of work people performed. The name Zając may have been originally given to someone who hunted rabbits. Who knows? Zając is pronounced as "ZAH"+"yontz" and eventually took on the Americanized spelling as *Zaiontz*.

The name Zając was recorded as early as 1464 in Syrokomla, Poland, and had become a notable family name by the early Middle Ages (16th and 17th centuries) with their own Achievement of Arms. In Poland, an Achievement of Arms did not belong to a single family but to an entire feudal clan known as an *herbu*. Many families with different surnames may have shared this same heraldic symbol. One of the famous Zaiontz descendants is Pat Sajac, the *Wheel of Fortune* television personality.

Ludwig Zając was born in Rzędowice, Poland, in 1825. He married Franciska Aniol in 1851 and they immigrated to the United States with their infant son, John, in 1855. Ludwig bought land on Martinez Creek—the future site of St. Hedwig, Texas, a Polish community fifteen miles East of San Antonio—in 1856.

The First Polish Americans, by T. Lindsay Baker, states that in 1856 or 1857 a church was built at St. Hedwig on land donated by Ludwig Zając. Ludwig was naturalized in Texas in 1865, and I believe that the spelling was probably changed to Zaiontz at this time. My daughter, Barbara, and I went to St. Hedwig and found his grave and also the grave of his wife, Franciska, my great-grandmother. In this same cemetery by the Annunciation of the Blessed Virgin Mary Church rest grandfather and grandmother, Albert and Albina Zaiontz.

The symbolism of the Achievement of Arms consisted of the following parts:
- the scrolls generally contained the motto. The Zając arms did not have a motto but simply listed the surname
- the crest is shown above the helmet. Plumes or feathers were often used.
- the torse is the twisted wreath of cloth on top of the helmet
- the helmet. An open-visored helmet represented nobility while the closed-visored helmet was used for untitled nobility or commoners.
- the mantle is the wreath of cloth draped from the helmet. This protective cloth was worn by a knight to protect him from the elements (wet, cold, and heat) and to guard him in battle. The red and silver mantle on the Zając arms is shown cut to shreds as if it had been torn in battle.
- the shield is the actual coat-of-arms. The background color of silver represents nobility, peace and serenity. Silver, the metal, is associated with the qualities of purity and chastity. The salamander represents a man of faith and is considered good luck. The flames signify passion or zeal.

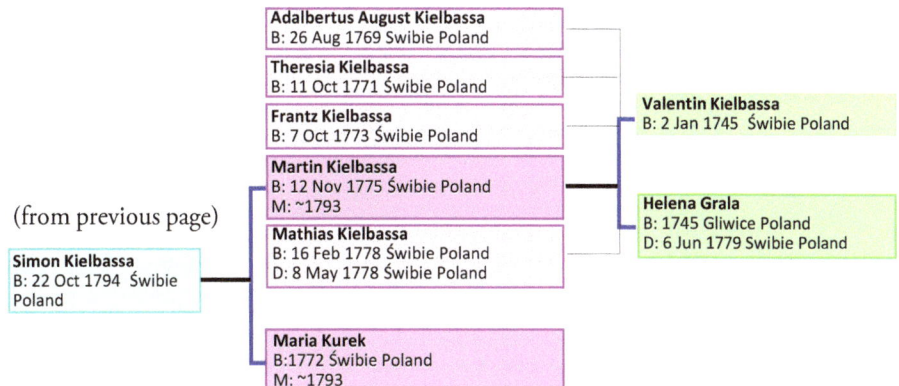

(from previous page)

Simon Kielbassa
B: 22 Oct 1794 Świbie Poland

Johanna Kozielski
(from previous page)

½ siblings (Franciszka Filla):

Anton Kozielski III
B: 14 Jan 1837 Strzelce Opolskie Poland
D: 21 Sep 1909 Yorktown TX
M: 2 Sep 1873 St. Hedwig TX
  Florentina Kosub
  (b: 7 May 1855 Poland
  d: 8 Mar 1929 TX)

Johann Kozielski
B: 16 May 1838 Izbicko Poland
D: 8 Jun 1838 Izbicko Poland

Emanuel Kozielski
B: 6 Aug 1839 Strzelce Opolskie Poland
D: 2 Sep 1839 Strzelce Opolskie Poland

½ siblings (Lucille Secock Fikus):

Paul Kozielski
B: 1850 Tarnów Opolski (?) Poland
US: 1 Oct 1855
D: 1898 TX
M: 1 Nov 1876 St. Hedwig TX
  Maria Ploch
  (b: 26 May 1850 d: 1877 TX)
M: 23 May 1883 De Witt C TX
  Hedwig (Jadwiga) Burda (Bunda)
  (b: 12 Oct 1863 Panna Maria TX
  d: 22 Feb 1951 TX)

Frances or Franciska Kozielski
B: 9 Mar 1853 Oschiek Poland
D: 30 Jan 1930 TX
M: 22 Jun 1873 De Witt C TX
  Simon C. Kolodzey
  (b: 9 Dec 1848 Poland
  d: 24 Oct 1926 TX)

John Jesse Kozielski
B: 11 May 1855 Oschiek Poland
D: 19 Jul 1936 Yorktown TX
M: 10 Jan 1882 **Florentina Golla**
  (b: 11 May 1858 Inez TX
  d: 28 Nov 1944 Yorktown TX)

Magdelena Maria Kozielski
B: 21 Jul 1859 Yorktown TX
D: 13 Oct 1948 De Witt C TX
M: 17 Aug 1885 Yorktown TX
  John Neslony
  (b: 14 Feb 1859 Panna Maria TX
  d: 19 May 1937 TX)

Frank Pete Kozielski
B: 16 Sep 1862 Yorktown TX
D: 13 Jan 1950 TX
M: 14 May 1889 Yorktown TX
  Frances Plasczyk
  (b: 22 Jan 1869 Lindenau (Lipniki) Poland
  d: 28 Feb 1958 TX)

Constantina Kozielski
B: 12 Sep 1866 Yorktown TX
D: 28 Jun 1941
M: ~1893 **Jesse H. Kozelsky**
  (b: 16 Aug 1866 Poland
  d: 12 Dec 1943 TX)

Anna Apolonia Kozielski
B: 21 Feb 1869 Yorktown TX
D: 25 May 1960 TX
M: 29 Jan 1889 Yorktown TX
  Louis J. Syma
  (b: 1 Sep 1865 TX
  d: 14 May 1927 TX)

Isadore (Isydor) Paul Kozielski
B: 10 May 1871 Yorktown TX
D: 16 May 1952 Yorktown TX
M: 1 Aug 1898 Yorktown TX
  Frances Florence Kaminski
  (b: 30 Sep 1877
  d: 1 Sep 1942 Yorktown TX)

Carolina Kozielski
B: 15 Jul 1876 Yorktown TX
D: 31 Mar 1957 TX
M: **Michael Plasczyk**
  (b: 6 Dec 1870 Poland
  d: 5 Jul 1960 TX)

Ludwig Zajac's grave marker

Franciszka Zajac's grave marker

Grandfather Albert Zaiontz married Albina Kiolbassa,[8,9] on November 18, 1890. I never knew Albina, as she died in 1921, five years before I was born. Albina's father, another of my great-grandfathers, was Ignacy (Ignatz) Kiolbassa, and his father, my great-great-grandfather, was Piotr (Peter) Kiolbassa. Piotr was born in Poland in 1814 and immigrated to the United States through New York in 1855. Somehow he found his way to the frontier in Panna Maria, Texas.

Albert and Albina had many children. The oldest boy in the family was Ignatz, followed by my father, Walter (Wadyslaw in Polish), Benjamin Joseph, Onufry, the twins Gregory and Alexander, Clement, Claude, and Helidor, and two girls, Sally (the oldest child), and Otilla (Tillie). Four of my uncles shown in the family tree are mysteries to me. I do not remember my father ever mentioning any of them. According to the US Census records, the oldest of these four, Benjamin Joseph, was a son living with my grandfather's family in 1910. Benjamin Joseph would have been close to my father in age so they would have undoubtedly played and worked together. My older brother was named Joseph, perhaps after Benjamin Joseph. I wonder why I never heard of him. Could he have been a cousin living with Albert and Albina and not one of my father's brothers?

Gregory and Alexander were twins who died on the same day when they were only three months old and before my father was five. He probably had no memories of them. They are also buried in the Annunciation of the Blessed Virgin Mary cemetery in St. Hedwig, although there is no marker. The fourth of the uncles unknown to me was named Claude. All I really know is that his birthday is in 1909 and that he is not listed with the family in the 1910 census. Dad never talked to me about him but named my younger brother Claude, after whom I do not know.

---

[8] In Polish, *Kiolbassa* means sausage. The Kiolbassa could have originally been makers or sellers of sausage. In fact, there is a company in San Antonio called The Kiolbassa Provision Company. They make and sell all types of sausage, including Polish sausage.

[9] Prior to immigrating to the United States, *Kiolbassa* was spelled *Kielbassa*. The spelling change is shown in the family tree.

Around 1900 my grandfather Albert moved his family to Panna Maria, about fifty miles southeast of San Antonio and some thirty-five miles south of St. Hedwig. The family lived in the country outside of Panna Maria, but, much to my regret, I do not know where. Once when Dad was driving us to Helena, he pointed to a place two or three miles east of Panna Maria and said that is where he used to live. This spot was just past Cibolo Creek. I presume Grandfather Albert made a living for his family by farming. Another of my many regrets is not asking my father where the family lived when he was young and how they made their living.

When World War I broke out in Europe many Polish immigrants volunteered for service. Others were drafted. My father Walter and his brothers Ignatz and Onufrey all served in France. Dad was a machine gunner in the 7th Division. Onufrey was in the Meuse region and in the Argonne Forest of France. Dad's younger brother, Clement, was too young to fight in World War I, but he enlisted in the regular army in the 1920s and served for thirty years, retiring as a master sergeant.

There were quite a few young men of Polish descent from Texas who gave their lives for America in World War I: Baranowski, Jankowski, Murski, and Gutowski. Ignatz Moczygemba from Panna Maria was killed in action.

The return of peace immediately following the war was filled with rising discrimination against the Poles by various organizations that were blind to the Poles' service and sacrifice. Chief among these was the Ku-Klux-Klan. They campaigned not only against the colored races but against anything foreign or Catholic. In their view, the Polish people qualified on both counts, even after generations of living in Texas. My mother told of disruptions during Sunday mass as late as the 1920s, when cowboys rode their horses into the church and terrorized worshipers.

THE SNOGA BRANCH

Because it has a profound bearing on my ancestry, I will give a brief history of Maximilian and his ill-fated sojourn into Mexico.[10] When Benito Juárez was elected president of Mexico in 1861, he inherited a bankrupt nation and a foreign debt of 80 million pesos. Most of this debt was owed to Britain, France, and Spain. When Mexico could not start repaying this debt, the three creditor nations agreed to the occupation of the port of Vera Cruz. By this action they were to take Mexico's customs receipts as repayment of the loans.

Confrontation was avoided when agreement was reached with the Juárez Mexican government. Britain and Spain withdrew, but the French forces stayed. Napoleon III of France wanted a foothold in the Americas. He well knew that the United States could not enforce the provisions of the Monroe Doctrine[11] as it was embroiled in a Civil War and was fighting for its very existence.

The French received reinforcements of 2,500 additional troops and marched inland. They were, however, defeated at Puebla on May 5, 1862, by Porfirio Díaz. Celebration of this victory is the origin of the *Cinco de Mayo* festivities, even in this country.

France was allied with Austria at the time and, in early 1863, received 30,000 fresh troops with which they seized Mexico City. The Archduke of Austria, Maximilian, was offered the title Emperor of Mexico, which he accepted and went to Mexico with the Austrian army. This Austrian army was also composed of men of Polish descent, many of whom had been forced into the Austrian army, tricked into service, or volunteered as mercenaries.[12]

After many defeats and rising Prussian pressures and saber rattling in Europe, Napoleon III withdrew the French troops from Mexico. This led to certain defeat of Maximilian's Mexican and Austrian forces. In May of 1867, Maximilian was defeated and subsequently executed on June 19, 1867.

I found during my research that more than a few

---

[10] *A Traveler's History of Mexico*, Kenneth Pearce, 2001.

[11] The United States policy of opposition to outside influences or interferences in the Americas. This was enacted after a foreign policy statement by President James Monroe in 1823.

[12] A professional soldier who agrees to fight for a foreign country for pay.

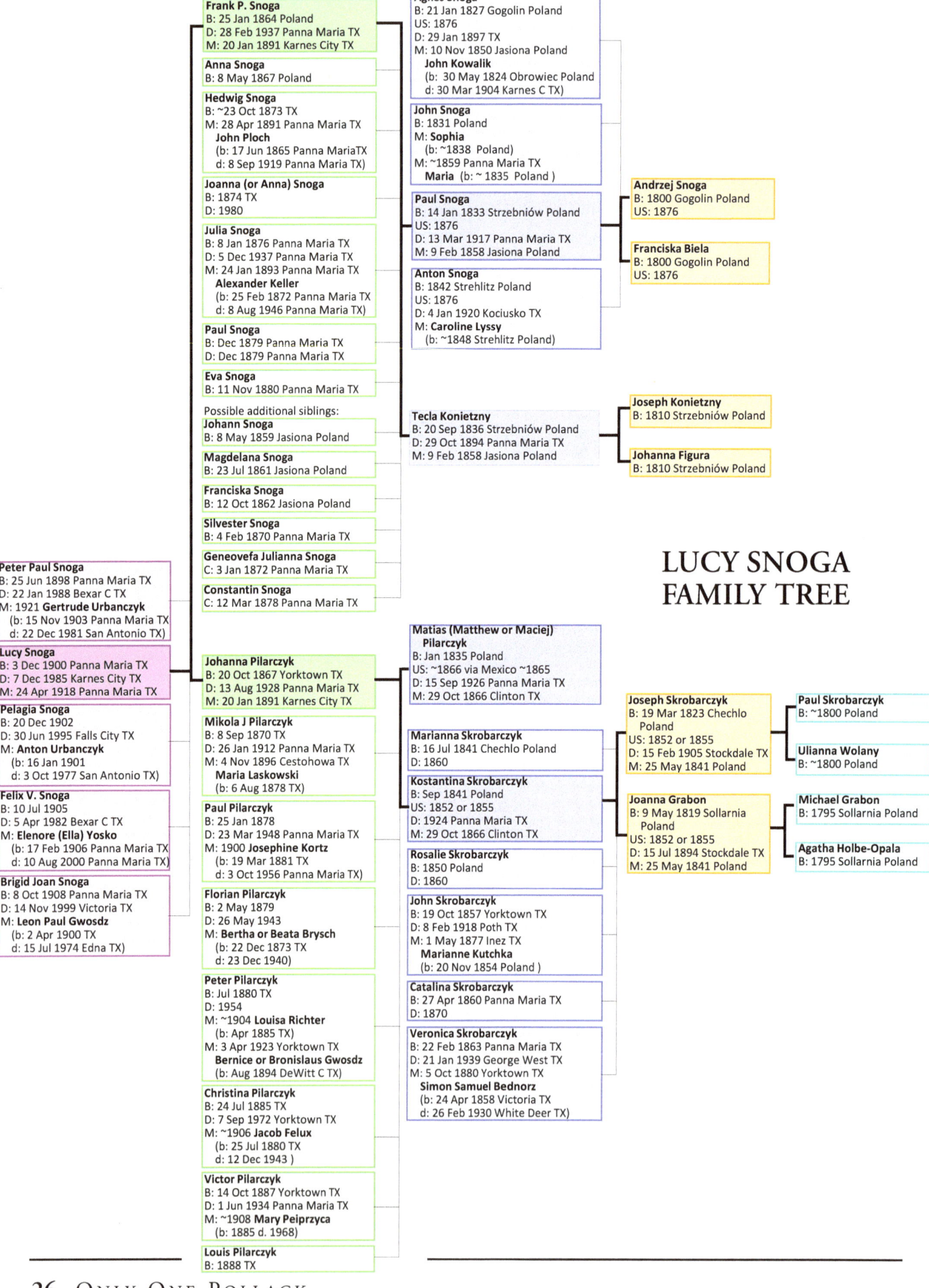

LUCY SNOGA FAMILY TREE

Poles deserted Maximilian's army, were set free after being captured, or escaped before being executed. When these men crossed the Rio Grande to safe haven in the north, they no doubt asked if there were any Polish people in Texas. Naturally they were directed to Panna Maria and St. Hedwig, the earliest Polish communities in the United States.

Among those Polish soldiers to escape Mexico was Mathew Pilarczyk. My mother's mother was Johanna Pilarczyk, who married Frank Snoga. Johanna was the daughter of the soldier Mathew Pilarczyk. My great-grandfather's story is related in *The Polish Texans*.[13]

My mother, Lucy Snoga Zaiontz, was born in Panna Maria into the family of Frank Snoga and Johanna Pilarczyk Snoga, who had three girls and two boys. She had an older brother, Peter, and a younger brother, Felix, and two younger sisters, Pelagia (Pella) and Brigid. I do not know when they bought the two-story, dog-trot house in Panna Maria but it was apparently after 1900. Frank and Johanna and the entire family continued to live in this spacious house.

As a boy, I spent some of my summers working in Uncle Felix's store or working on Uncle Anton's farm. (Uncle Anton Urbanczyk married Mother's sister Pella.) In the summer of 1935 or 1936, I was in Panna Maria while my Uncle Felix Snoga was helping Father Edward J. Dworaczyk do research for his book, *The First Polish Colonies of America in Texas*.

Uncle Felix asked if I wanted to tag along while he interviewed some people for the book. I said "Sure." We went to see some man in his eighties. I do not remember his name or where he lived, except that it was in the country. When my uncle introduced me as Alphonse Zaiontz, the old man's eyes lit up. He related that he had known my grandfather Ludwig Zając very well. (Actually Ludwig was my great-grandfather.) Oh, what a missed opportunity! I should have paid more attention and asked questions. I could have learned so much about my great-grandfather Ludwig. He was born and married in Poland, immigrating to St. Hedwig shortly after Texas joined the Union. Regrets. Great are my regrets.

Shortly after my mother and father married on April 24, 1918, Walter parted for military service in the army. Lucy continued to live in the two-story house with her parents. When Walter returned from France, he also lived with the Snogas.

My grandmother, Johanna, developed cancer about 1915, dying in 1928, two years after I was

---

[13] *The Polish Texans*, T. Lindsay Baker, 1982, University of Texas Institute of Texas Cultures-San Antonio.

A COLORFUL PAST

Another of the exiles from Maximilian's imperial army was Mathew Pilarczyk, who settled in Karnes County. He also came from Europe to Mexico in the army supporting the French-backed Austrian emperor. After Maximilian's fall Pilarczyk was captured by the liberals and, according to the stories he later told, he was due to be killed by a firing squad. "The instant the Mexican gunners started shooting," he related, "one comrade and I broke away and ran. Good fortune attended us while almost all the others were shot down." Pilarczyk continued his tale: "We reached the river and plunged in and swam it with Mexican horsemen on our heels anxious to cut us down." The two men crossed the river and came upon a Mexican teamster hauling wood and offered to give him whatever objects of value they had if he would conceal them. "He saved our lives, for when the horsemen came galloping up asking to be put on the track of fleeing men this teamster directed them away from us and without question saved our lives." Pilarczyk and his friend plodded on day after day until they reached the Rio Grande and safety in Texas. Hearing that there were Poles at Panna Maria, Pilarczyk made his way there, where he settled. In later years he married into one of the Silesian families and became a substantial member of the agricultural community. His grave today lies at the Panna Maria cemetery, and his descendants enjoy telling visitors about the colorful ancestor.

– *The Polish Texans*

Corporal Walter Zaiontz and Lucy shortly after he returned from the war, ca. 1918.

born. Mother took care of Johanna for thirteen years while making a home for grandpa, Dad and her own growing family. Of course she had help from her sisters, Pella and Brigid, and her mother contributed as she was able. Can you imagine keeping a household running while caring for a cancer patient and all her needs, as well as a toddler? My brother Joe was born in 1919 and I was born in 1926.

Late in 1928, after Grandmother died, Grandfather Frank Snoga decided to retire from the many years of making his living by owning and operating Snoga's store. In those days, there was no such thing as Social Security, which was not created by congress until 1935. People had to provide for their own retirement.

Apparently my father helped with the grocery store, so Frank turned the store over to him. I do not know what was behind this change. Perhaps it was confidence in Dad. Perhaps it was because Mother took care of his Johanna and the family all those many years. Perhaps it was a combination of many things. I presume the title to the two-story house was given to my father at the same time. Grandpa continued to live in the house with us and, even though he considered himself retired, he still worked in the store with my father.

I never knew my grandmother Johanna, but I knew my grandfather Frank very well. In fact, I spent more time with him than I did with my own father and mother. I remember riding to San Antonio with him every Saturday to gather stock for the grocery store. Without a doubt these trips were a relief to Mother since I was out from under foot and in good hands.

Frank probably had other automobiles in the 1920s and early 1930s, but I remember a Model A Ford with what was known as a rumble seat[14] in back, where the luggage compartment would otherwise be. Only the driver's and passenger's seats were covered by the cab. The rumble seat was in the open air. To my great disappointment, I was never allowed to ride back there.

For a five- or six-year-old boy, the ride to San Antonio was very long, at least four or five hours over dirt roads. Now this fifty-mile trip takes less than an hour. We approached San Antonio on what is now Goliad Road, passing right by Brooks Field with its huge hangers and many dirigibles. What technology; I had never seen anything like that before, certainly not in Panna Maria, Texas!

Continuing toward the city, we eventually reached the five-way intersection where Gevers Street and Fair Avenue met Goliad Road. Today, this area that was once open fields hosts a dense residential neighborhood including St. Margaret Mary's Church and School, where my wife, Mary, and I

---

[14] A rumble seat is an upholstered exterior seat which opens out from the rear deck of a pre-World War II automobile and seats one or more passengers. In America, this type of seating became largely obsolete in the mid-1930s when cars became too fast and streamlined for the comfort of passengers in such a seat. Their popularity was further diminished by frequent injuries, including decapitation that sometimes occurred in accidents. Rumble seat passengers were essentially seated out in the elements, and received little or no protection from the regular passenger compartment top. Folding tops and side curtains for rumble seats were available for some cars (including the Ford Model A) but never achieved much popularity. Source: wikipedia.org

Lucy & Walter Zaiontz's 50th anniversary, 1968, Immaculate Conception of the Blessed Virgin Mary Church, Panna Maria. (L-R) Brigid Snoga Gwosdz, Aunt Christina Pilarczyk Felux, Felix Snoga, Ella Yosko Snoga, Gertrude Urbanczyk Snoga, Peter Snoga, unknown maid of honor, Lucy Snoga Zaiontz, Walter Zaiontz, Otilia Zaiontz Hannah, Ignatz Zaiontz, Anna Ramzinski Zaiontz, Helidor Zaiontz, Flordene Jackson Zaiontz, Pelagia Snoga Urbanczyk, Anton Urbanczyk.

now worship.

Turning north on Gevers Street, we passed between what were probably the remains of the stone pillars of a gate. There was little other evidence of San Antonio for another two or three miles whereupon houses became more numerous and perhaps only a quarter mile apart. Finally, we entered San Antonio proper.

Grandpa and I loaded candies, tobacco products, notions for sewing, medications, and other odds and ends for the store. The rumble seat was packed full with the products that were to be delivered directly to Snoga's store, as was the front passenger seat. As little as I was, there was hardly room for me to squeeze in beside my grandfather. Exhausted, I mostly slept on the long drive back home.

Dad was no longer running Snoga's store and we were living in Kenedy, Texas, again when my mother and father were summoned to Uncle Felix's house in Panna Maria in February 1937. Frank had suffered a massive stroke and was dying. On February 28, at the age of seventy-three, Grandpa died. Mother told me he came to America from Poland when he was just four years old.

Three days later the funeral was held in Panna Maria. I had not the slightest inkling of how well-known and liked my grandfather was. It seemed as if everyone in Karnes County and even beyond knew Frank Snoga. More than half of the people who came for his funeral stood outside the church because there was no room inside. There were no parking spaces in Panna Maria. Cars were parked on both sides of the road well past Uncle Felix's house. I had no idea there were so many automobiles in the entire county. Certainly there were between 300 and 400 cars in Panna Maria that day. To this day, I have never seen a funeral with larger attendance, save for some televised funeral for a dignitary.

This young boy ached that day. I had a tight feeling in my chest. Grandpa was not ever coming back.

A TREE FROM STRONG ROOTS

My mother and father worked very hard all their lives. But never were they able to buy a new car. I am sure that Dad had other cars, but the first one I remember was a 1932 Buick bought about 1934. It looked like a hearse. Next came a 1934 Plymouth, again bought previously owned in 1936.

Even though my parents owned the house in Panna Maria, provided by Frank Snoga, they rented it out when they lived elsewhere. Other than this house, they always rented wherever we moved. While we were living in Kenedy, they rented two different houses at two different times. In Beeville they rented two different houses as well as again in Cuero. My father used to say that he did not want to be tied down in case we had to move again. The first house my parents actually bought was the third house they rented in Cuero. This happened after World War II when Dad was in his fifties.

My father only finished the eighth grade. He did, however, teach himself penmanship, and he could converse with anyone in Polish, English, or a Tex-Mex version of Spanish. He also had some knowledge of French and German. Most importantly, my father never met anyone he did not consider a friend. And oh, how he loved to laugh. His sense of humor exceeded that of anyone else I have ever known. I can still see him sitting by the radio listening to the likes of *Amos and Andy* and *Fibber McGee and Molly*, laughing so hard he would be on the verge of tears.

The decade of 1929 to 1939 found the United States in an awful depression. The family of Walter and Lucy Zaiontz was not able to have the best of food during the depression but we never went hungry. My father saw to that. The staple in our house was corn bread and beans—pinto, red, or large

Walter with one of his cars.

limas, also called butter beans. Occasionally my mother sent me to the butcher shop to buy hambacon, now known as Canadian bacon, for 15¢ a pound. If we asked, the butcher would give us a soup bone for free.

I do not know where my mother learned it all but she was talented in many ways. She was an excellent cook and baked cakes and pies, and made bread every day. Her musical talent extended to the organ. My grandfather Frank bought an organ and donated it to the church where my mother played it every Sunday. (Apparently when it became obsolete in church, it was given back to grandfather. He put it in the side room, where I saw it in the 1930s. I do not know what happened to the organ when the house was rebuilt in 1948.) Needlework and crocheting were favorite pastimes. She was also a nurse when she had to be, and she always knew what to do to make us feel better. However, sometimes her remedy included castor oil in orange juice or Black Draught, a powerful laxative.

It is inconceivable that she found the time but Mother made most of her dresses and those of her sisters. She made a lot of the clothes for my dad, for me, and for my brothers. And now allow me to brag a little. These were not just quickly made garments. When I discharged from the army in 1947, Mother made some civilian shirts for me. I still had two of them in the year 2011. How is that for "home-made in the USA" quality products?

Role models, love, and social interaction are powerful molders of character. Joe, Claude, and I benefitted immensely from our close-knit rural upbringing around extended family. I believe this environment instilled in us the qualities of frugality, responsibility, perseverance, humility, kindness, mercy, compassion, and an enduring work ethic.

Research for recording these chapters of my life brought the realization that not all in my family were born in the United States. Were it not for Maximilian's army and Polish citizens seeking freedom through immigration, Joe, Claude, and I, and all of my cousins, aunts, and uncles would have been born in Poland. We would not have had the opportunities afforded by being born in the United States of America. We would have had to endure all of the trials and tribulations the people of Poland have had to endure for the last 150 years—World War I, World War II, the brutality of German occupation and persecution, Soviet occupation, and the Cold War.

We would all, my whole family, be speaking fluent Polish. The Polish that is spoken in Panna Maria, St. Hedwig, and elsewhere in Texas today is now interspersed with English, Spanish, and some German. It is now difficult for us to understand visitors from Poland. While gaining our freedoms, we have lost something else from the old mother land.

But the sun has shone on Zając, Aniol, Kiolbassa, Kozielski, Snoga, Konietzny, Pilarczyk, and Skrobarczyk family members; shone on their lives, their fortunes, and their fields. Polish blood runs strong and pure in our veins and the traditions and pride of our Polish heritage swell our hearts, but we are Americans by choice. Proud and strong Americans!

I always believed that Ludwig Zając came over in Maximilian's Army in 1863. Since he was born in 1825, he would have been thirty-eight years old and, I assume, an officer of some kind. In all of my research, I have not found any corroborating evidence that he came over with Maximilian. However, I do have some circumstantial evidence:

1. He was not naturalized as a citizen until 1865, long after the original settlers were naturalized. I assume that it did not take eight or ten years for naturalization to take place, especially when immigrants were welcomed.
2. Of two different family tree sources, neither one goes back beyond Ludwig Zajac. This is also true of Matthew Pilarczyk.
3. My father sometimes said that his grandfather came to Mexico in Maximilian's Austrian Army. He also said that the Zaiontz family in Falls City, Texas, were a different family and no relation to us. The only way that this could happen was if they emigrated from Poland at a different time and they were a different part of the family tree.
4. It is possible that both my father and the man interviewed by my uncle were actually referring to Matthew Pilarczyk. It is my hope that further research will one day disclose that Ludwig was actually also in Maximilian's Army.

chapter 4
ALPHONSE IN THE MIDDLE

I, Adrian Alphonse (pronounced "*awl funz*" in Polish), was the middle of three boys born to Lucy Snoga and Walter Zaiontz. I was a younger brother to Joseph Peter and an older brother to Claude Charles.

My mother's youngest sister, Brigid, was born in 1908, being seventeen when I was born. According to my mother, Brigid did a lot of babysitting of me, which, as we shall see, is why Alphonse became an important name for me. While I was a toddler, Brigid dated a boy named Adrian, whose last name shall not be given for obvious reasons. They had a falling out and she did not like him thereafter. Henceforth, Brigid refused to call me Adrian and instead persisted in calling me by my middle name, Alphonse. Thus began a trend and eventually even my parents called me Alphonse, as did my aunts, uncles, cousins, and eventually all who knew me. Alphonse Zaiontz, that was my name. All through school I did not know that my first name was actually Adrian. Both my grade school and high school diplomas identify me as Alphonse Zaiontz.

In the middle of my junior year in high school,[15] Mother and I applied for Social Security numbers and cards. She produced my baptismal certificate showing my first name as Adrian and not Alphonse. I was flabbergasted.

In the late 1920s or early 1930s, Aunt Brigid married Leon Gwodz and moved away to Edna, Texas, about eighty miles from Panna Maria. Even though she was gone, Brigid was always my favorite aunt and remained so. I wonder why?

YOUNGER BROTHER CLAUDE

Mother always wanted a daughter, but instead was blessed with three sons. My younger brother Claude and I played together constantly, and I

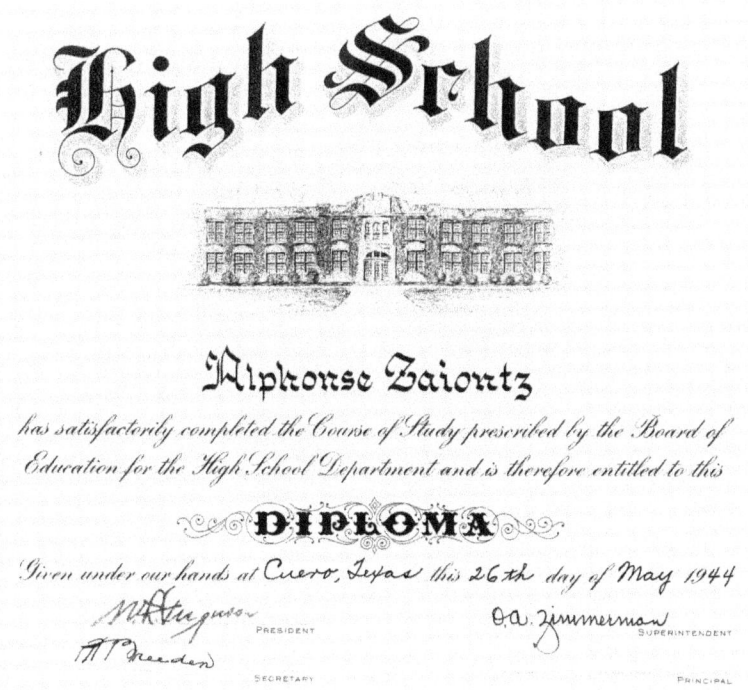

Alphonse's high school diploma

probably led him astray many times. He and I used to jump off the second story porch in Panna Maria. Actually the ground was only about six or eight feet from where we climbed the railing and jumped to level ground. Claude is three years younger than I but even at this early age was already smarter that I was. He used the pillar to launch himself from a slightly lower, and therefore, less dangerous position before he jumped. Mother always feared we would break a leg, arm, or worse, but we never did. She was also concerned when we wrestled each other. Nevertheless, we survived our childhoods mostly unscathed.

Claude is a veteran of the US Air Force. When his enlistment period was up, he was honorably discharged from the Air Force just as the Korean War was ramping up in 1950. The Air Force had sent him to several aircraft maintenance and mechanical schools. In 1947, he served as a crew chief for an F-80 Shooting Star. Claude was one of the first jet engine mechanics in the USAF, ending his enlistment

---

[15] On Sept. 8, 1941, three months before the Japanese attacked Pearl Harbor, the Texas Department of Education put in place new requirements for graduation from high school. Students had to complete twelve grades instead of eleven.

Claude Zaiontz

Claude, ca. 1950

as a sergeant.

Claude was contemplating re-enlistment, but, wanting to make the best choice, investigated his alternatives. As he had no means of transportation, he asked me if I could take him to places where he could apply for jobs. Claude applied at Slick Airways, an air freight carrier, Alcoa Aluminum, and Dupont Chemical. Because of his excellent training, as listed on his applications, he was offered positions at all three companies on the same day. He chose Slick Airways because the work there was more in line with what he wanted to do: aircraft maintenance.

Claude worked at Slick Airways as a lead mechanic until 1958 when the company moved from San Antonio to California. Opting to stay in San Antonio, he then went to work for Howard Aero as an accessories[16] mechanic. Claude worked his way up to accessories foreman. In 1964, when Howard Aero was sold to Business Aircraft Company, Claude switched employment to Gary Aircraft Company as their accessory shop foreman.

When Gary Aircraft Company moved to Hondo, Texas, Claude started his own accessory business. In the early years, Claude's company had two full-time employees besides himself: Bob Hay and Eugene (Red) Harlos. They were both very competent accessory repairmen. While I held a full-time job at the post office at night, I worked for Claude two afternoons a week, doing payroll and other office work. During these early years, Claude worked twelve to fifteen hours a day, including weekends. Later, when I got a job as a substitute teacher with

---

[16] Aircraft accessories are the pumps and many other components that constitute the many subsystems in an aircraft.

the San Antonio Independent School District two or three days a week, I left my job at Claude's business.

In 1966, he incorporated the company as the Zee Company, Inc. Dee Howard was in the aircraft refurbishing business at the time, renovating aircraft for large private and business aircraft owners. Claude made Dee Howard a full partner later in 1966 and gained his financial backing and access to additional equipment. Dee's own refurbishing company became Claude's best accessories customer.

In 1976, Claude bought out Dee's share of the Zee Company. Two years later, Claude started ZEE Systems, Inc. with two new partners. ZEE Systems was and still is separate from the Zee Company. ZEE Systems, Inc. manufactures air conditioner systems for aircraft. In 1988, Claude bought out his two partners. ZEE Systems is now operated by Claude's oldest son, Kevin.

ZEE Systems, Inc. has installed approximately 500 A/C units in twenty-five different types of aircraft. In addition to its commercial customers in the US, the Zee Company Inc. has had foreign aircraft customers and United States government contracts for its A/C components and accessories. Hard work, a focus on excellence, and a sense of fairness have resulted in growth and success for Claude's companies. As the 21st century began, the companies had twenty-five full-time employees and occupied three large buildings at 123 Braniff Drive in San Antonio, Texas.

Although he never attended college, Claude is an inspiration. Look what can be accomplished with discipline, determination and honest, careful hard work. Claude is past eighty now and still goes to his office every day and oversees the general operation of the Zee Company.

The worst tragedy that can befall a parent is the loss of a child. I have seen that sense of devastation hit my younger brother Claude and his wife Laurie twice. Their daughter Moira, nicknamed Buggy, died in an automobile accident in 1979. Then in 2001 another daughter, Lanie, committed suicide. Yet another daughter, Lorna, suffered the near drowning of her son in 1999. Now age 18, Claude's grandson, Lani Mejia, has been in a coma ever since. Claude, Laurie, and Lorna care for him at home. Claude often talks about his grandson Lani and says that he looks as if he is just sleeping and will wake up at any time.

OLDER BROTHER JOE

My older brother Joe was my mentor and my savior in many ways. He was seven and a half years older than I, and I always looked up to him. He could do things of which I could only dream.

About the time I started school in Panna Maria, Joe had antennas strung from the mesquite trees to our two-story barn and back again. He had a crystal radio purchased with his own money from working odd jobs. I did not understand how this radio worked, but from time to time Joe would hand me the earphones to listen. Depending on how he tuned the radio to the short-wave frequencies, people would be talking in different languages. When he wanted to change frequency, he just moved a wire that touched the crystal to a different part of the crystal. I was amazed.

Joe also had a single-shot .22-caliber rifle which he taught me to aim and shoot. Always the big brother and proper mentor, Joe taught me firearm safety as well. Once we found a dead armadillo and Joe showed me how .22 bullets bounced off the armadillo's "armor."

Joe, the athlete in the family, was quite gifted: football, baseball, track, gymnastics. There seemed to be no end to Joe's natural talents. I remember him demonstrating his gymnastics stunts. He performed cartwheels, back flips, and front flips, and walked on his hands. Mind you this was long before pep squads did these stunts while cheerleading. My athletic big brother was also the shortstop on the Panna Maria baseball team, which played on Sunday afternoons.

Joe's gift for athletics seemed to be endless. I remember watching him play tennis with his high school friends. They were coached by Jay Poth, the principal of Panna Maria High School. There were two tennis courts next to the narrow, two-story school building. I participated by shagging balls hit

Joe's high school records

off the court.

When the high school closed in the late 1930s, the hard surface of the tennis courts became an open air dining pavilion, including a roof that was added. Since those early days, the dining pavilion has been rebuilt twice. Each time the old tennis courts were the floor. Finally a cement floor was poured. Then air conditioning was added in about 2008 or 2009.

The high school building was where the new auction pavilion is now, next to the parish hall. The front was only about twenty feet wide and there were high wooden steps leading to the second floor classrooms, while the library was on the first floor.

Sadly, Joe was one of the last students attending Panna Maria High School. Apparently following the spring semester of 1935, the school closed and its students were absorbed into the high school in Karnes City, about five miles away. I obtained Joe's transcript from the Karnes City Independent School District. The front shows his courses completed and the back is a hand-written record of the seven and a half credits transferred from Panna Maria High.[17] What a shock this change of scholastic environment was to Joe. In Polish-speaking Panna Maria, Joe was a B and C student, second year Spanish being the exception. But in Karnes City it was all English and Joe's grades dropped a letter.

When Joe enrolled in Karnes City High School, he was taught to shower after physical exercise. We, of course, did not have a shower at home, so Joe decided to build one.

On the ground floor of our home was a room used for storage. There were a few wooden packing crates, which Joe opened and stacked to form walls for the shower. Nailing rubber from old inner tubes on the bottom of the lower crate provided a floor for the shower. So that it would drain, Joe drilled holes in the wooden floor. This shower was in the southwest part of the house which was three to four feet above the ground level with the ground sloping to the outside. Water from the shower drained nicely and never pooled under the house. As we had no running water in the house, Joe hung a pail with small holes in the bottom and placed a large tub which he could tilt to pour water into the pail. This made his shower. As far as I know, my father neither objected to this construction nor to the holes through the floor of the storage room.

When we moved from Panna Maria to Kenedy in 1932 or 1933, Joe stayed behind. To his credit, Dad allowed Joe to live with Uncle Felix and remain with

---

[17] Few of the older residents of Panna Maria even remember there ever being a high school there. I found mention of it in the *Centennial History of Panna Maria 1854-1954*, but no real substantive information, history, or pictures of it.

36 ONLY ONE POLLACK

all of his high school friends in Panna Maria, attending school there, then later in Karnes City. Joe's best friends were Justin Johnson,[18] Ben Gawlick, Joe Kyrish, and Robert "Rap" Kaczmarek, who was several years older. Robert earned the nickname "Rap" because he seemed to always be able to deliver a hit, or rap, when the Panna Maria baseball team most needed one.

There was a New Year's Eve tradition in Panna Maria that something outrageous would occur. When we went to church one New Year's Day—for Catholics this was a holy day of obligation—the congregation discovered a Ford Model T automobile sitting atop the porch roof of Uncle Felix's store. After the great laugh, everyone marveled and wondered how this could have been accomplished. I listened to all of the speculations and it was suggested that my brother Joe and his friends were involved. But Joe was mum and never admitted or denied his involvement.

While we lived in Kenedy, we saw Joe every Sunday when we attended Mass in Panna Maria. (My father is listed in records as a parishioner in Panna Maria until 1937.) When we later moved to Beeville, we were only able to see Joe about once a month. The distance was now about forty miles instead of merely the ten miles from Kenedy.

After graduating from Karnes City High School in May 1937, Joe enlisted in the United States Navy. He had several friends who were already in the Navy, including his high school friend Justin. Joe enlisted for four years and after basic training in San Diego, California, was assigned to a destroyer[19] based at Pearl Harbor. Joe came home on leave twice during his enlistment period and told us all about his adventures in the Pacific and of all the countries he had visited.

When his enlistment was up, Joe was discharged and came home. He was considering going to work for the post office as a route carrier. But clouds of

Joseph Peter Zaiontz

war hung over our country and the draft[20] was in full swing. After only a month at home he decided to reenlist in the Navy. This time he was sent to the east coast to await the commissioning of a new destroyer. In the meantime, he went on training cruises, spending a lot of time visiting Maine on these cruises. In one letter home, Joe said Maine was beautiful and that he would like to live there someday.

While not yet at war, the United States was allied with Great Britain and many other countries against Germany, Italy, and their allies. We should not forget that in 1941, Great Britain and her allies had already been at war for two years. Lend-Lease[21] was in full swing. The British and their allies were suffering

---

[18] Justin Johnson's brother was Lambert Johnson who married Helen Yosko. Helen was a sister of my Aunt Ella Yosko Snoga, Uncle Felix's wife.

[19] Destroyer - a fast and maneuverable yet long-endurance warship intended to escort larger vessels and defend them against small attackers such as submarines.

[20] Draft - to select and draw from a group for some unusually compulsory assignment such as military service.

[21] Lend-Lease was an aid program during World War II through which the United States provided food, munitions, and other materials to countries whose defense against Germany and Italy was necessary to the United States, according to the Lend-Lease Act passed on March 11, 1941.

USS Ingraham destroyer

horrendous losses, many of which were due to Germany's U-boats (submarines). A victorious outcome of the war was in grave doubt.

Then on December 7, 1941, Pearl Harbor was attacked by Japan, an ally of Germany. War was declared the next day against Japan, Germany, and all who were allied with them. On December 8 when we declared war, the United States of America was in dire straits, as were our allies. Germany was winning in Europe, Africa, Russia, and at sea with its U-boats. In the Pacific Japan invaded the Philippines and other countries and spread its influence across the entire Pacific. Our Pacific fleet was in shambles as a result of the attack on Pearl Harbor and, undoubtedly, Japan had the strongest navy in the world at the time.

I remember my mother and father being very happy that Joe was not at Pearl Harbor when it was attacked. Joe's destroyer, the *USS Ingraham*, was commissioned late in 1941, just before Pearl Harbor, being immediately put in service on convoy[22] duty delivering war supplies to our European allies. The Ingraham made several crossings with Joe aboard, escorting convoys to England.

After the draft was instituted in 1940, a great number of new recruits came into the navy and the other services. Joe was considered an "old salt." Promotions came fast for those having previous service.

By August 1942, he was a petty officer first class, a rank of considerable responsibility just below that of chief petty officer.

After the American declaration of war, Germany did not waste any time shifting a great number of its U-boats into American waters. From January 11, 1942, to August 13, 1942, U-boats sank 259 ships off the US mainland and in the Gulf of Mexico. There was a tremendous loss of life and materials. Against these losses, Germany suffered relatively minor losses: seven U-boats and 300 men.

In late August 1942, the USS Ingraham, eight other US destroyers, a battleship[23] and a heavy cruiser[24] were escorting seven troop ships to Great Britain. The convoy was given the code name AT-20, escorted by Task Force 37. At this time in the war, none of the war ships in Task Force 37 were equipped with radar[25] but all were equipped with sonar.[26] Ordinarily battleships and heavy cruisers were not assigned to convoy duty; however, they were equipped with floatplanes.[27] These aircraft could be used to scout for enemy submarines and therefore afforded the troop ships a greater level of protection.

At 2200 hours (10 P.M.) on August 22, 1942, fog descended on the convoy. It was described as nasty and cotton thick. All ships in the convoy were capable of at least 15 knots,[28] but the commander was forced to slow the convoy.

---

[22] Convoy - A number of ships grouped together for mutual support and protection. The US Navy provided additional protection with accompanying war ships.

[23] Battleship - the largest of warships with the heaviest caliber guns firing shells twelve to eighteen inches in diameter. Battleships were larger and better armed than cruisers and destroyers.

[24] Heavy cruiser - a warship many times larger and much less maneuverable than a destroyer but smaller than a battleship. Its largest guns were of eight-inch caliber.

[25] Radar - a method of detecting distant objects and determining their position, velocity, and other characteristics by analysis of very high frequency radio waves reflected from their surfaces. Radar was not only beneficial in locating enemy ships but also tracking friendly craft.

[26] Sonar - a system using transmitted and reflected acoustic waves to detect and locate submerged objects such as submarines.

[27] Floatplane - a type of seaplane with slender pontoons for landing on the water. In the early years of World War II battleships typically carried four floatplanes while cruisers carried one or two. They were launched from catapults and, after landing on the sea, recovered by cranes.

[28] Knot - a unit of speed equal to one nautical mile per hour, approximately 1.151 statute miles per hour.

In this photo of the USS Ingraham's crew, the officers are seated. Behind the officers the chief petty officers are standing, wearing visored caps. Behind them are the first class petty officers. My brother Joe is the fifth one from the left, standing between two chiefs.

In this fog and without radar, the destroyer *USS Buck* collided with the troop ship SS Awatea. A 300-pound depth charge[29] exploded, damaging Buck's propeller. Buck was helpless in the water but still afloat. There were many casualties. The *USS Ingraham* was ordered to investigate the collision and pick up survivors. The Ingraham itself then collided with the Navy oiler[30] *USS Chemung*. The *USS Ingraham* was lying on its side when a tremendous explosion ripped the ship. Presumably the powder magazine had exploded. There was no time to give the order to abandon ship. According to later eyewitness accounts, as the *USS Ingraham* was sinking, its depth charges exploded.

Of the Ingraham's crew of about 260, there were only eleven survivors—nine enlisted men and two officers. Twenty-three-year-old Petty Officer First Class Joseph Peter Zaiontz of Panna Maria, Texas, was not among the survivors.

On August 24, 1942, my mother and father received the dreaded telegram that Joe was "missing in action."

It was unbelievably hard on my parents. We all went to Panna Maria to notify our relatives. Uncle Felix and Aunt Ella took the news especially hard because Joe had lived with them for four or five years. I was sixteen. To me it was a heart-wrenching loss that seemed to drive the breath from me. I just wanted to be by myself so I left everyone and went to Uncle Felix's store, which he had closed, and sat on the sidewalk for hours, overwrought that the war with Germany had taken the life of my brother. I seethed for revenge. My first step was to get into the military and extract payment from the Germans. Boy! Was I naive at the age of sixteen.

What happened to our family was repeated some 250 times as telegrams went out for every lost member of the Ingraham's crew. Almost the entire crew had perished. Yet, there was no mention of this in the press, except that the destroyer *USS Ingraham* had been lost. Although the sinking of the *USS Ingraham* was not a direct result of the German U-boat campaign, it was an indirect result of it. The *USS Ingraham* would not have been in that situation otherwise. (Walter and Lucy did not actually learn the details, circumstances, and full magnitude of the disaster until sometime after the end of the war.)

It was especially heart-wrenching to receive a telegram with the status of missing in action. My mother held out hope that Joe was still alive until the day she died in 1985. One time in the 1950s, she claimed she saw Joe on television. It was a news story about how American sailors were captured by Russians and they were going to be released. She asked me to find out more about this news story.

At the height of World War II, there were 16,000,000 men and women wearing uniforms of the United States. There were well over 400,000 deaths, reaching every corner of America. Staggering

---

[29] Depth charge - an anti-submarine warfare weapon designed to explode under water at a preset depth and destroy or cripple a targeted submarine by the shock of the explosion. Depth charges were launched from a destroyer deck and used against submarines located by sonar.

[30] Oiler - a combat logistics ship that replenished other ships with fuel, and perhaps other supplies, while at sea.

JOE ZAIONTZ MISSING NAVY REPORT SAYS

Cuero Boy Serving Second Enlistment Unaccounted For

FATHER IS HOPEFUL

Walter Zaiontz, Cudahy Shift Foreman, Believes Son Is Alive

Joseph Peter Zaiontz, son of Mr. and Mrs. Walter A. Zaiontz, 407 E. Morgan Avenue, is missing in action with the United States Navy, the navy department has notified his parents in this city.

Zaiontz, who was 23 years of age February 23, was born in 1919 while his father was serving in France in World War No. 1. He was with the American Navy in the Atlantic and was serving his second enlistment which he began on May 24, 1941. He holds the rate of Coxswain.

Mr. Zaiontz, who has been a resident of Cuero for more than four years and is a shift foreman at the Egg Drying Plant of the Cudahy Packing Company, held high hope today that his son may still be alive and that he has been picked up by some outside vessel. Details are lacking and Zaiontz was requested not to divulge the name of his son's ship or its location in the telegram received from the navy department.

Following is the wording of the telegram reaching Zaiontz.

The Navy Department deeply regrets to inform you that your son, Joseph Peter, Coxswain U. S. Navy is missing in the performance of his duty and the service of his country. The Department appreciates your great anxiety but details are not now available and delay in receipt thereof must necessarily be expected. To prevent possible aid to our enemies please do not divulge the name of his ship or station."

Although he was serving his first enlistment in the Navy when his father moved to Cuero in 1938 young Zaiontz spent nearly two months at his parents home here prior to his re-enlistment last year.

Left: East Coast Memorial in Battery Park

Below: Sharon Keller beside Joe's name on East Coast Memorial

numbers of our service personnel were wounded. Some still suffer today. We must never forget the sacrifices made by these heroes and their families. We must never forget the sacrifices made during World War II nor any of the other conflicts of our history. We owe a debt that can never be repaid. Our country is free because of those who have served it. Freedom is not free.

Today, the men who lost their lives in the Atlantic during World War II are memorialized in New York City at the East Coast Memorial in Battery Park. Battery Park is the departure point for boats leaving for the Statue of Liberty. In 2007 my youngest daughter Sharon Keller and her family visited Battery Park. At the base of the eagle laying a wreath, a black granite slab holds this inscription:

1941-1945
*

ERECTED BY THE UNITED STATES OF AMERICA
IN PROUD AND GRATEFUL REMEMBRANCE
OF HER SONS
WHO GAVE THEIR LIVES IN HER SERVICE
AND WHO SLEEP IN THE AMERICAN COASTAL
WATERS
OF THE ATLANTIC OCEAN
*

INTO THY HANDS O LORD

If you are ever in New York, be sure to go to Battery Park to see this memorial.

My younger brother Claude and I greatly regret that our collective thirteen children never knew their Uncle Joe. He would have been a truly great uncle.

Parents suffering the loss of a child: Claude and I witnessed that wrenching shock to our parents when our older brother Joe was lost at sea. Walter, Lucy, Claude and Laurie all suffered this terrible kind of loss. How fortunate my wife Mary and I have been. We still have all five of our children, all five of our grandchildren, and all eight of our great-grandchildren, and four step-great-grandchildren.

Alphonse in the Middle

Chapter 3
SCHOOL YEARS IN CUERO AND SUMMERS ON THE FARM

Cuero, Texas, is the origin of the famous Chisholm Trail. From April to October of 1866, Thornton Chisholm drove 1,800 head of cattle from near what is now Cuero to St. Joseph, Missouri, for Crockett Cardwell, a wealthy merchant, rancher, and entrepreneur living north of the present town site. *Cuero* is Spanish for leather made from animal hides, an early local industry, for which the town was named in 1873.

Cuero is where I did most of my growing up. Our route to get there was circuitous. From the time my father was discharged from the army in 1919, he worked odd jobs, farmed a little, and worked for my grandfather Frank Snoga in his grocery store in Panna Maria. Dad took over the store in 1928. At that time, it was customary to give farmers credit against their groceries—sometimes for a year or longer. Then, when the farmers sold their crops, they paid off their debts. But during the early 1930s there was a terrible drought that lasted for a couple of years. Crops failed and the farmers could not pay dad what they owed him. He, in turn, could not pay his debts. Many of the farmers tried to give him land in exchange for what they owed him. But he said no because he could not have paid the taxes on the land, so he would still go bankrupt. My father would say in his later years that he could have owned half of Karnes County. (Oh! what a missed opportunity! Today the Eagle Ford oil and gas boom is going full swing in Karnes County and the surrounding counties. The standard lease rate for an acre of land is $1,500 for three years and prime acreage is leasing for $10,000 for three years.)

So, in 1931, Dad declared bankruptcy and went to work for the Cudahy Packing Company in Kenedy as a turkey buyer. Every farmer raised a few turkeys as a side cash crop. Cudahy was a nationwide meat packing company with headquarters in Des Moines, Iowa. Dad bought turkeys from the same farmers who were his customers when he ran the store. He drove a big truck, picked up the turkeys, and delivered them to the Cudahy plant in Kenedy.

Late in 1932, he was transferred to the Cudahy plant in Beeville as a truck driver. He drove all over the middle and southern United States, being gone sometimes as long as two weeks. I remember lying in bed at night thinking that with Joe in the navy, I would be the man of the house if anything happened to Dad. As far as I know, my father never had a vehicle accident until after he retired. And then it was a minor one.

He continued driving when he was transferred back to Kenedy in 1935. In 1938 he was transferred to the Cudahy plant in Cuero and promoted to shift foreman. He stayed with Cudahy in Cuero until he retired in 1959. Social Security did not pay him enough to live on, so he worked part-time as an attendant at several auto service stations. Later he worked at Merchants Storage and Mission Provision Company in San Antonio and lived with my wife and me for a while, going home to Cuero on the weekends.

So the family arrived in Cuero in the summer of 1938, whereupon our state of affairs ameliorated immediately. We were accepted into the neighborhood, church, school, and the entire community very quickly. This is not to imply that we were not accepted in Kenedy, Beeville, and again in Kenedy, but in those places it took more time than it did in Cuero.

First we rented a house at 407 Morgan Avenue. There were two huge hackberry trees in front, each with a circumference of at least ten feet. The trees had been topped, but I do not know why. The house was owned by a Mr. Dreyer, who owned a dry goods (clothing) store called The Fair. It was located at Main and Esplanade streets in the center of the business district. Our rent was $18 per month, which does not sound like much, but my father was earning only $25 per week even with the new promotion.

Mother and Father purchased a Servil Electrolux refrigerator, which ran on natural gas. They had first bought one, while in Kenedy, that mother really loved, so wherever we moved, Mother always insisted on the same make. Many people like one of our new neighbors, Mrs. Schmidt, did not want the newfangled gadgets and preferred an icebox. The top compartment of an icebox held a fifteen- to twenty-five-pound block of ice. From this compartment the cold would flow down to the lower portions of the icebox where the food was stored. Once or twice a week, an ice man would deliver the ice. This was only feasible in town because of the delivery costs. I always wondered how Mom's refrigerator could get so cold from burning natural gas.

Our landlord, Mr. Dreyer, lived only about a block from us in a huge, two-story house on the corner of Morgan Avenue and Stockdale Avenue. Mr. Dreyer wanted to sell us the rental house for $2,000. He said Dad could pay it off like rent but Dad declined because he did not want to be tied down in case we needed to move again.

Our house was about four blocks from the middle of downtown, which was very fortunate because we could walk to downtown for all of our needs. The house had two bedrooms with a bathroom in between. Claude and I shared one bedroom and my parents had the other. Our new home also had a big living room, a dining room, a large kitchen, and a big back yard. There was electricity in Cuero and we had a radio, but it was a source of news, not entertainment.

Neighbors living in the same block were a widow, Mrs. Schmidt, and her daughter Margaret, who was a senior in high school, and a Miss Marshall, who was an eighty-year-old spinster. There were only three houses and two garages in this entire block. We understood that Miss Marshall had owned a millinery shop in downtown Cuero. She had closed her shop several years before, but had a lot of hats left over. She occasionally wore these hats, which were very colorful.

Morgan Avenue was at least sixty feet wide. There was an alley between our house and the large two-story house in which a retired doctor, Dr. Grunder, lived. Directly across Morgan Avenue from us lived the Simons. Rollie Simon was one of Claude's friends as was Jimmie Grunder—no relation to Dr. Grunder.

I also had good friends in Cuero, but none of them lived close to us. Two of them were Edward J. (E.J.) Fuchs and Blas Hernandez. E. J. was a year older than I and lived four or five blocks north of the high school while Blas lived on the west side of town.

St. Michael's Church and School were less than five blocks from our house and within easy walking distance. Father William Jansen, from Holland, was the priest in charge of both the church and the school. I entered the sixth grade there. I remember the sixth and seventh grade, with nuns for teachers, as being my best years, undoubtedly due to Sally Sweiger's tutoring back in Beeville.

During recess, we played softball. There was a ten-foot-high fence about five or six feet beyond second base. The fence truncated the field so anyone hitting a fair ball over this fence and into the street had hit a home run. I got my share of home runs.

I grew in faith while attending St. Michael's and during the seventh grade was nominated for the Junior Holy Name Society.[31] We had eleven members and met once each month in the rectory. I was elected president! Father Jansen was our leader and spiritual advisor. I was also an altar boy at St. Michael's, helping the priests during masses.

For Christmas of 1938, at the responsible age of twelve, I received my first bicycle. Before then, Claude and I walked everywhere. I had my one and only accident while riding that bicycle. An elderly lady hit my bike when she severely cut the corner at an intersection near the fire station. Some of the firemen were outside and witnessed the accident. I was not hurt, just scared, and she agreed to pay all

---

[31] The Holy Name Society honors God and Jesus Christ. Its members are expected "to assist in parish ministries by performing the *Corporal Works of Mercy*: to feed the hungry, to clothe the naked, give drink to the thirsty, shelter to the homeless, tend the sick, visit those in prison, and bury the dead; as well as the *Spiritual Works of Mercy*, to convert sinners, instruct the ignorant, counsel the wayward, comfort the sorrowing, bear adversity patiently, forgive offenses, and pray for the living and the dead." [From the Mission Statement of the National Holy Name Society]

Because its members must be eighteen or older, many Catholic churches introduced a Junior Holy Name Society for younger people. With adult leadership, the members are encouraged to organize both spiritual and service projects. They are expected to be role models in their schools and must be recommended and endorsed in order to join.

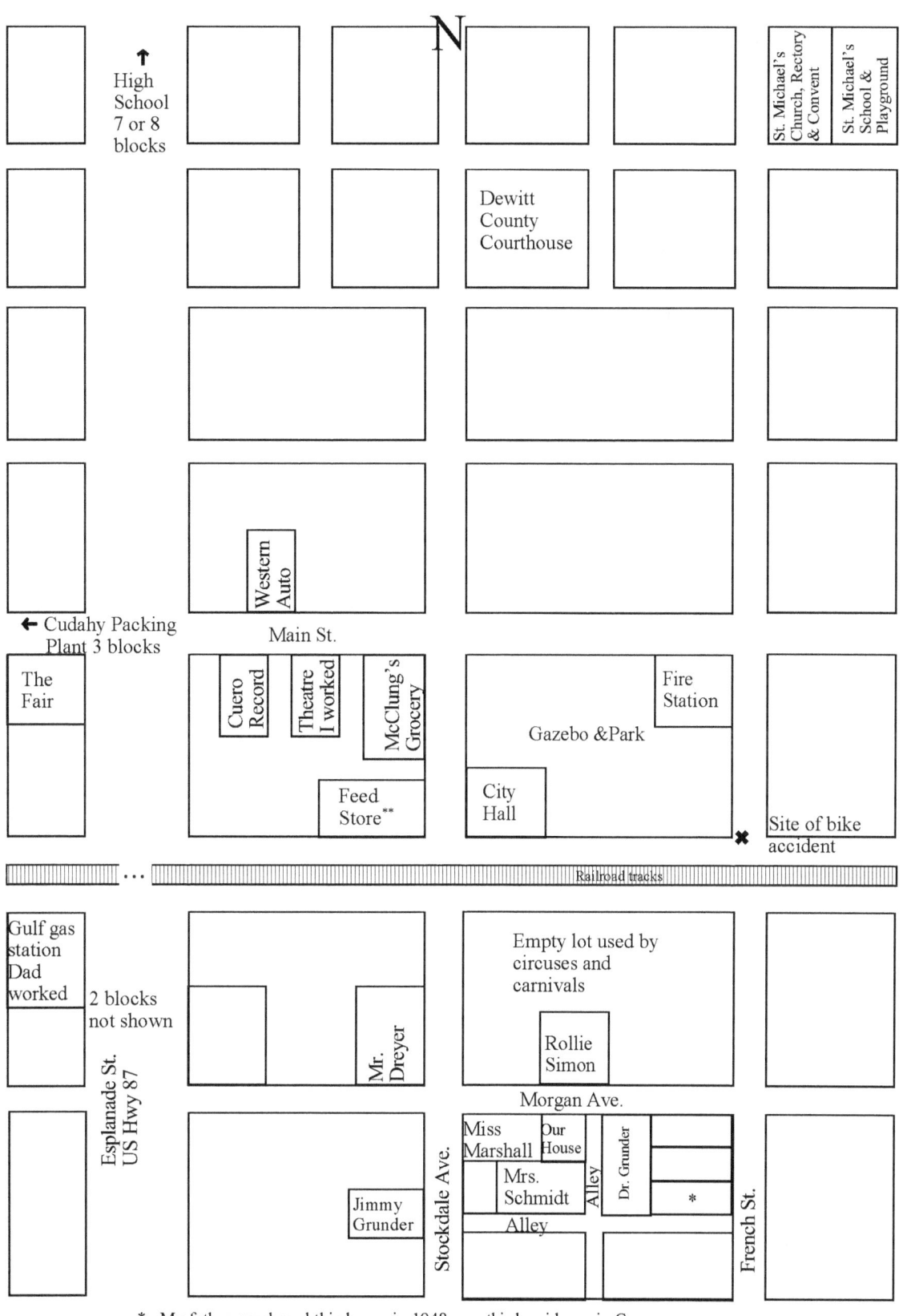

* My father purchased this house in 1948, our third residence in Cuero.
** The Feed Store bought our extra eggs.

the costs to repair my bike. The front wheel was bent ninety degrees. The firemen took my bike to Western Auto, where my bike had been purchased. When it was ready, the lady paid the bill and it was as good as new.

My friend E.J. was working at the weekly newspaper, the *Cuero Record*, as a type setter, and he arranged a paper route for me. It was several miles long. Every Thursday morning before school, I delivered about fifty papers for which I was paid $1. Our parents never gave us spending money or an allowance; rather, Claude and I were expected to earn it ourselves.

Every Saturday, I worked about three hours for Mrs. Schmidt at odd jobs like pulling weeds for which she paid me 15¢. Back then, 15¢ paid for my movie ticket (9¢) and a bag of popcorn. The movies were always westerns supplemented by a weekly chapter of *Flash Gordon*. I usually stayed to watch everything at least twice. Life was good.

About a year later, E.J. enlisted my help with the popcorn machine at the movie theater, and I was required to have a health card from the doctor to show I had no communicable disease. I worked one day a week for six to eight hours for 50¢ and never even got to watch a movie or eat any of the popcorn. This job meant standing at the machine the entire day. Now, when you stand in one place for very long periods, your feet begin to hurt. Really hurt! Right then, in my very early teens, I learned that I did not ever want another job requiring me to stand in one place for hours.

Claude and I also helped deliver the *Houston Chronicle* newspaper every Sunday morning, working with a Mr. Laake, who owned the *Houston Chronicle* franchise in Cuero. Mr. Laake owned a car. Claude rode inside with him and rolled the papers while I rode on the running board throwing the papers. We had to pick up the papers at the Greyhound bus station at midnight and deliver them right away. I threw about 100 papers in all areas of Cuero. One Sunday morning the temperature was below freezing and I got a touch of frostbite on my toes. I remember Mother warming my feet afterwards. She heated a pan of water so I could put my feet in to help thaw them. (Amazingly, this is the same treatment used today for minor frostbite.) It was a big-time job, picking up the papers at midnight, riding that running board in all weather conditions, and a hundred pitches—all right over the plate, of course—for $1 a week.

To my lifelong delight, the genes of my ancestor farmers became evident when, just before entering high school, I developed a love of working the soil and watching plants grow. I asked Mrs. Schmidt if I could use a small plot on her land behind our house for a little garden. She gave her permission and I used a spading fork to turn over the soil. Then I planted three rows of corn, each row about ten feet long, and a few squash. Practical me, I selected corn and squash primarily because their seeds were readily available and nothing else was to be had. Never did I plant tomatoes or cucumbers because my Dad knew some farmers from whom we got abundant tomatoes and cucumbers every spring, canning eight to a hundred quarts of each to last all year.

My corn grew six to eight feet tall with two or three ears per stalk and sometimes four. Occasionally people stopped and looked over the fence and marveled at how tall and green my corn grew. I had a secret I never told anyone: When Mrs. Schmidt's husband was alive he kept eight to ten horses on this property. After he died, Mrs. Schmidt had several cows in that pen. My corn and squash were properly fertilized. Manure. Nature's fertilizer. Happy vegetables.

Mrs. Schmidt, a Lutheran, and my mother, a Catholic, became good friends. She gave us milk and butter and we gave her eggs and chickens. My mother and father raised laying hens and fryers in the back yard. Sometimes some of our chickens got into Miss Marshall's yard next door, which always aggravated her. Mrs. Schmidt also had several huge pecan trees in the area. We would thrash these trees for her and pick up the pecans in exchange for half of them.

Claude and I were quite fortunate growing up, in that we had lots of family close by and were able to interact frequently with all of our first cousins, plenty of them—about thirty-five. It seems that every weekend we visited family. If no one drove to Cuero, we drove to visit someone. We usually made

SNOGA COUSINS

Peter Snoga & Gerturde Urbanczyk	Lucy Snoga & Walter Zaiontz	Pella Snoga & Anton Urbanczyk	Felix Snoga & Ella Yosko	Brigid Snoga & Leon Gwosdz
Sally †	Joseph †	Lucian	Ivan	Emmanuel †
Lucy †	Adrian	Ermit †	Elsie Jane (Bootsie)	Evelyn
Alvin	Claude	Andrew (Jack)	Anna (Hannah)	Leon (Gene)
Gladys †		Adeline	Bertille (Deka)	Patricia †
Emil †		Frank		Clarence †
Bennie		Patricia		Virginia
Mary		Anton Jr.		Mary Elizabeth
Peter				Kathleen

ZAIONTZ COUSINS

Sally Zaiontz & Felix Moczygemba	Ignatz Zaiontz & Anna Ramzinski	Onufry Zaiontz (batchelor)	Otilia Zaiontz & James Hannah	Clement Zaiontz & Fern Morse	Helidor Zaiontz & Clara Williams
(We had no contact)	Sophie		Proxie	(In Army, married later)	Roberta Lee †
Clara †			Albina (Beanie)	Frances	
Theodore †			Victor	Loretta	
Lottie †			Frances	and perhaps	
Alex †			Silvern	others	
Vincent †			Ralph †		
Florien †					
Victor †					
Isabel †					
Elizabeth †					
Walter †					

† Deceased

arrangements, by mail or word of mouth, weeks or months in advance, scheduling when we would visit or when we would be home to have visitors.

We would go to Panna Maria where Uncle Pete Snoga and Uncle Felix Snoga and their families lived. Uncle Pete and his family lived in our old two-story house. Uncle Felix lived next door. Uncle Anton and Aunt Pella Urbanczyk and their family lived in the country twelve miles farther north towards San Antonio, between Kosciusko and Poth. In the other direction, about fifty miles east from Cuero towards Houston, Uncle Leon and Aunt Brigid Gwosdz and their family lived in the country close to Edna, Texas. Occasionally we went to San Antonio, where my father's brother, Uncle Ignatz, and his sister, Aunt Tillie, lived with their families. Uncle Clem Zaiontz served in the Army for thirty years, at times stationed in Colorado. Uncle Unofrey was a bachelor living in the Continental Hotel close to Santa Rosa Hospital in San Antonio. Uncle Hilly Zaiontz had no children at this time and we had no contact with Aunt Sally.

School Years in Cuero and Summers on the Farm

SUMMERS ON UNCLE ANTON URBANCZYK'S FARM

Previously, I had generally spent my summers working in Uncle Felix's store in Panna Maria. (Felix had taken over Snoga's grocery store when my father went bankrupt.) Felix also had a farm where I helped when I was twelve. When I turned thirteen, I started helping on Uncle Anton's farm and continued to do so until I was sixteen. (Anton Urbanczyk was married to my mother's sister, Pelagia [Pella].)

Uncle Anton and Aunt Pella had three sons about my age. Lucian was two years older than I, Ermit was a little younger than I, and Andrew was about Claude's age. His oldest daughter, Adeline, was just a few years younger still. There were other children as well, but they were much younger.

Andrew was never called by his given name. Even today we all know him as "Jack." Sometime before moving to Cuero, while visiting Uncle Anton's, our departure was delayed until Monday morning. Uncle Anton was plowing his fields with his mules, who he constantly coaxed by hollering and even cursing. The lead mule was named Jack, and was exceedingly stubborn. "Jack," being shouted along with other words, was heard frequently. Uncle Anton's third son, Andrew, was also very stubborn when he was little. So Uncle Anton started calling him "Jack" and the name stuck. Just as my middle name Alphonse stuck to me, after a while everyone sort of forgot that Andrew's real name was not Jack. During the latest Snoga reunion, I asked Jack if he knew where he got his name. He answered, "Dad must have told everybody that story."

During those summers with the Urbanczyks, I was just one of their family, treated as another of Anton's sons. I was expected to work and pull my weight like one of his boys. I picked cotton, shook out peanuts, harvested corn, fed cattle, cut pigweed[32] for the pigs, cut sugar cane, milked cows, and did a myriad of other jobs that kept the farm profitable. But we found time for recreation. Ermit and Lucian would ride the calves that were penned up—no saddles, bare back. If they wanted to make the calves buck, as in the rodeo, they would grab the calf's tail and twist it. That would make them buck and it would be great fun, if you could stay on. When bucked off, they would shake off the pain and climb back on. As for this particular form of juvenile entertainment, I had better sense. I never rode a calf. Uncle Anton would have been quite angry if he had known of such treatment of his calves.

The boys also had a pony. We saddled the pony and took turns riding it, pretending to be cowboys on the open range. One time I rode this pony to a neighbor's farm about a mile away. I said "hello" to the neighbor. Then as I was leaving, a big dog jumped from behind a tree and scared the pony and off we went! I barely managed to hang on but finally settled the pony down. If I had been dumped, we could have spent a very long time finding him.

Another time, Ermit and I were riding that pony double in the pasture when the pony bucked and threw us both into some cacti. Perhaps the pony thought it had seen a snake, I don't know, but we were both picking cactus needles from our back sides for at least two weeks. Some were so tiny as to be almost impossible to see and would only be detected when the protruding ends rubbed against clothing. Requiring help with their removal was extremely embarrassing for a self-conscious teenager.

Some Sunday afternoons were spent swimming at our favorite places in the San Antonio River, Cibolo Creek, or Marcelinas Creek. None of our favorite swimming holes were near Panna Maria because the banks of the San Antonio River there were ten feet high and hard to climb. There were places where we swam that the water was eight to ten feet deep. Occasionally the sons of one of Uncle Anton's neighbors, Emil and George Dziuk, went with us. The Dziuks lived about two miles east of Uncle Anton. Of course we had no swimming trunks, so we played and swam naked. There was a rope tied to a limb of a huge tree. This swing took us out over the deepest part of the river where we dropped into the water. I could swim, having learned at the Cuero Municipal Park swimming pool. I discovered that if I filled my lungs with air and held my breath, it was impossible to sink.

---

[32] Pigweed is a quite formidable weed. It can grow up to three inches a day, and at its base it can be as thick as a baseball bat.

Many evenings we played cards by lamplight. Pinochle or double pinochle—played with two pinochle decks—was our favorite game. Cousin Lucian was a whiz. He could remember which cards had been played five or six hands before. Guess who usually won. There was no electricity at the farm so we had no TV, no computers, no electronic games. (It took the REA a long time to get electricity to the rural farm areas, but I do remember them having it shortly before World War II.) As a consequence, when we had time to play during daylight hours, we played outside and we played hard. Sometimes we wrestled; sometimes we played baseball; sometimes we hunted.

Across the county road from Uncle Anton's property was a huge pasture. Lucian and Ermit called it McDonald's Pasture and said it contained at least 10,000 acres. Lucian, Ermit, and Jack made extra money by trapping and killing small animals such as raccoons, badgers, opossums, and even skunks, but not rabbits. They skinned these animals and stretched and nailed the pelts to a board. They sold these for a dollar. A good pelt, especially without any bullet holes, brought more, as much as $1.50.

I hunted on McDonald's Pasture with them several times. As far as I know, they never asked for permission. Each of my cousins was armed with a .22 caliber rifle and I used a 20 gauge shotgun. The boys' dogs went with us and when the dogs found an animal burrow, we dug the animal out. If it turned out to be a skunk we had to be extra careful and just let the dogs do their job. Amazingly we never got lost in this huge pasture, even though we walked for miles.

When we hunted at night, each of us carried a carbide lantern, food, water, guns, ammunition, and a shovel. Leaving at dark, we stayed out until after midnight. When we shined the carbide lights into the trees, if an animal was there, light was reflected back from its eyes. This gave away its location and one of my cousins would shoot a .22 bullet between the shining eyes.

A good source of extra meat in the late 1930s and early 1940s was jack rabbits. If you shot a jack rabbit, it was either young and good or old and very tough. If it was old, you could not eat it unless you ground the meat and made chili out of it. One summer morning, I decided to go and get us a jack rabbit or two. I arose before others, fetched the 20 gauge shotgun and slipped into a nearby cotton field where I had seen jack rabbits. Sure enough a few minutes later I saw movement in the cotton bushes, perhaps fifteen to twenty yards ahead. I aimed and fired, then ran to get my jack rabbit. To my shock, I found a dead grey and white cat. The cat had been stalking something when I shot it.

My cousins heard the blast from the shotgun. I never told anyone that I had killed a cat, but instead I said that I missed the jack rabbit. Luckily for me, the cat did not belong to the Urbanczyks and, as for the neighbors, no one ever mentioned a missing cat. I learned my lesson: Never shoot unless you can clearly see your target and know exactly at what you are shooting.

One day Jack took me aside to show me something. As he removed his right shoe I could see that his big toe was swelling terribly. He related that he had been carrying a semi-automatic .22 rifle with the barrel down. When he touched the .22 with his foot it went off. The bullet went through the shoe, through the fleshy part of his big toe and grazed the bone. It also did a little damage to his second toe. Jack swore me to secrecy because he did not want his parents to know. He said if his daddy knew about it, he would give him a whipping for the careless handling of a firearm, whereupon he would have pain in another part of his body as well. As far as I know, none of his brothers ever knew about this. I respected his wish even though I thought it was wrong for him not to seek help. I remember fearing that if he died, it would be my fault for not saying anything. He treated the wound himself with alcohol and bandages and apparently was successful. As far as I know, Jack never suffered any adverse effects. I asked Jack about this at the last Snoga reunion and he said that that gunshot wound was the most pain he had ever experienced in his entire life.

Uncle Anton leased several different pastures and many acres of grazing land for his cattle. Once he needed to move his cattle back home some three or four miles along the county road. The herd included about thirty cows, some with calves, and one big, mean bull. Uncle Anton, Lucian, Ermit, and I walked behind them for two or three hours and when we neared the farm, Uncle Anton directed me to run ahead and open the gate. I opened the gate, then boldly stood in the middle of the road to guide the cattle through the open gate. With the big bull leading the way, they did not need much guidance, but I made quite sure that every cow was herded through that gate. I was quite proud of myself until told that I had, unfortunately, opened the wrong gate. Uncle Anton had intended for me to open the second gate which was to the pasture. The first gate, the one which I had opened, led to his corn field—a nine-acre corn field—nine acres of corn almost ready for harvest and the entire herd of cows. Uh oh!

When those cows reached the corn, they thought they were in cow heaven! The four of us tried and tried to shoo them from the field, but to no avail. Uncle Anton finally decided to leave them alone because we were doing more damage to the corn than the cattle were. I knew he was very angry with me but he never said a word. I guess he realized that he never said to open the second gate and that I was just a dumb city kid from Cuero. As it turned out, getting them out of the corn field was really easy. The next morning all of the cattle were standing next to the pen where the water troughs were. Walking for hours down the road then gorging on corn had made them very, very thirsty.

Lucian and Ermit used to tease me constantly because I was a city kid and not very quick with farm chores. I could never pick cotton as fast as they could. No matter how hard I tried, I always had less in my cotton sack than they did. We weighed the cotton at lunch time and again in the late afternoon when we quit for the day. If they each had seventy or eighty pounds, I had sixty or less. The most I ever picked in a single day was 170 pounds and even this did not top their picking.

To me, picking cotton was the hardest job imaginable. The dreaded cotton boll had sharp ends on the bottoms. These ends would stick me in the cuticles of my finger nails to the point of making them bleed. One morning I decided yet again that I was going to pick more cotton than my cousins. I started early, at six instead of seven o'clock, while they were still eating breakfast. When I started the cotton had a little dew on it and was wet and consequently a little heavier. I also put some green cotton balls, a few dirt clods, and an occasional small rock into my sack. When it was time to weigh in, I still did not have as many pounds in my cotton sack as either Lucian or Ermit. Boy, what disappointment. Of course, my cousins were immune to cuticle soreness because their hands were toughened and the dried cotton balls had no effect on them.

There were other jobs on the farm that I disliked besides cotton picking. The number one dirtiest job was shaking out the peanuts. Uncle Anton usually had about a quarter of his fields in Spanish peanuts—also known as redskins. When they were ready for harvest, Uncle Anton plowed them up.[33] Then Lucian, Ermit, "Jack," and I, in teams of two, would go down each row, pick up the stalks, and shake the sand and dirt out of the peanuts. Next we stacked eight or ten stalks together, peanut side up. A few days in the hot Texas sun and raw peanuts were dried out, after which they could be separated from the stalks by a thrashing machine. This thrashing machine was contracted by Uncle Anton. The peanuts were then put in sacks and the stalks baled up like hay. This "hay" was used to feed the livestock during the winter months.

In the 1930s and early 1940s peanuts were graded by how many "pops" there were. The man doing the grading reached into the middle of each sack and pulled out one peanut. When he had gathered samples from ten sacks, he put each of the ten peanuts, one at a time, between his thumb and forefinger. He pressed them and each time he found one that was not full, he called it a pop. The percentage of pops from the sample set the price the farmer got for his crop.

---

[33] After pollination, the peanut flower stalk elongates, causing it to bend until the ovary touches the ground. Continued stalk growth pushes the ovary underground where the mature fruit develops into a legume pod, the peanut. Source wikipedia.org.

One evening after a long day's work and after supper, a heavy lightning and thunder storm started rolling in from the south. There were no weather reports back then, so this came as a big surprise to us. Uncle Anton shouted for all of us to get into the pickup and go with him to haul the fifty- to sixty-pound sacks of peanuts into the barn so they would not get wet. In fifteen minutes we made four or five trips moving over 100 sacks out of the rain to keep the peanuts from being ruined. Then we had a downpour. Perhaps an inch of rain fell in just the first ten minutes. We saved the peanut crop, but I was exhausted. I had never been so tired in my young life. I remember sleeping really well that night.

Another job that I hated immensely was cutting and stripping sugar cane for making molasses. Molasses was the main sweetener in those days. After going into the cane field and cutting the stalks, we had to strip the leaves from each stalk by hand. Sugar cane leaves are almost as sharp as razor blades. If you were not careful, you would be severely cut on the hands, arms, and even on the face. Working carefully while wearing gloves was a necessity.

After the sugar cane was cut and stripped, we loaded it on wagons and hauled it to a spot by Marcelinas Creek. A man owned a mule-powered sugar cane mill, which was set up at this location. Families from all around brought their sugar cane to this mill. The mule went around and around the mill turning a long arm attached to rollers in the middle of the mill, which crushed the sugar cane, extracting its sweet juice. The men took turns feeding two or three stalks at a time into the crushers. I remember feeling sorry for that mule because he never got to the end of his path. All day long, for family's after family's sugar cane, that mule plodded along, turning the arm that drove the mill that crushed the cane, two or three stalks at a time, wagon load after wagon load.

Once the juice was extracted, it was poured into kettles and cooked for several hours, the final result being molasses. The molasses was then divided up in proportion to how much sugar cane each family brought to the mill. Molasses time was fun time for all the children. The creek had a sand and gravel bottom and was very shallow here. We played in the water for hours while the menfolk fed the mill and the women fixed dinner and gossiped. This went on all day.

Another multiple family coalition was the butchering club. Rural homes had no refrigeration at the time so this association insured that everyone had fresh meat. If a family butchered a calf by themselves, a lot of the meat would spoil before it could be consumed. Six or seven families could, however, get together maybe every other Saturday and take turns providing a calf for butchering, then dividing it up. No family took the same portion of the calf twice in a row. A family would get a front quarter this time, a hind quarter next time, then perhaps organs like the heart, liver, and brains. No meat of any kind was wasted. While the men butchered and divided the calf, the children played or got haircuts. There was always someone there who cut hair. If you had a nickel or dime, you paid; if not, you got your hair cut for free.

Ice cream was a special treat when I was a boy. When Uncle Anton brought the Urbanczyk family to Cuero for a visit, he would go to the Guadalupe Valley Creamery and buy a five-gallon container of ice cream for $5. This was after dinner, of course, and everyone could eat all the ice cream they wanted. Mother had her refrigerator with a small freezer but there was rarely much left. No wonder Uncle Anton was my favorite uncle.

Guadalupe Valley Creamery ice cream was almost as good as the homemade ice cream we made when we visited the Urbanczyks. Homemade ice cream was a joint effort. Everyone took turns at the crank of the one-gallon home freezer. Adding rock salt to the ice to lower the freezing point made the liquid ice cream freeze faster, but still required about an hour of cranking. And the closer to freezing it came, the harder and harder the cranking got. And, with so many of us and being such big ice cream eaters, we made several gallons, one right after the other.

I was in Panna Maria one Saturday when a retired army colonel came to town. He owned some land, had a field of cotton that was ready to pick, and was trying to recruit pickers. He was willing to pay double the prevailing wage, which was about $1 per 100 pounds, but there was a catch. The reason his field workers would not pick his cotton was an infestation of black widow spiders. My cousin Gladys Snoga, after much discussion, recruited me, her brothers, and some friends to pick his field. It was not nearly so bad as everyone thought it might be. If you were careful, you could avoid the spiders. As far as I know no one was bitten. Later I learned that the spiders were more afraid of us than we were of them.

My cousins and I made our own fireworks for July 4 and other occasions. Using an empty can with a lid, such as from baking powder or coffee, we would pierce a small hole in the back with a nail then place calcium carbide crystals inside. Now calcium carbide reacts with water to produce flammable acetylene gas. So, we spit on the carbide, closed the lid tight and waited about thirty seconds for the gas inside the can to build up. Then we put a foot on top and pressed it down. Applying a lighted match or candle to the hole in the back of the can would ignite the gas causing an explosion like a large firecracker and sending the lid flying. Miraculously all feet stayed attached to legs, legs to torsos, and so forth on upward. Although we were never hurt, there were a lot of things which could have gone wrong with this homemade explosive. It would be best if this 1930s technology were forgotten and not revived by my great-grandchildren.

When our family visited Uncle Leon and Aunt Brigid in Edna we had different adventures. One of the most notable was when the irrigation canals had several feet of still water in them. Manuel, their oldest child, showed us how to catch crawfish—now called crayfish. You tie a tough string to the end of a pole or large stick, then tie a piece of bacon or meat to the other end of the string. Once a crawfish grabs the bait with its claws it will not release it even when pulled from the water. We had great fun catching the crawfish and putting them into a five-gallon bucket without getting our fingers pinched by the claws.

When we returned to the house, everyone marveled at the size of our catch. But, we did not know that they were good to eat. Cajuns in Louisiana eat them and now you can buy them in grocery stores and restaurants. But this was a different time and place. We did not know what to do with them. I said we should take them back and turn them loose, but the first canal was at least a half mile away and it was suddenly deemed way too far to go. So we turned them loose in the chicken yard. The chickens made short work of the crawfish even though some of the chickens were caught in the crawfishes' claws. Chickens will eat anything, even feces if you let them.

Speaking of things we did not know were good to eat: Once we journeyed to the coast of the Gulf of Mexico with Uncle Felix to fish. From the piers we caught Gafftops (also known as gafftopsail catfish, *Bagre marinus*), red fish, and trout. But, we also caught several small sharks in the five- to ten-pound range. A small shark will put up a good fight before you can land it. Of course the fun you have fishing in the first place is that battle while landing a fish. We did not keep the sharks but let them die out of the water on the piers. Uncle Felix said that they killed the good fish. Now, however, shark meat is sold in restaurants and grocery stores at premium prices. Just like the crawfish, another bonanza missed.

Uncle Anton was also a good fisherman. Occasionally, we went fishing on his brother-in-law Charlie Pollock's farm along the San Antonio River near Hobson, east of Panna Maria. Uncle Anton would look at the surface of the water and tell us whether we would or would not catch fish there. His predictions always came true no matter how many trotlines[34] or throw lines[35] we set out.

At this place on the river, my cousin Lucian would

---

[34] A trotline is a heavy fishing line with baited hooks attached at intervals by means of branch lines called snoods. A snood is a short length of line which is attached to the main line using a clip or swivel, with the hook at the other end. A trotline can be set so it covers the width of a channel, river, or stream with baited hooks and can be left unattended. There are many ways to set a trotline, with most methods involving weights to hold the cord below the surface of the water. They are used for catching crabs or fish (particularly catfish). Source: wikipedia.org

[35] A throw line is a line that is tied to a tree or rock on the bank. A rock or heavy weight is tied to the other end of the line. In between three or four hooks with bait are on the line. Then the heavy weight is thrown into the water.

wade close to the bank. When he found a large hole with his foot and felt a large catfish there, he would put his hand in there and grab the fish. I remember him landing several twelve- to twenty-pound catfish by hand. But on a sad note, my mother told me that a long time ago she lost her Uncle Pilarczyk fishing that way. I believe this must have been Louis Pilarczyk. He went into a large hole under a bank of the river for a large catfish, but he could not find his way out, got tangled in roots and drowned. My father was with the crew that recovered his body. Dad related that the only way they could retrieve the body was to dig through the bank from the top.

In 1942 or 1943, Uncle Anton had an opportunity to buy a grocery store and meat market in Poth, between Karnes City and San Antonio. Lucian went with him to work as the butcher. This left Aunt Pella, Ermit, Jack, Adeline, and me to work the farm, harvesting all the crops, feeding the cattle, hogs, and chickens, milking the cows, and all of the other myriad of chores done on the farm. Cream was separated from the milk and sold. If milk soured it was not wasted. It would turn to clabber (curdled milk) that the pigs loved. They even fought over it. Another name for this bacterial fermentation of milk is yogurt, but we never ate it. During those years working on the farm, I never had trouble sleeping when bedtime finally rolled around.

Saturday mornings found Ermit, Jack, and me in Poth, with no particular good intentions in mind. We went to Bomba's, next to Uncle Anton's grocery, changed our hard-earned "spending money" into pennies and shot pool and played the penny slot machines. Then we would adjourn to the Plantation and do more of the same. Amazingly, we eventually lost all our pennies. Yes, unfortunately, slot machines were legal in Texas at the time.

Uncle Anton had a cellar in the middle of the house, but you could not find it unless you knew where the access was. And there, he stored his homemade wine. Taken into confidence by the Urbanczyk boys, we sampled his stash on several occasions. Just recently I bought some grape Sangria. It tasted just like I remember Uncle Anton's wine.

About a week before school started in the fall, Uncle Anton would drive me back home to Cuero then give Mother a $20 bill for my nine or ten weeks work on the farm. Now before you scoff at this measly amount for all my work, you should know that this was enough to pay for all my new clothes for school, including two new pairs of high-top tennis shoes at $1 per pair—Mother got a discount at The Fair. Furthermore, there was the significant savings to my parents from not having to feed me all summer! As you can imagine, my appetite was considerable at the time. Now get up out of that chair and go finish your day's chores.

Chapter 6
THE HOME FRONT

In 1940, when I graduated from the seventh grade at St. Michael's School and entered the eighth grade, I suddenly found myself a freshman in Cuero High School, a totally new experience for me. No longer would I stay in one classroom the whole day, but only an hour, for a single subject. There was also an hour in home room, another in physical education and one for study time in the library. Bertha Marquis, Shirley Voelkel, Ethel Clair Burns, Blas Hernandez, Fritz Gohlke, E.J. Fuchs, and Anna Lea Miller—most of whom were also from St. Michael's—were among my school mates.

Effective September 8, 1941, just three months before the Japanese attack on Pearl Harbor, the Texas Department of Education made it mandatory for all students to complete twelve grades rather than eleven. Those of us already in school entered the eighth grade as freshmen and graduated as seniors from the eleventh grade, typically at age seventeen. But then we still had to attend one more year of school to satisfy the new requirement. Subsequently, elementary schools such as St. Michael's began instructing through the eighth grade and the freshman class in high school was shifted to the ninth grade.

The high school was about ten blocks from home, six blocks or so farther than St. Michael's, but on my bicycle it only took a few minutes longer to get to school. I would give Claude a ride to St. Michael's on the bicycle frame, then continue to the high school.

One morning just past St. Michael's, I noticed smoke coming from a second floor window of the nuns' home. I anxiously knocked and rang the bell. Finally a nun came to the door. I warned her of the smoke, whereupon she came out and saw it for herself. Charging me to go to the fire department about two blocks away, she returned to the house to evacuate the other nuns. I raced to the fire department and within minutes they were at the scene. Now already late for school, I continued on my way.

Apparently the fire was not serious. There was no visible damage to the outside of the structure. I speculate one of the nuns was cooking in her room and things got out of hand. This was probably a very embarrassing situation for the nuns. I never heard any more about it.

I was a fifteen-year-old sophomore on Monday, December 8, 1941. Like most of my classmates I was stunned to hear of the attack on Pearl Harbor the day before. I do not recall our family activities that Sunday but we must have never once turned on the radio that day. News of the attack was an incomprehensible jolt. That Monday, with a single dissenting vote, Congress passed and the president signed, a declaration of war against Japan. As the days passed and reports came in, we learned that US casualties were almost 3,000 dead and that our Pacific fleet was decimated. Thursday of that same week, America declared war on Germany and Italy, which were allied with Japan.

A Japanese submarine shelled Ellwood, California, and the west coast states, Alaska, and Hawaii were bracing for an imminent invasion by the Japanese. Our Japanese American citizens were forcibly placed into internment camps in the interior of the country. This was a terrible affront to American citizens but, under the circumstances, it was deemed prudent. To understand why this action was taken, you just had to have lived at that time and witnessed the mood of the American people. You had to have felt the intense fear for our safety and the future of our country and the magnitude of the anger toward the Japanese people.

As the weeks and months passed, the mood in school changed and became somewhat somber as the full gravity of being at war crystallized. The draft to fill the ranks of our armed forces had started the year before so nearly everyone had close relatives in some branch of the service. Students with immediate family members away at war grew particularly despondent.

My brother Joe was originally stationed on a destroyer out of Pearl Harbor, but six months before the attack he was transferred to the East Coast to await the commissioning of a new destroyer. But Joe

CUEROS CITIZENS KILLED IN WWII

Name	Age	Branch	Rank	Status	Location	Notes
Harold Green*	22	Navy	Fireman First Class	KIA, 4-26-42	Off Coast of Florida	Destroyer USS Sturtevant - under water explosion
Herbert Tieken		Army	PFC	7-24-42	Bataan, Philippines	Died in Japanese prison camp
Joseph Zaiontz	23	Navy	Coxswain PO First Class	MIA 8-22-42	North Atlantic	USS Ingraham sunk in collision with USS Chemung - only 11 survivors
Jesse O. Rodriguez		Army	PFC	KIA, 11-8-43	North Africa	In an armored division (tank)
Samuel Lane		USMC	Lieutenant	KIA	Pacific	Tank commander
Kenneth Thigpen		Army		KIA, 4-1-43	Italy	Member of Texas 36th Division- Medical Detachment
Alton Schaffner		AAF	Staff Sargent	KIA, 8-6-44	Over Europe	Ball turret gunner on B-17
John Ellzey		Army	Lieutenant	Wounded & died, 4-44	France	Infantry platoon leader
John R. Goldman		Army	PFC	KIA, 7-18-44	France	In Normandy
Willard H. Green*	26	USMC	PFC	KIA	Guam	Buried in cemetery on Guam
Charles L. Ryan		Army	Tech Sargent	KIA	France	Killed in Normandy invasion
Elden Mueller		Army	Flight Officer	Killed	France	His airborne unit glider crashed
Joe Wayne Milligan		Army	PFC	KIA, 3-27-45	France	Killed in a paratrooper assault
Edgar C. Hehgst		Army	Staff Sargent	KIA, 1-1-45	Belgium	Sniper fire
Fritz Gohlke, Jr.	19	Army	PFC	KIA 5-45	Germany	Enlisted in August 1944 - in Army 9 months when killed by sharp shooter in Infantry unit
Harold G. Keseling		Army	PFC	KIA, 3-3-45	Germany	Killed in invasion of Germany
J.T. Newman		Army	Lieutenant	KIA,12-22-44	Germany	Jeep ambushed by German troops

*Brothers

still had many friends at Pearl Harbor on December 7.

The telegram arrived on Monday, August 24, 1942: Joe was MIA, missing in action. We had been at war for a little more than nine months. Our neighbor, Mrs. Schmidt, called her Lutheran minister who came over to console Mother. Mother and Dad took the news very hard, but held out hope that Joe was still alive.

Ours was not the only family in Cuero to suffer a loss. It seemed that every week or two another Cuero son became a casualty. I kept a scrapbook of losses from Cuero cut from *The Cuero Record*. I know there were more, but I only kept the ones listed in the weekly newspaper. Some of those who made the ultimate sacrifice are listed here and some of them were friends of mine. My friend and classmate Fritz Gohlke entered the army about the same time as I did.

When we had lived in Beeville, my mother had a friend named Rosie Biemer, who worked as an *au pair*.[36] When she visited Mother, she brought Claude and me the comic books that her charges had finished.[37] Rosie's brother was killed in action. No city, town, community, village, or hamlet was spared when the casualty reports came in.

Rosa Lee Moczygemba, Mother's neighbor once she moved back to Panna Maria in 1973, lost a brother. Two other distant Zaiontz cousins also lost their lives: John Andrew Zaiontz and Stanley J. Zaiontz Jr., from San Antonio. Yet another Zaiontz was wounded.

Mother and Claude continued to keep the scrapbook after I went off to war. Here are a few of my friends, classmates or close relatives of theirs who were lost.

The intensity was overwhelming! Everything took a back seat to the war effort. Everything was salvaged to contribute: old farm equipment, junk automobiles, scrap metal of any kind. There were drives for scrap metal from which ships, tanks, and munitions were manufactured. The Japanese had been buying our scrap metal, all that we had, for many years. Now they were sending it all back to us in the form of bombs and bullets. But our turn was coming.

There were drives to sell war bonds to borrow the money needed to finance the war. Hollywood celebrities promoted and attended the bond rallies. I remember three or four starlets at one such rally. They were all very pretty, but I thought Gale Storm was the prettiest. As planned, huge crowds were drawn to these rallies.

Tin was a strategic war material. We had tin drives. Tooth paste tubes and other containers were made of tin. Plastic was in its infancy and plastic containers for food and other commodities were not yet practical. Milk and other liquids came in glass bottles. Some commodities came in paper bags or paper cartons, but many things which needed soft packaging were packaged in tin.

In time there were shortages of almost everything. Many "necessities" were rationed: meat, sugar, coffee, butter, shoes, automobile tires, gasoline, and oil. We had to save and present ration coupons to buy these items. I remember my father standing in line for hours to obtain our family's allotment of ration coupons. Our allotment of gasoline was two gallons per week. People living on farms were allotted more gasoline than city dwellers because they were, after all, raising food and fiber for the war effort. Uncle Anton bought his first tractor in early 1942, either a John Deere or a Farm All—I do not recall which— to increase his production.

Rationing severely curtailed our weekend visits to relatives. We saved our two gallons a week for a month or more so we could make an occasional trip but, like all citizens, we took these shortages in stride. We were contributing to the effort to save our country! All that we sacrificed and did without went to our troops or to our allies who were suffering much more that we were.

As part of the war effort my father worked overtime at Cudahy Packing Company. The company operated twenty-four hours a day, six days a week drying eggs by dehydration. The yolks were separated from the whites and then dried separately. The entire plant output went to the government either to feed our military or to ship to our allies.

The war was always there, but life and school did go on. High school athletics were austere but continued. I went out for football in my junior year. Our uniforms consisted of shoulder pads, hip pads, knee pads, helmets, and very little else, and the helmets gave very little protection. There were no face guards. There was only one football coach for the

---

[36] A young person who is employed to take care of children, do housework, and other chores in exchange for room and board. From French *au pair* meaning "on a par" or "equal to," indicating that the relationship is intended to be one of equals. The *au pair* is intended to become a member of the family, albeit a temporary one, rather than a traditional domestic worker. Source: wikipedia.org

[37] Another missed fortune! I learned recently that an original copy of Superman Comics sold for one million dollars. I am sure Claude and I had many of the original comics.

entire high school: Coach Shinn. There was no junior varsity team playing a different schedule than the varsity team. We all scrimmaged and played together. Coach Shinn assigned me as a guard because I weighed between 200 and 210 pounds. There was no such thing as a specialty defensive team or offensive team. When someone was good enough, he played both sides of the ball. Had I had not needed to wear glasses while practicing I could probably have made the varsity team. But there were other things that also interfered with my football career, like my job, which I will discuss later.

Two of my favorite teachers were Ms. Green, my English teacher, and Ms. Sutherland, who taught history and civics. Ms. Green was in her seventies and Ms. Sutherland more than fifty. I remember Ms. Green kept me after school one day because I used a double negative in class. I do not remember the specific thing I said but it was something like "I didn't have no pencil." She had me write on the black board, "I will not use double negatives." Not just a few times, but I had to cover every space on all the black boards. The next day, after the entire class had seen what I had written, I was allowed to erase it. Thanks to Ms. Green, I really learned correct English. I could diagram any sentence as well as anyone in class. I think Ms. Green was an aunt to Willard and Harold Green, listed in my chart of those killed in the war. Everyone lost someone close.

Ms. Sutherland, on the other hand, was easier but still took no nonsense in class. I liked Ms. Sutherland and history became my favorite subject. Early in my junior year we were each assigned a topic on which to write a 250-word report and read it to the class before submitting it. We had one month to finish. I was assigned the "Sutton-Taylor Feud." I had never heard of this feud and neither had my classmates.

My first study period in the school library failed to be of much help to my research. There were many references to the famous Hatfield and McCoy Feud, but virtually nothing about the Sutton-Taylor Feud. With no public library in Cuero at the time, I was running up the proverbial blind alley. What was I to do? More than 200 words with no apparent sources of information.

Now it just so happened that in those days, in the 300 block of Morgan Avenue, next to Mr. Dreyer, our landlord, was the Dubose residence and next to that was a grocery store. This grocery was not like any other grocery. There were no signs identifying it as such and it needed repairing and repainting badly and probably had needed it for twenty-five years. A frail, stoop-shouldered gentleman of more than eighty years of age ran this store. His name was Mr. Kuester. He kept no certain hours. When you wanted something from the store, you had to summon Mr. Kuester from his home next door. He carried only the basic staples: flour, sugar, beans, rice, noodles, lard, dried fruit, hard candy, and a few other items, but was always appreciative of the business and always greeted you with a smile even if you came late at night. Everything came in wooden barrels or large boxes. I would go to Mr. Kuester's grocery for my mother and watch him very meticulously weigh my order, place each item in a brown paper bag, then tie it with string. If I did not buy any hard candy, he would always give me a piece anyway.

Mother sent me to the store at least once a week, so I became well acquainted with Mr. Kuester. One day, by chance, I ask Mr. Kuester if he had ever heard of the Sutton-Taylor Feud. Suddenly his eyes lit up and he began to speak of it eagerly. On he went and would not let me leave, but Mother was waiting for the groceries and I had not brought my note book to record any of this. So I came back later for the tale.

The feud itself is not relevant to my story. Suffice it to say that over many, many years, a lot of members of both extended families were killed. As for Mr. Kuester, he related that in his younger days, he had been caught in the middle of a fight between the Taylors and the Suttons right there in Cuero. Several men were killed and he had thought that he, too, was going to die.

I returned again and again to hear him talk and gained a wealth of information about the subject feud. Thanks to these sessions with old Mr. Kuester, I wrote my report and received an A. I remember thinking that Ms. Sutherland was an excellent teacher because she exposed all twenty-five to thirty of her students to all kinds of subjects that would never be covered in a normal history class. So English, civics, and history were my favorites. I will not be speaking very fondly of algebra, physics, and trigonometry, nor will I be explaining why.

Many things happened when I was sixteen and a junior in high school. Mother wanted me to learn to drive a car, so I studied for my license. The Department of Public Safety office was in the Dewitt County Courthouse but only open one day a week. I passed my written and eye tests and a trooper asked me if I was ready for the road test. I said, "Sure." The first thing was parallel parking. I passed that with ease. Then he said to take a right turn at the next corner, which I did, then he said to go around the block and park in front of the courthouse. I failed the test because I did not stop at the stop sign on the first corner. He said, "Better luck next time." Needless to say I stopped at that sign on my next try and got my license.

Another thing I remember vividly was that my mother wanted me to have Hermann Sons Life Insurance. Mom and Dad had it, as did Joe. The prerequisite was to pass a physical examination. But I failed. The doctor said I had high blood pressure and that I would not live past forty. This did not bother me too much as I still had twenty-four years to go. In those days there were no medications to control high blood pressure and many other common diseases. Life expectancy was not what it is today.

At the end of the summer when I was seventeen and Uncle Anton brought me back to Cuero to await the start of school, Mother learned that Guadalupe Valley Cotton Mills was looking for workers to expand operations to twenty-four hours a day. The two of us walked into their employment office and were both hired immediately, pending both of us receiving Social Security cards. Off to the Social Security office for cards and, low and behold, from my birth certificate, produced by Mother, I learned that my first name was Adrian and not Alphonse! We received consecutive Social Security numbers, hers ending in 97 and mine 98.

Mechanic's helper was my job title and Mother worked in the thread room. I was assigned and reported to a man of about fifty who looked almost like Santa Claus, minus the white beard. My job was to help keep the twenty carding machines oiled well and running smoothly.

Carding machines have two main parts. In the back is the gin saw with thousands of teeth. It is five feet wide and about nine inches in diameter. The function of the gin saw is to tear the raw cotton as it is fed into the carding machine. To do this, cotton is first pulled from the bale and shaped into rolls one inch thick and five feet wide.

In front of the gin saw is a huge, slowly-rotating drum also about five feet wide and five feet in diameter. This drum has many thousands of sharp points, about twenty to thirty per square inch.

These points are sharpened at an angle (◣) and pick up the torn cotton fibers as fine fuzz or lint. This fuzz is picked up by the front of the drum as it rotates at a slow speed. The cotton fuzz is formed into a "rope" (for lack of a better word) about one inch in diameter and output into canisters about three feet high and a foot wide. The canisters rotate slowly, accepting the cotton "rope" in small circles to prevent tangling. After an hour, when a canister is filled, it is replaced with an empty one. The full canister is then taken to the next department for spinning into cotton thread.

The fine points on the large drum must be sharpened from time to time. First the machine is taken out of production and then the twenty-four-hour sharpening process is started. The actual sharpening is accomplished by a rotating emery wheel three or four inches wide and is automatic once the emery wheel is properly set up. The wheel moves across the whole drum while the drum is turning at a slow speed. The trick is in the proper setting of the emery wheel, a technique I never really mastered.

Forty hours a week for 54¢ cents an hour, I worked in the mill. Most workers were paid 40¢ per hour. Mother made 44¢ cents an hour working in the thread room.

Work at the mill did not conflict with school because I already had enough credits for graduation. I was just finishing that newly required extra twelfth grade. I picked the easiest subjects: Gregg shorthand, typing, Spanish, and P.E. and got out of school at 1 P.M. to go to work at 2 P.M. My shift ended at 10:30 P.M. five days a week.

My first day on the job stands as testament to my extensive knowledge of mechanics and to how badly Guadalupe Valley Cotton Mills needed workers. Mr. Folsom sent me to the blacksmith shop to retrieve his left-handed monkey wrench, which the crew there had borrowed. The head of the blacksmith shop said that the electrical shop now had it. I went there and they said the transportation shop had borrowed it from them. After an hour of this dog chasing his tail, I finally caught on that everyone was having a lot of fun at my expense. I went back to Mr. Folsom and he confessed that there was no such thing as a left-handed monkey wrench. But it had apparently been worth 54¢ of Guadalupe Valley Cotton Mills' operating funds to provide a morale boost to the old timers.

I worked alongside Mr. Folsom making quick repairs to the carding machines when they ceased to function properly. When necessary, we even fabricated our own gears and replacement parts. Once each day the points on one carding machine were sharpened. As we had time, we performed routine maintenance on other machines.

Once, while trying to remove a particularly stubborn gear, a spark flew from the punch when Mr. Folsom hit it. The spark landed in some cotton rolls and started a fire. Without thought, I snuffed out the fire with my bare hands. Moving my hands very rapidly, I did not get burned. Mr. Folsom said that we could have had a serious fire if not for my quick reaction.

If we had a lot of spare time on our hands, we made real cotton rope. There was a rope-making machine out of the way in the carding room. It used the same type of thread also used to make cotton duck. I still have some of this rope—now almost seventy years old and still as good as new.

There were other incidents involving me while working at Guadalupe Valley Cotton Mills. The line of carding machines was powered by a series of large, wide pulleys along a drive shaft near the twelve-foot

This illustration is of a row of similar carding machines but probably much older models than ours. It shows women with long hair and loose clothing running the machines. This is a formula for disaster with all those machines running. At Guadalupe Valley Cotton Mills, women were not allowed to run the carding machines as it was considered too dangerous. The picture also shows a large pulley at the ceiling and smaller pulleys on the carding machines. Our machines each had two large pulleys with a smaller pulley near the ceiling.

high ceiling. A ten-foot loop of belt ran each machine from its pulley at the ceiling to a pair of pulleys on one end of the machine. The two pulleys on the carding machine were side by side and about two feet in diameter. The first pulley was a neutral pulley which could spin without driving the machine while the second pulley was the one that actually drove the machine when the belt was in that position.

One of my jobs was to put a machine back into production after completing repairs. While a machine was idle for repair the belt was off of both lower pulleys and sat loosely over the drive shaft at the ceiling. The sequence of putting a carding machine back in service was to apply starch to a portion of the loose belt, then work that section over the top pulley. The starch allowed the belt to slip while it was being tensioned and forced onto the neutral pulley—a process which required both gloved hands and pushing with a hip. Next, tar was applied to the belt to stop the slipping. The belt was then forced with gloved hands onto the adjacent drive pulley, a very dangerous operation.

The operators of the carding machines were not allowed to move the belts, as this was deemed too dangerous for them. One day, I had starched a belt so it would slip until tightened, put the starched part over the ceiling pulley, held the belt in both hands,

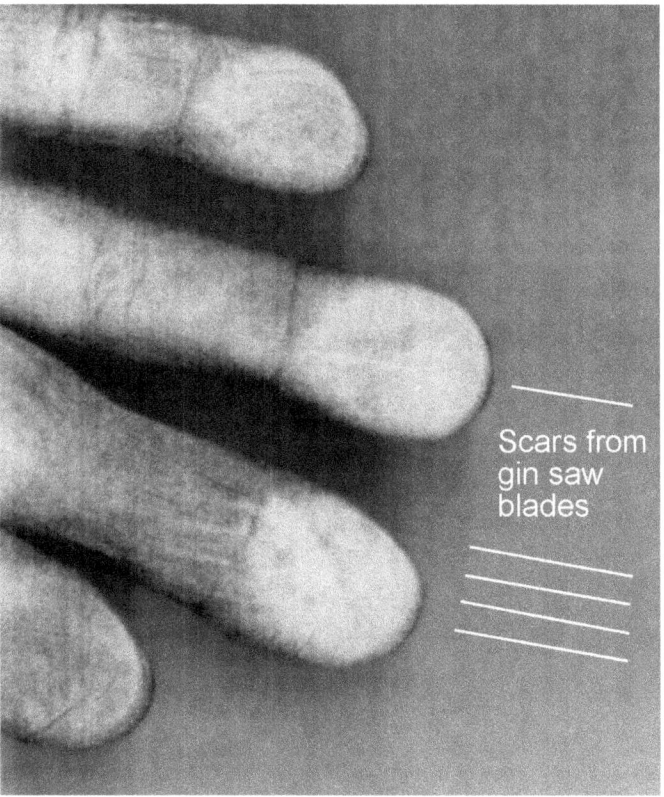

Hand scars

and was using my left hip to slide the belt onto the neutral pulley. Something went wrong. Suddenly the belt grabbed the top of my pants above my belt and tore off exactly half of my pants! They parted at the middle seam. Fortunately the pants were worn out and that seam was very weak, otherwise I could have been seriously injured. So there I stood, pants covering my right side and on full display on the left side. I was greatly embarrassed, and you know what the word embarrassed means: being in a bare assed state, and that I was. I quickly tied my sweater around my waist and, after telling Mr. Folsom, I raced home for a whole pair of pants.

Another memorable, though more unfortunate, incident involved me and a gin saw at the back of one of the machines. There was trouble with the gin saw so I moved the belt off the driving pulley, onto the neutral pulley and then off the neutral pulley to completely stop the machine for servicing. Waiting for a few minutes for the machine to come to a complete stop, which I was sure it had, I opened the back and put my fingers on the gin saw. But it was still turning. Surely this was testimony to the terrific job I did when oiling all the machine parts. It ran as smoothly and quietly as a Swiss watch.

With a severe injury to my hand, I was sent to the Guadalupe Valley Cotton Mills' doctor. He stated that I had tried to make hamburger out of the middle finger on my right hand. There was nothing left to stitch up, so he put medicine on it, bandaged it and instructed me to come every other day so the nurse could change the dressing. I was off work for two weeks. Now being a young lad, I thought that being off for two weeks while still getting paid was the greatest thing ever. Wow! But I still had to go to school, and everyone there was quite interested in my wrapped hand and wanted to know what had happened.

Shortly after my mother and I started at Guadalupe Valley Cotton Mills, we decided to move closer to all of our jobs. We rented a house on French Street. The mill was only two blocks from our new house while Dad was just four blocks from Cudahy. I had my bicycle but Mom and Dad walked due to the rationing of gasoline, oil, and tires.

In January or February 1944, there was an announcement at the Mills that the company would start a softball team to play other teams in Cuero. Along with about fifty other men, I decided to try for the team. On try-out day the coach put me in center field. Right away it was evident that I could not judge where a high fly ball would come down. Then, when he asked me to throw the ball from center field to home plate, my throw cleared the back stop by twenty feet. My try-out was over. I played a little baseball during P.E. at school and I think it is possible to make the transition from baseball to softball but it takes time.

I graduated that year from the only graduating class in history that had more than enough credits to graduate. Because the twelfth grade was added for the first time, most people in my class had twenty or more credits when normally you only needed sixteen to graduate.

In 1945, Mother joined the Gold Star Mothers organization. This is a nationwide group of women who have lost sons or daughters in the service of our country. Some of these ladies lost several children. Mother was an officer and held various positions in the organization from time to time.

Above: Cuero High School graduating class of 1944; Adrian is in the second row, far right.

Right: An unidentified colonel visiting the Gold Star Mothers of Cuero in 1945. Lucy Zaiontz is standing to the colonel's left in the polka dot dress. The back of the photograph credits John H. Berning, Service Office, Dinter Post #3, The American Legion, Cuero, Texas.

The Cuero chapter of the Gold Star Mothers helped raise money for the War Memorial erected on the grounds of the DeWitt County Courthouse. This memorial honors all the men and women of DeWitt County who gave their lives for our country in World War I and World War II.

Upon turning seventeen, I told Dad that I wanted to follow Joe and enlist in the navy. The navy was taking enlistees at seventeen. After Mom and Dad discussed this at length, they finally agreed. Dad took me to the navy recruiter in San Antonio but I was turned down because of my high blood pressure. The next month, he drove me to the navy recruiter in Victoria, thirty miles to the east. They also turned me down but this time because of my farsightedness. After this, I resigned myself that I would never be in the military so I began thinking of the alternatives. The draft was in full swing. A new quota had to be filled each month with eighteen- to forty-five-year-olds, but I knew they probably would not take me. The United States Merchant Marine was recruiting seamen to man the cargo ships and tankers that supplied our military and allies. The Merchant Marine functioned as an auxiliary to the Navy and likewise suffered tremendous casualties from sinkings by Nazi U-boats. With several options, none very promising, what should I try for my next step to serve my country?

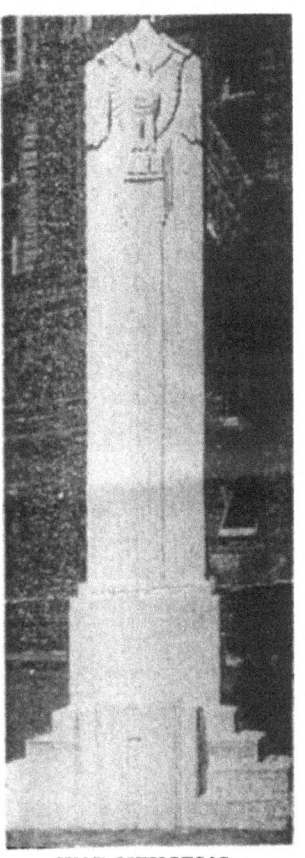

WAR MEMORIAL
County lists dead

The Home Front 63

Chapter 7
CITIZEN SOLDIER OR PFC
(POOR F___ING CIVILIAN)

Upon turning eighteen in August, 1944, I went before the draft board in Cuero and volunteered to be drafted. In September, my draft order was issued with the notation that I had volunteered for the draft. When I told Mr. Folsom that I had been drafted, he was devastated because he would have to train somebody new to fill my job. The management of Guadalupe Valley Cotton Mills assured me that my job would be waiting for me when I completed my service. I told Mr. Folsom and the Guadalupe Valley Cotton Mills that I was not gone yet as I might not pass the physical.

A bus was waiting on the morning the local draftees departed for Fort Sam Houston in San Antonio. It was filled with draftees, but only one other man was a volunteer as I was. Upon arriving at Ft. Sam, we were taken to a huge building and told to strip naked for our physicals. Our clothes and possessions were put into lockers and the keys handed to us. Each of us was given a length of string with which to tie the key around our necks while we were standing in line. There I stood, clad only in a key string and a new pair of glasses made by Dr. Doyle, an optometrist located on East Commerce Street in San Antonio.

Being thirsty and sighting a water fountain I proceeded to drink about a quart of cold water. My new glasses corrected my farsightedness and, amazingly, my blood pressure was within limits. I had passed the physical examination! I was in the service of my country! To this day I believe that my blood pressure was low enough because I drank all that cold water.

I was informed that since I had volunteered for the draft, I would be given several choices. The first choice would be which branch of service I preferred. I said "the navy," and they said the navy was full. My next choices were which theater and what occupation. I said Europe and the infantry, and they looked at me as if I were crazy. At this time I still had revenge on my mind because of Joe's death. They were only too happy to give me my third choice.

All who passed our physicals and were bound for the army were sent to Dodd Field, a northern part of Ft. Sam. Here there was a huge tent city where we were assigned sleeping cots. We were sworn in declaring that we would protect the Constitution and our country from all enemies, domestic and foreign. Then we were congratulated on becoming members of the United States Army.

Next we were marched to an immense building which was a quartermaster depot to be issued uniforms (fatigues only), underwear, socks, and caps. No measurements were taken. The PFC (private first class) issuing the clothing, some new and some reconditioned, took one look at each new soldier and started throwing the clothing at him from different bins at his back. There were hundreds of draftees there so everyone was in a hurry. If the clothing did not fit, it was possible to exchange it for the proper size later. The rest of our uniforms were issued within the next few days.

We were free for the rest of that day, but were confined to the tent area. Later that day a call went out for recruits that knew how to handle a rifle. I volunteered as did about ten others. We were given 1902 vintage, single-shot Springfield rifles and told that we would be going on guard duty that night, augmenting the regular guard force. We were instructed by the sergeant on codes of conduct and duties of a guard.

My guarding assignment was the Ft. Sam Houston finance office which was only a stone's throw from the historic Ft. Sam Houston Quadrangle. I was told that I would be on guard duty for three hours, to walk around the finance building and to challenge all trespassers. I mentally noted a problem. We were not issued bullets for our rifles. I guess they did not want us to shoot anyone, or perhaps ourselves.

A day or two later we were allowed to go home,

take our clothing and possessions, and await further orders. My orders came in a few days to report to the Southern Pacific Railroad station on East Houston Street in San Antonio at a certain hour on a specific date. Dad delivered me there at the appointed time. Seven or eight other soldiers were there awaiting transportation to California and I became acquainted with William C. Favor from Pearsall, Texas. He was also going to Camp Roberts in California. At least I had someone with whom to share my apprehensions about going into the great unknown. This was a terrifying experience for an eighteen-year-old boy who had never been more than 100 miles from home.

The journey to Los Angeles was uneventful, seeming to be desert most of the way. Passing through West Texas, New Mexico, Arizona, and Southern California, I had never appreciated just how much of the United States was barren.

Arrivals in Los Angeles were met by contingents from all the different basic training bases in California. Transportation to Camp Roberts was awaiting those of us in the army. New sailors and marines had transportation to San Diego. I wished I had been bound for San Diego. That is where Joe took his basic training.

BECOMING A SOLDIER

Upon arrival at Camp Roberts we were met by a sergeant who marched us to the parade ground, where we were met by a colonel, the camp commander, who stood on a huge dais. He welcomed us and then he said that he had never seen a sorrier bunch of "sad sacks" in his life. But he said not to worry because by the time we finished our basic training we would be proud soldiers in the greatest army in the world.

Training started almost immediately. Wake up call was at 5:30 A.M. and breakfast was at 6:30 A.M. We had to be in formation after having shaved (for those of us who had something to shave), brushed teeth (I had never brushed my teeth before), taken care of all bodily functions, and fully dressed. We double-timed everywhere, even to breakfast. (Double-timing can be best described as a running walk.)

Our company commander was Lieutenant Jansen. Our barrack commander was Sergeant Horner. The sergeant was a combat veteran who explained that his job was to teach us all he knew about how to stay alive once we were in combat. He said that we would have many other instructors, specialists in various weapons and combat tactics. We would receive instruction and training with heavy weapons like 81-mm mortars, .50-caliber machine guns, flame throwers, bazookas, Browning automatic rifles (a light machine gun called a BAR), and Thompson submachine guns. I could not hit the side of a barn with a Tommy gun because after the first shot, the barrel kicked up and it took all of my strength in my left arm just to keep the barrel down.

Every man received sufficient target practice with each weapon so that he could step in and operate that weapon when another soldier was killed or wounded. Our twelve-week course also covered other essentials like close-order drilling, hiking with our rifles, proper saluting, hiking while loaded with a backpack, gas mask training, hiking uphill, bayonet fighting, hiking at double time, using hand grenades, and endless hiking and other exercises with our rifles.

After being issued our boots and leggings, we went through a line where a specialist made sure that each man had a proper fit. As testimony to properly fitting boots, I never developed blisters even with all of the hiking and marching we did.

Next each of us was issued a brand new M1 Garand semi-automatic .30-caliber rifle. I was trained to very rapidly apply the safety, insert a clip of eight shells into the magazine[38] using my thumb, remove the safety, and commence firing. Failure to properly manipulate my thumb would result in the bolt slamming on the thumb and severely injuring it. This happened to soldiers often enough that it became known as M1 Thumb.

This new rifle came packed in grease called cosmoline.[39] Every part of the rifle was covered with it

---

[38] A magazine is the ammunition storage and feeding part of a repeating firearm. A clip holds multiple rounds of ammunition together for rapid loading into the magazine.

and the only way to get it off was with gasoline. The factory packed all new fire arms with this stuff and each soldier had to clean it off of his own rifle. That rifle became a part of me and was carried on all hikes, drills, and parades.

As mentioned before, I never developed blisters on my feet; however, I did develop a severe case of athletes' foot. This is a fungal condition that develops when feet sweat. It causes the skin to crack between the toes and is very painful. I went on sick call to have it treated. The doctor who saw me, a colonel, gave me some salve and three pairs of white sox to wear instead of the Army-issued olive drab socks. He said the dye in the Army-issued ones was part of the problem. I was to come and see him again if the problem persisted.

The next morning when we fell in formation for roll call, Sergeant Horner said "Zaintz, (rhymes with 'saints') go and change socks. You are out of uniform." I did. The next time I went on sick call with athlete's foot, I told the doctor that my sergeant said I could not wear white socks. He wrote a note to give to Sergeant Horner who never gave me any more static about socks.

I will note here that I did make a concession to the olive socks. I wore my white socks for hikes, everyday training, and exercises, but not for close-order drilling and parades. I certainly did not want my white socks to call attention to me or any mistakes I might make.

About midway through our training, we had instruction and demonstrations of fighting with bayonets. Sergeant Horner said that the bayonet sometimes got stuck in flesh and bone and you would not be able to pull it out. In that case, all you had to do was fire your rifle and that would loosen it so it would come out easily. I raised my hand and Sergeant Horner said, "Yes, Zaintz?" "If I have a shell left in my rifle, why am I using my bayonet on the guy?" He answered that there could be many reasons and left it at that. I do not know if my question was the cause, but the next day I found my name on the KP[40] list. However, no one really minded being on KP. We usually got plenty to eat, but more important, we got out of that day's training, including hikes and exercises.

While neither side had yet used poison gas as a weapon of war, we did not know what the Japs might do if they got desperate. Thus, we received training in the use of gas masks. We were required to go through a hut full of some kind of gas. I never found out what it was. We had to check our gas masks and carefully put them on. I do not know what I did wrong but I almost passed out before I made it out of the hut. Either the mask had a leak or it was not capable of keeping out the gas they used. Many of us were coughing and choking before we got to fresh air.

Hand grenade training was also included. I was the only one in my group of fifteen or twenty recruits that could consistently put an eight-ounce hand grenade into a six-foot circle seventy to eighty feet away. During one of our sessions, our instructor was demonstrating how to pull the pin when the grenade slipped out of his hand (probably on purpose). He hollered "grenade" and everyone scattered and hit the dirt. Nothing happened because it was a dud.

Those in our group who smoked never had a shortage of cigarettes. I suppose the tobacco companies gave the barracks hundreds of cartons, trying to get those of us who did not already smoke hooked on nicotine. The longtime smokers grabbed the Camels and Lucky Strikes[41], not wanting the Old Gold, Raleigh and Chesterfields brands. The citizen soldiers were left with the three less desirable brands. But those Old Gold and Raleigh individual packs became useful missiles in a war between one side of the barracks and the other. Beds and foot

---

[39] Cosmoline is a type of rust preventive which meets demanding military specifications. It is wax-like, has a slight petroleum odor, and is brown in color.

[40] KP stands for Kitchen Police, a misnomer, as it has nothing to do with policing the mess, unless you call picking up stuff policing. Those assigned to KP had to get up at 3:30 A.M. instead of 5:30 A.M. to do all of the menial tasks required in preparing the meals for the unit—peeling potatoes, washing pots, stirring pots, etc. —all under the supervision of the cooks.

[41] "Lucky Strike Green has gone to war!" was an advertisement heard on radio. After changing its packaging from green to white, the war was used to help market the new look.

lockers were overturned for fortification against the sailing packs. If you threw the pack in the manner of a frisbee, it sailed beautifully.

Barracks inspections occurred regularly and we failed several times for dirty floors. So we cleaned the barracks thoroughly. With a water hose from outside we put two to three inches of water over the entire floor. Everyone scrubbed the area around his bed and foot locker, then we swept out the dirty water and mopped up. We never failed another inspection for dirty floors.

Our grueling basic training continued through November and December of 1944. Then on the 20th of December, we were told that we would be given leave until New Year's Day. We could go home if we had money for transportation. Fortunately, I had saved enough money out of my $50 per month pay.

I do not remember the amount of the train fare, but for members of the services a round-trip fare was not very much. When the Southern Pacific train got to San Antonio, I was supposed to change trains to get to Cuero. Being a dumb country boy, I did not know that. When we left San Antonio, the towns we passed did not look like the towns on the route to Cuero, so I asked the conductor when we would arrive in Cuero. He said "never" as we were on the way to Houston. He said I could either continue on to Houston and catch the morning train to Cuero, or get off at the next town, which was Flatonia, and hitchhike to Cuero. Not wanting to waste another day, I chose to get off and hitchhike.

Carrying my duffel bag, I walked out to the road to Cuero which was about forty-seven miles away. For two hours I waited, but not a single vehicle came by. I had forgotten how the strict gasoline rationing had limited civilian driving. So I walked

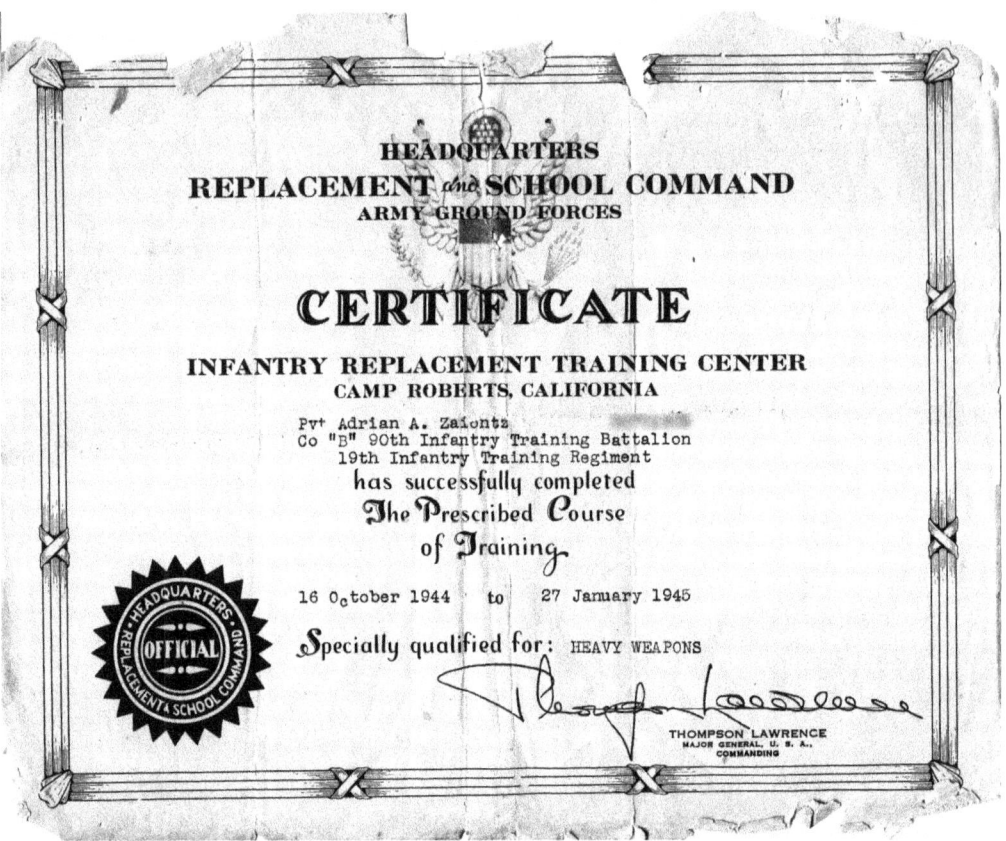

Certificate of heavy weapons training.

back into Flatonia and found an open café. It was now about 9 at night and dark. Explaining my situation to the café owner, I asked if he knew of anyone who would take me to Cuero and stated that I would pay $20. Finally a middle-aged gentleman who overheard the conversation said he would take me. Now the trouble was that I did not actually have $20. Luckily, when we arrived in Cuero at 10:30 P.M., my father lent me the money to pay for my ride.

I spent Christmas Eve and Christmas day with my brother Claude, Mom, and Dad. I was even able to visit with some of my aunts and uncles and their families. My leave was wonderful and I enjoyed every minute, but I had to start back on December 27 in order to report in at Camp Roberts by New Year's Day.

Intensive training resumed. One of the scarier hazards we endured was crawling fifty yards, with our rifles, while live machine-gun fire zipped six inches above our heads. After three more weeks the final test was to hike twenty-five miles in eight hours carrying a forty-five-pound field pack, a nine-pound rifle, and three clips of ammunition. But the

Camp Roberts Infantry Replacement Training Center, 17 January 1945
Front, kneeling: Douglas Trodahl, Harold Snograss. Front row: Moncel Tas, Jerry Vance, Richard Smith, Edward Zolot, Cpl. MacDonald, Cpl. Johnston, Lt. Jansen, Sgt. Horner, Cpl. Garcia, ___Willis, Donald Scubert, George Schmier, David Vacarro. Second row: William Sutton, George Stone, Robert Whaley, William Strangeways, Richard Schlichter, Robert Wright, Hugo Walfred, William Webb, Gilbert Urian, Rosalito Solis, Donald Shutley, Harry Weslowski, **Adrian A. Zalontz,** Peter Simon. Third row: Thomas Simpkins, Audrey Schram, John Schirmer, Raymond Schuh, Robert Walforth, Edwin Willie, Franklin Starl, Cecil Woods, Wennen Sadenberg, Richard Stoll, Walter Wegmeuller, James Stevens, Hiliberto Tellez, Johnnie Wahl. Top row: Albert Serradel, William Thompson, Lawrence Taylor, James Stephenson, Pedro Vasquez (would also be assigned to 38th Division with me), Donald Schmidt, Gerry Scheffel, Eugene Szpot, Jerome Vallens, Soo S. Won, Robert Wilming, Kenneth Stork, Johnie Sellice, Herbert Walker

incentive was great! Those who failed would have to repeat the basic training course again. No one wanted to repeat twelve weeks of misery and everyone from our barrack made it, although some had bleeding blisters on their feet by the end.

The United States has been described as one big melting pot of people from all over the world forging one nation. The army exposed me to recruits from all parts of our country. Many had different accents and spoke differently, but we were all Americans. Some came from New York and Chicago, some from Minnesota, Oklahoma, Georgia, and Puerto Rico, and one came from Cuero, Texas. We melded together. We watched out for each other. We depended upon each other. And we had one common cause: the welfare of our country and of each other.

On one hike, I fell down in a small creek and knocked my right knee out of joint. My buddies picked me up and pulled on my leg until it popped back into place. I started basic training weighing 220 pounds and finished at 180.

I did well at target practice with the M1 rifle. Having been taught to zero it in on a target and allow for wind and elevation, I qualified on the fifty-yard, 100-yard, 200-yard, 500-yard, and 1000-yard ranges. I could hit a target over a half mile away. Then came the one-mile range. I told my buddy next to me that I could not even see the man-sized target I was supposed to hit. He said to shoot between two trees. After adjusting for wind and elevation, I got a hit on my target and qualified as a sharpshooter, but I suspect one of my buddies hit the target for me that day.

FACE TO FACE WITH WAR

We parted ways and left for our various overseas assignments at the end of January 1945. Departure was from Camp Stoneman, which was close to Oakland on San Francisco Bay. As we passed under the Golden Gate Bridge most realized that many of us would not be coming back home. The Pacific Ocean voyage was uneventful except that after only one day out, I got very seasick and I stayed that way until I got off that ship more than a month later. I remember thinking how fortunate I was that I did not get my wish to be in the navy!

Our ship had 5,000 army replacements on it, encompassing every type of military occupation specialty (MOS). We had infantrymen, engineers, artillerymen, medics, ordnance, quartermasters, and on and on. For at least 1,500 miles we sailed due south before turning westward. There was no navy escort and we were avoiding areas with Jap submarines.

After about a month at sea, we arrived at Finschhafen, New Guinea, but were confined to ship. We assumed (ass-u-me) our captain was awaiting further orders. While we waited, some military personnel would come out from Finschhafen in small boats and ask if anyone had 5¢ candy bars. They said they would pay us $1 for each one. I knew that they would sell them on shore for twice that.

After about three days, we left Finschhafen and headed north to the Philippines. En route we drilled about what to do if we were attacked by Jap *Kamikazes*.[42] If we had to jump overboard to abandon ship, we were instructed to unbuckle our helmet chin straps, lest our neck be broken when we hit the water.

We arrived at the island of Leyte in the Philippines and disembarked. Three hours later our ship and home for over a month was hit by kamikazes and sunk. All of our duffel bags and personal be-

---

[42] Kamikazes were explosive-laden suicide planes which were modified from conventional aircraft with the sole intention of destroying ships by crashing into them.

Higgins boat, a type of LCVP

longings were lost as they had not yet been unloaded. We were issued new clothing and equipment and could put in claims for cameras, radios, watches, and other things that were lost. I claimed nothing because everything that I had was army-issued. No one believed that any compensation would ever be realized. But lo and behold, about six months later most everyone, except for me, received reimbursement, some for nonexistent personal items. Some received as much as $600.

We stayed ashore about ten days, then boarded another ship headed for the main island of Luzon. We disembarked at Subic Bay, north of the Bataan peninsula and stayed in a tent city for a few days. Then we boarded yet a third ship that was bound for we-knew-not-where. (There was a considerable amount of grumbling about the army not knowing what it was doing.) After another day of travel, we transferred to a "landing craft vehicle personnel" (LCVP) and went ashore a few miles south of Manila. Manila Bay was full of sunken ships. Most had hulls and masts sticking out of the water and were creating hazards to navigation.

A replacement depot was set up where we landed, complete with yet another tent city. A replacement depot is commonly known as a Repple Depple. The Repple Depple was where all army units drew their replacements for casualties or for soldiers sent home for various reasons. The Repple Depple had replace-

Mitsubishi A6M Zero

ments for all military operation specialties (MOS).

We were still under potential attack by kamikaze pilots flying Zeros[43] manufactured by Mitsubishi. Even today, I cringe when I hear the word Mitsubishi or see a vehicle with the Mitsubishi logo.

Finally, after sitting around the Repple Depple a few days, an officer from the 38th Infantry Division arrived asking for replacements to fill vacancies in many units of the 38th. Three of us were assigned to A Company (a rifle company), 1st Battalion, 152nd Infantry Regiment. I had trained in heavy weapons, including .50-caliber machine guns, 81-mm mortars, bazookas, flame throwers, and Browning automatic rifles. Under ordinary circumstances, I would be assigned to the heavy weapons companies in a battalion (D, H, or M Companies). But, alas, these companies did not need replacements. Evidently the brass correctly surmised that if I could handle heavy weapons, I could handle lighter arms such as .30-caliber water-cooled or .30-caliber air-cooled machine guns and the 60-mm mortars placed in each rifle company's weapons platoon.

ORGANIZATION OF THE 38TH DIVISION

The three of us for A Company and a dozen more replacements for B and C Companies climbed into trucks bound for the 1st Battalion positions in the Sierra Madre Mountains about fifty miles east of Manila. As we drove through the outskirts of

---

[43] The Mitsubishi A6M Zero was a very formidable long-range fighter aircraft. There were more Zeros built during World War II than any other type of aircraft.

Citizen Soldier or PFC 71

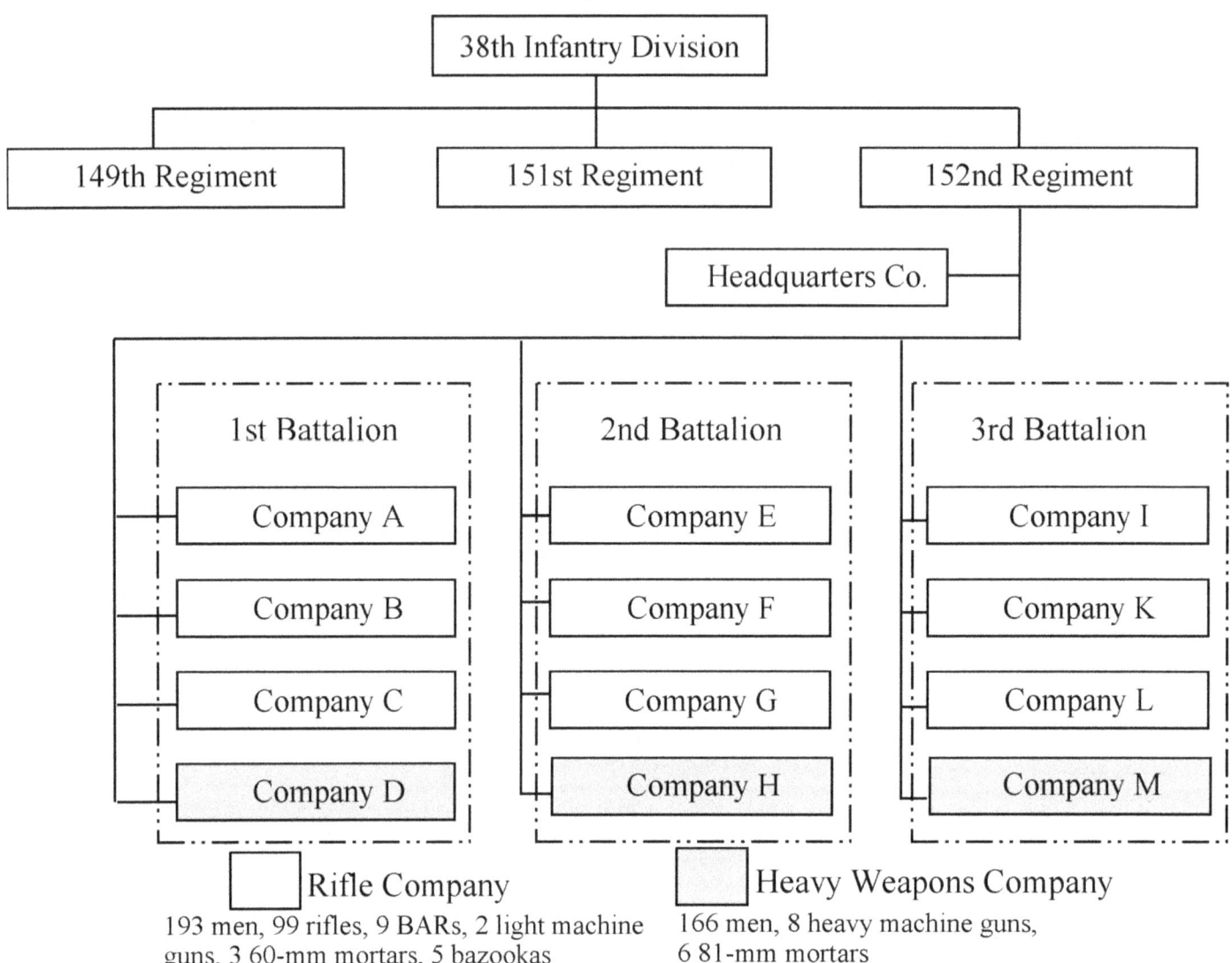

Organization of the 38th Division

Manila, we were amazed at the three or four miles of tent cities filled with military personnel. There were about 500,000 Allied and US personnel on Luzon at this time. Stationed nearby in Biak, New Guinea, was S.Sgt. Mary Catherine Lukawitz.[44] Quite unknown to me at the time, but four years later, Mary would become my lovely bride.

We came to the foot of the Sierra Madre Mountains. These mountains run along the east coast of Luzon for more than 100 miles. After a couple of hours of riding on rough roads and following a heavy rainfall, the truck began sliding toward a cliff. In a panic, one man in the back jumped out, but the rest of us did not have time to react. The truck struck a tree and came to a stop. Had it not, we would all have been killed or badly injured. The only injury suffered was the soldier who jumped and broke his leg. Shaken, we hiked the last few miles to the battalion's position. Not a gripe was heard.

As we arrived about 10 A.M., the three of us assigned to A Company were immediately put into the fight for Woodpecker Ridge. The remaining twelve replacements proceeded to their new companies' positions. Woodpecker Ridge was named for the sound of the slow-firing 6.5-mm air-cooled machine guns used by the Japs. Someone suggested that they sounded like woodpeckers hammering for bugs in a dead tree.

---

[44] Mary Catherine Lukawitz joined the Women's Army Auxiliary Corps (WAAC) in 1942 and was sent to Biak, New Guinea. While serving there, the WAAC was converted to the Women's Army Corps (WAC) on 1 July 1943. When the war ended, the WACs were moved to Luzon and given priority on transportation home. She both arrived in New Guinea and was transported home on the SS Lurline, along with 1000 other WACs.

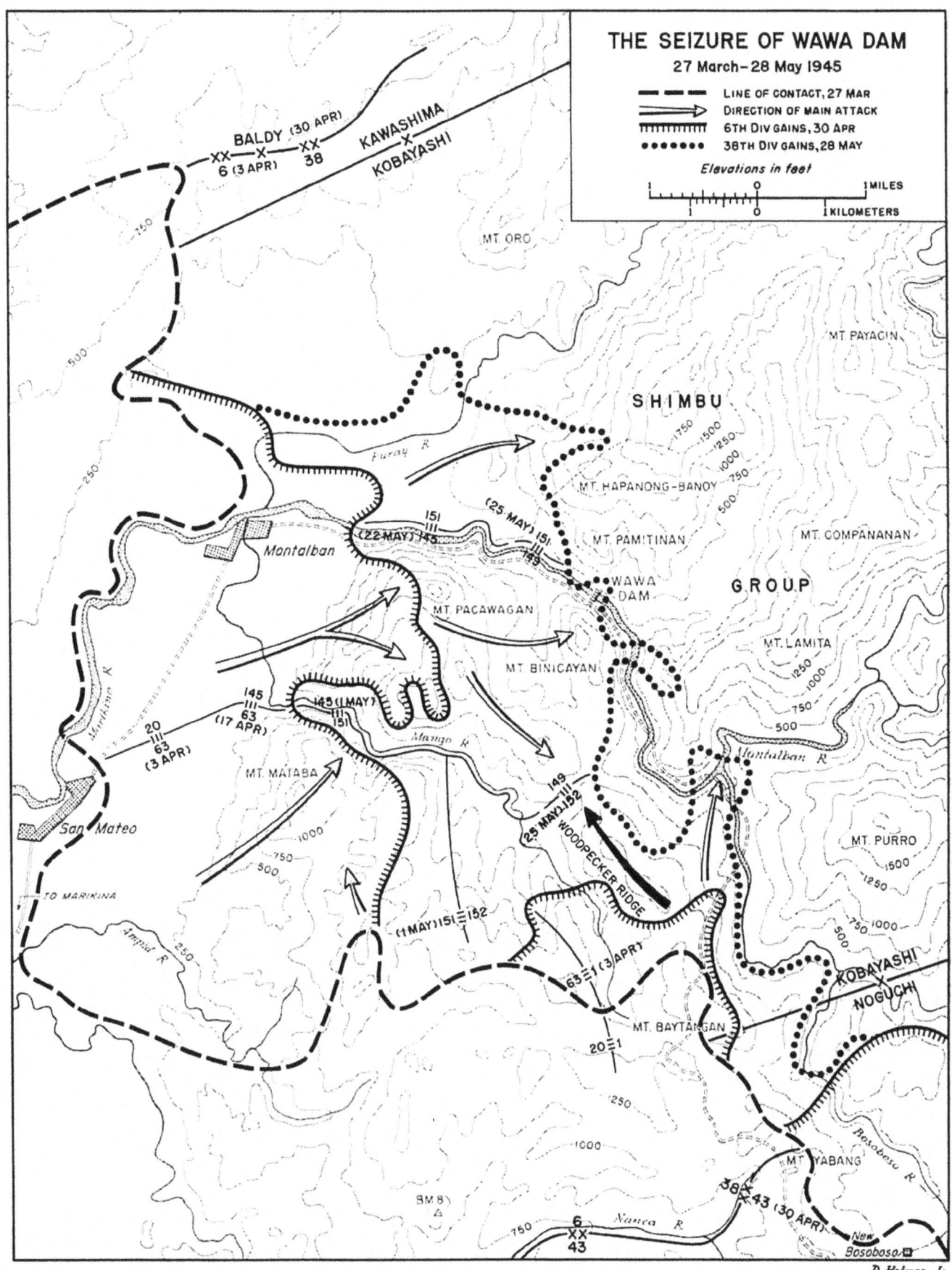

Capturing Woodpecker Ridge – the black arrow is the path of the 152nd after I joined them.

Citizen Soldier or PFC 73

ARMY MORTARS EXPLAINED

Every Army in the world has mortars and they all work the same way. This has not changed much since the mortar was first introduced in the 15th century. The 60-mm mortar shell is about the diameter of a baseball and about 10 inches long including its fins. The 81-mm shell is about the size of a softball and over a foot long. The 60 mm has a normal range of 200 to 500 yards. The 81 mm has a normal range of up to 1000 yards. With the addition of leaf powder attached to the fins with paper clips, the range can be increased. Each shell has two safety pins and a plunger on the nose of the shell. Even after the first pin, the wire pin, is pulled and the nose is depressed the shell will not explode. I have first-hand knowledge of this because I depressed plungers several times and nothing happened. Another process has to take place before the shell is fully armed. When the shell leaves the barrel and is ten to fifteen feet high, the set back pin flies out because of inertia. Once this pin is out, the shell is fully activated and anything that depresses the plunger will detonate the round.

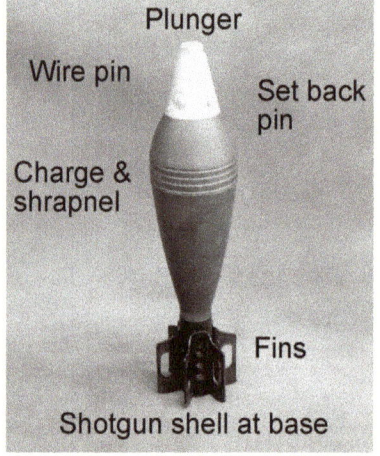

There is a small propelling charge at the bottom between the fins which looks similar to a 20-gauge shotgun shell. When the round is dropped down the barrel of the mortar, it strikes a firing pin at the bottom exploding the propelling charge. The shell is launched back up the barrel at tremendous speed.

Mortars are aimed by driving three stakes in the ground at set distances in front of the mortars. Each mortar has an eyepiece attached to it. A forward observer is essential to effectively aim and hit a target. The forward observer calls for a white phosphorus shell to mark where the first round hits. He then calls for so many degrees up or down, left or right. The mortar sergeant is following these instructions by peering through the eyepiece at the stakes in front of the mortar and making adjustments to the pointing of the barrel. If the next few rounds hit the target, the forward observer calls to "fire for effect." Because of the tremendous force placed on the mortar base plate by the propulsive charges as the shells are fired, periodic aiming adjustments are necessary.

Company A had been attacked the night before and the bodies of three Japs lay ten or fifteen yards in front of our perimeter. As near as I could tell, A Company had suffered no casualties, or, perhaps, they had already been evacuated earlier. I just remember thinking, "What did I get myself into?"

Upon reporting, the company commander directed that I be taken to the 60-mm mortars in the weapons platoon and introduced to all the members of the three mortar squads. Sgt. Oscar Neukam was my squad leader. The other members of my squad were Clem Miller, Roy Brockriede, Jesse Wilhite, and Ernest E. Popp, all from Indiana, and Willie Cribb, a previous replacement from West Virginia. No one told me whom I was replacing and I really did not want to know.

The original men were members of the 38th Infantry Division of the National Guard from Indiana, mobilized in 1941. Quite a few of them had been wounded in earlier fighting but their wounds were not severe enough to be sent home. Sergeant Neukam showed me the scars in his left biceps. The A Company roster from 1945 (shown at the end of this chapter) lists nearly all its members as being from states other than Indiana. They were brought in as replacements because most of the original members from Indiana were casualties. Sergeant Neukam, Brockriede, Miller, and Popp took me under their wings. I think there were many occasions in which I owed my life to them.

Sgt. Neukam said that during the previous night's fight, the mortar barrels had been pointing almost straight up when fired. The higher the angle, the shorter the lateral distance the mortar shells travel. The Japs had been in really close. Of course the great danger in using mortars at short distances is that if there is even a slight breeze, the shells could drift and start dropping back on our own positions.

Mortar crew firing

Some of the older members of A Company searched the three Jap bodies, then dragged them into shell holes and covered them with dirt. Their decomposing bodies would start to smell by noon.

Over the next eight hours of my first day with A Company, our three 60-mm mortars fired more than 2,000 rounds at the enemy positions on Woodpecker Ridge. I found out later that these rounds cost $38 each, so our company dumped about $80,000 in mortar rounds on the Japs that day. During the next two weeks, thousands more rounds were fired into and around Woodpecker Ridge. This was in addition to all the artillery and machine gun fire and other weapons including napalm[45] from navy aircraft carrier planes.

---

[45] Napalm is a gelling agent added to petroleum or other fuel to produce an incendiary fluid. "Napalm" is a combination of the names of two of the constituents of the gel: naphthenic acid and palmitic acid. The term is used generically for flammable liquid weapons. Source: wikipedia.org

On about the fifth day of this battle, we were firing as fast as we could. There was a team of three men on each side of the mortar with the teams alternating rounds with the mortar. The first man removed the mortar shell from its transport carton, the second pulled the wire pin, and the third dropped the shell into the barrel. The third men of the teams alternated dropping shells into the tube as soon as the other man's shell had fired. Firing continued with a "whomp . . . whomp . . . whomp" eight to ten rounds per minute for hour after hour. Once an hour, the three of us changed jobs.

Willie, an earlier replacement to the squad, was on the left side of the barrel and I was on the right. After almost an hour of me dropping a shell in, then Willie dropping his in, a bad thing happened. My round had not yet cleared the tube when Willie dropped one in on top of it. Luckily, neither shell was armed yet, as the set-back pins require the inertia of launching to fall free. Both shells came out at such tremendous speed that it was impossible to see where they landed. But on the way out the fins on my shell tore three fingers on Willie's right hand. One finger was almost severed and Willie got to go to the hospital for almost a month. Boy! Was he happy!

Over the next eight or nine days, each mortar squad fired thousands more rounds at the enemy's positions. We were not immune to sniper, machine gun, or mortar fire ourselves if our positions were located. Fortunately, a mortar can be put into any depression, creek, or otherwise below ordinary ground level. For the enemy to locate our mortars, they had to have a clear view of us from the higher ground, a view we did our utmost to deny them.

After about two weeks, our riflemen finally dislodged the Japs from the mile-and-a-half-long Woodpecker Ridge and we took possession. Each unit was assigned a position on or near the ridge and an area to defend. We dug three-man fox holes all around the perimeter and facing all directions. We never knew from which direction the next attack would come. Every night, one man would be awake at all times so that at least a third of the men on the perimeter would be on guard at any time. Each guarded for two hours then slept for four hours, rotating times each night. Every hole had an army watch issued just to track the guard times. When it was his time to sleep, each man just stretched out in his portion in the three-man hole, ready to fight immediately upon being awakened.

The order was that if we saw or heard any movement inside the perimeter, we were to consider it a Jap sapper[46] or infiltrator and to fire and kill him. Needless to say no one got out of his hole from dusk to daylight. And no father-figure sergeant came around at night to check on our position as depicted in the war movies.

The Japs only attacked at night and they seemed to attack a different unit every night. If they did not attack infantry units, then they attacked artillery, quartermaster, or supply units in our rear.[47] Even if

[46] A sapper is a soldier who builds tunnels, lays or clears minefields, and in general helps forces move forward or impedes enemy movement.

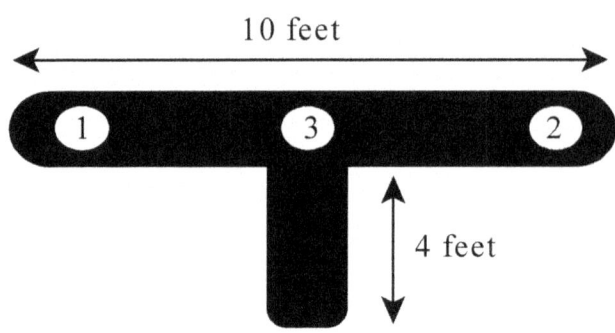

Three-man foxhole

the attack was a mile or more away, every man was awakened by the gunfire and was fully alert. If an attack on us was deemed imminent, our own artillery shells would be whizzing over our heads and exploding forty to fifty yards in front of our position. Occasionally our artillery hit on or near our positions. Once a shell struck half way up a seventy- or eighty-foot pine tree right on the edge of our perimeter. Our captain wasted no time getting on his walkie-talkie to have the artillery adjust their fire. The explosions were constant and the ground was always vibrating. Need you wonder why I do not like fireworks to this day?

After the battle for Woodpecker Ridge, we had more stable positions. And with attacks only at night, we could do anything we wished during the day—anything that needed to be done. Patrols were out every day and sometimes two or three times each day. We needed to know enemy locations, activities, and strengths. Everyone took their turn on patrol. If a mortar was taken out on patrol, the mortar squad carried the three main pieces with two members carrying shells. Each rifleman accompanying us carried two more shells. Members of the mor-

[47] "By delaying the progress of the 152nd Infantry along Woodpecker Ridge, the Japanese had also delayed the capture of Wawa Dam, for Maj. Gen. William C. Chase, commanding the 38th Division, believed it too risky to push the 145th Infantry to the dam until the 152nd had cleared Woodpecker Ridge. The period of the counterattack – roughly 4 through 18 May – cost the 145th, 151st, and 152nd Infantry Regiments approximately eighty-five men killed and 305 wounded; the [Japanese] Kobayashi Force had almost 1,300 men killed during the same period." *U.S. Army in World War II, The War in the Pacific, Triumph in the Philippines* by Robert Ross Smith.

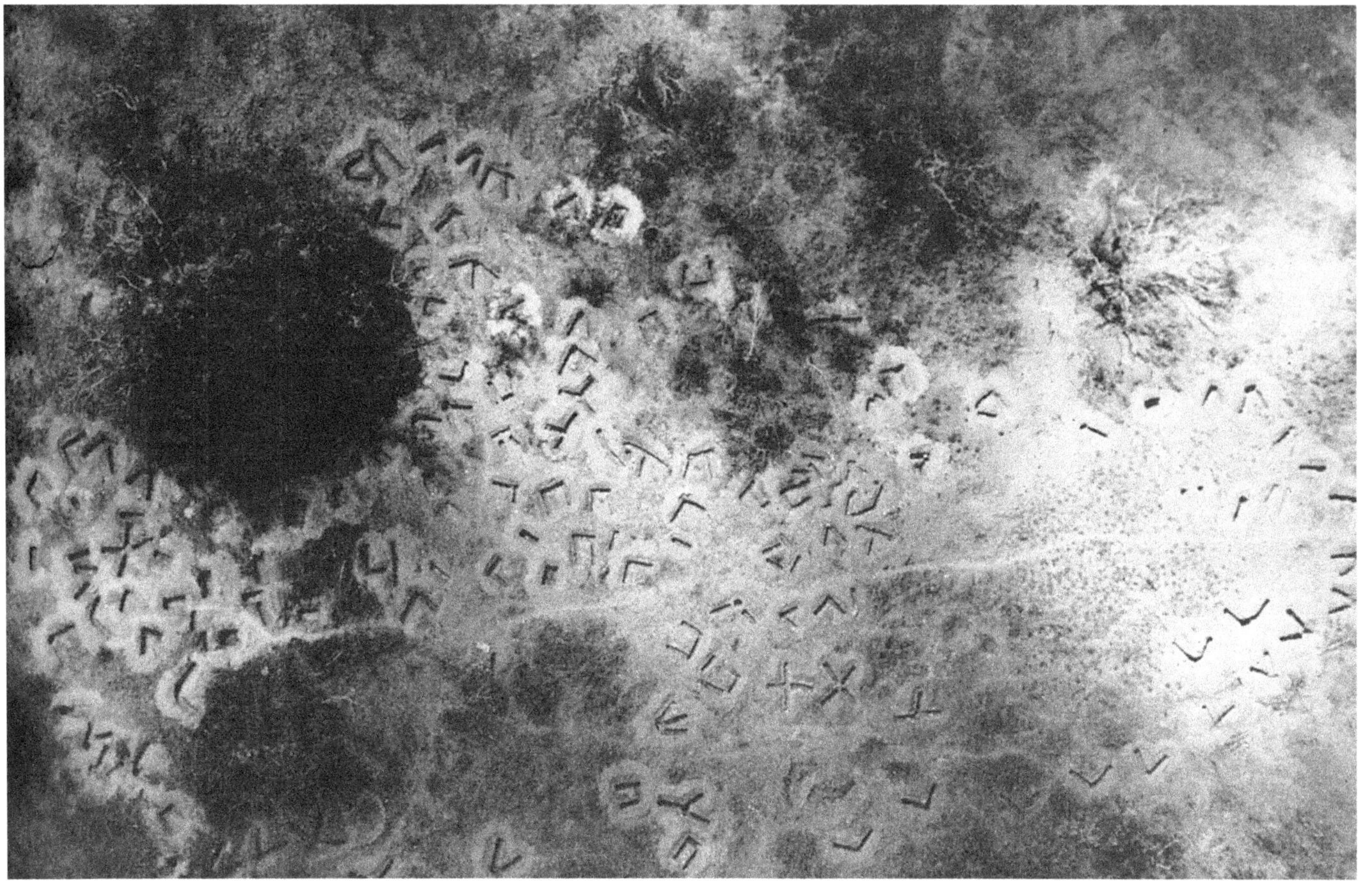

Above: Foxholes on the perimeter

Right: Group of riflemen from Company L who helped take Woodpecker Ridge. Company commander Capt. Wayne Sandefur, who earned a Silver Star at ZigZag Pass, is in the back row, second from the right.

tar squad were issued .30-caliber M1 carbines, except for the squad leader who had an M1911 semiautomatic .45-caliber pistol. The M1 carbine was not nearly as powerful a weapon as the M1 Garand rifles we had during basic training, but was half the weight and still semiautomatic—firing as fast as you could pull the trigger. The carbine also had a fifteen-round magazine rather than the eight-round magazine of the M1 rifle.

On days when we were not on patrol we cleaned our weapons, did laundry, and when we had extra water, took baths—this was not a frequent luxury. We wrote letters, received mail, read books, played cards, ate our C-rations[48] at leisure, and slept. Some-

---

[48] The C-Ration, or Type C Ration, was an individual canned, precooked, or prepared wet ration issued to US military land forces when fresh food (A-ration) or packaged unprepared food (B-Ration), prepared in mess halls or field kitchens, was impractical or not available, and when a survival ration (K-ration or D-ration) was not

```
                    HEADQUARTERS, 152d INFANTRY
                              APO 38

                                              22 May 1945

GENERAL ORDERS  )
                )
No..........27  )
            1. For exemplary performance of duty in action against
the enemy, the following named enlisted men of this command are awarded
the Combat Infantry Badge, under the provisions of WD Circular 408, 1944:
                                                   Effective:
Sgt Albert L Friesendorf                Co A     14 May 1945
Pvt Ivey L Allbritton                   Co A     14 May 1945
Pvt Leslie T Anderson                   Co A     14 May 1945
Pvt Ronald C Butler                     Co A     14 May 1945
Pvt Leland P Carpenter                  Co A     14 May 1945
Pvt Glenn R Carlson                     Co A     14 May 1945
Pvt Harold W Clark                      Co A     14 May 1945
Pvt Jake M Clowers                      Co A     14 May 1945
Pvt John Comeaux                        Co A     14 May 1945
Pvt Vittorio Cornacchione               Co A     14 May 1945
Pvt Howard L Dahlstrom                  Co A     14 May 1945
Pvt Richard F Hartley                   Co A     14 May 1945
Pvt Carrol Holcomb                      Co A     14 May 1945
Pvt Thomas A Majerowski                 Co A     14 May 1945
Pvt Lee J Mullikin                      Co A     14 May 1945
Pvt Richard D Woodruff                  Co A     14 May 1945
Pvt Adrian A Zaiontz                    Co A     14 May 1945
Pvt Malvern H Adams                     Co H     13 May 1945
Pvt Dale E Grove                        Co H     13 May 1945
Pvt John B Meadows                      Co H     13 May 1945
Pvt Floyd R Ullrich                     Co H     13 May 1945
Pvt Arlington N Wastman                 Co H     13 May 1945
Pvt James W Wells                       Co H     13 May 1945
Pvt Carl H Williams                     Co H     13 May 1945
Pvt Melvin L Willis                     Co H     13 May 1945
Pvt Theodore H Wilson                   Co H     13 May 1945
```

Above: Award of Combat Infantry Badge
Right: Combat Infantry Badge

times in the field, we did not change our clothes for periods as long as thirty days. Everyone had a body odor, but it did not bother us because we all smelled the same.

Then, just before dusk, we set out booby traps with green trip wires—the same color as the vegetation—all around the perimeter. These devices were called Bouncing Bettys. When triggered they popped about three feet above ground before exploding and sending deadly shrapnel in all directions. One night just as it was getting dark and after

78 ONLY ONE POLLACK

our booby traps were set, a runner[49] from one of our other units tripped one of our Bouncing Bettys. Fortunately, on the way up it hit him in the butt and did not reach its full height before exploding. The shrapnel struck his legs only, severely wounding him, but he did survive.

As soon as a Bouncing Betty was set off, everyone would be fully awake, expecting an imminent attack. Frequently an animal would set one off with the same result on the men of the 152nd. The Japs were very adept at avoiding our trip wires and sometimes other noises were heard outside our perimeters. In these instances an officer would fire off a parachute flare. As the flare descended, even bushes looked like advancing troops in camouflage. A lot of native bushes and small trees were cut to pieces by machine gun and rifle fire on Luzon.

With typical American ingenuity, someone figured out that if powerful search lights were aimed at low-hanging clouds—and low-hanging clouds were always there in the mountains—they would illuminate vast areas of the battlefield. This simulated a night of a full moon. Search lights were first used this way in the European theater but were in use in the Philippines while I was there. These lights could be set up many miles away and still do the job. But they also provided Japs another desirable target in the rear.

The helmet was one of our most valuable tools. Though very inadequate at its primary function of head protection, it functioned well as a wash basin for baths and laundry, a bailing vessel for water in our holes, a digging tool to move large amounts of loose soil, and, yes, a toilet when necessary. While confined to our hole at night, if you had to defecate, you did it in your helmet, without the helmet liner of course.

We used our ponchos as covers for the three-man holes, trying to keep water out from the frequent hard rains. Though they were totally inadequate for this purpose, we had nothing better. (Raise up three ponchos—so much for not letting the Japs know our exact positions!) Once near midnight, one of

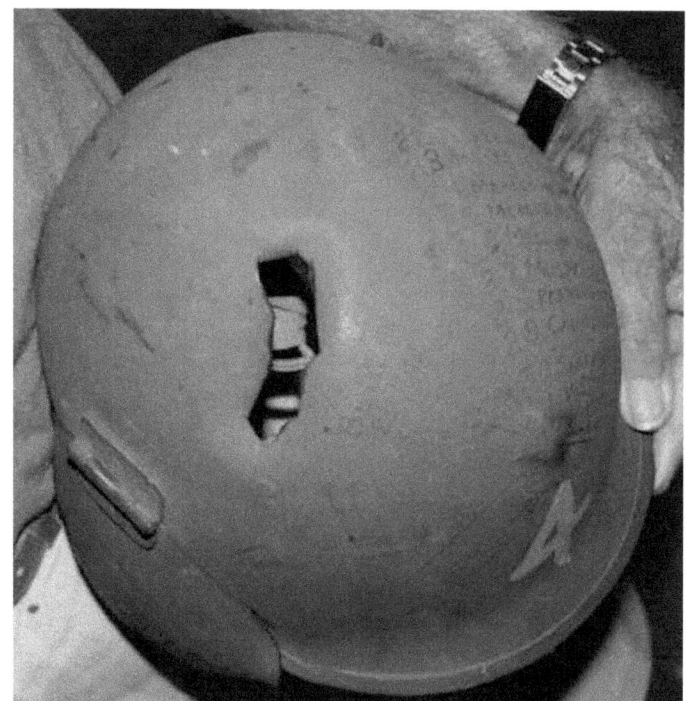

Steel helmets usually did not stop much more than fragments.

my buddies said he had to defecate—not using those exact words. Our hole held two or three inches of water from a previous heavy shower. I told him he could not get out of the hole. In the moonlight, he used his helmet sans the liner. As it bobbed in the water, this struck me as funny and I could not stop laughing. Next morning everyone in the perimeter also thought it was hilarious. Tensions eased, if only for a little while.

At night when it was my turn for guard duty, I was constantly hearing noises and imagining a Jap soldier sneaking up on me. Were these noises innocuous or perhaps completely fabricated in my brain? Before Luzon, it had been my misconception that I would be a cool person under fire and here I was a quivering mass of apprehensions and anxiety with intermittent jolts of pure fear. At the first light of dawn, an opposite feeling warmed me—a feeling of lightheadedness and elation. Everyone in the unit felt it. We had survived another night.

Finally, at the end of the first week of June, we were notified that we would be pulled back for rest. We were taken out and a reserve unit took up our positions.

---

[49] Using a human runner was another means of communication between units.

A tent city.

LIVING IN THE LAP OF LUXURY

The tent city was unbelievable: Real cots! Hot meals! Unlimited water for showers and uninterrupted dry sleep at night! Sometimes we showered two or three times a day using the only soap available, Sweetheart soap. It was a perfumed soap but believe me, no one complained. There were movies every night. The company clerk did his best but the films broke frequently, taking ten to fifteen minutes to splice back together. Our seating was on the hard ground and we sometimes just left the unfinished movie and went to bed. Dry, quiet sleep. No gun fire, no patrols, no Bouncing Bettys, no hunkering in a wet hole in the ground like an animal, just restful sleep.

Mostly we created our own entertainment. I know that everyone has heard of Bob Hope and his Entourage and the many other groups that entertained our troops. The front-line troops never got this kind of amusement. At least 90 percent of the rear echelon troops being entertained by such shows had never been in combat. In all my time overseas, I never saw one of these shows.

For our recreation, some officer at Division decided that we would have boxing matches to determine a divisional champion in each weight class. As I was the heaviest in the mortar platoon, I was talked into boxing. When I declared that I did not know the first thing about boxing, some sergeant said he would teach me. We had twenty-four hours. At 190 pounds I had to go into the light-heavyweight class.

Boxing matches went on from 9 A.M. until noon, then for a little while each afternoon. Each match was three rounds of two minutes each.

Unfortunately for me, I could not box with my glasses on, but in my first two fights I landed a few lucky punches and won both by decisions. Then came my third match. I lost to a trooper who was at least a foot shorter. I could never see his punches coming. After three rounds, each of my twelve-ounce gloves seemed to weigh fifty pounds. I could not keep them up to cover my face. I was sore from that pummeling for six days—the remainder of our rest time. The guy who beat me went on to win the regimental championship for the light-heavyweight class.

At the rest camp, everyone received two cans of free beer every day. I did not like beer so I gave mine to the old-timers. Now there was no ice to be had for cooling of the beer but there was American ingenuity. A dozen or more cans were put in the bottom of a garbage can and gasoline was poured in to cover the cans, then after a few minutes of running compressed air through the gasoline to accelerate evaporation, the beer was cold enough to drink. Talk about living dangerously! Any spark or cigarette could have set off an explosion and created an inferno. As far as I know, nothing ever went wrong. (If you ever have an ice shortage, don't do this. Just drink the warm beer.)

Having nothing better to do and as our rest time drew to a close, I decided to give my carbine a good cleaning. I took out the fifteen-round magazine and broke down the carbine. When I finished the cleaning, I put all the parts together, including the magazine but without the shells. I wanted to pull the trigger, cock it, and pull it again to insure that everything worked properly. The first time I pulled the trigger, the carbine fired, missing fellow mortar squad member Roy Brockriede's foot by inches. Roy proceeded to berate me for missing. He exclaimed that could have been his ticket home! (I still do not know whether this was in fun.) The shell must have been lodged in the magazine and this eighteen-year-old kid failed to see it.

The Philippine Government went into exile after the islands were invaded by the Japs in 1941. The Japs confiscated all hard currency, issuing their own locally-printed currency for the occupied Philippines. This Japanese occupation money was in use until early 1945 when the United States began liberating the Philippines, putting the Japs on the run. Once the Philippine government returned to power, they brought back their own currency and declared the Japanese occupation money worthless. When we were rotated from the front lines to the rear for rest, this money was no longer legal tender and it was everywhere, especially in the trash.

FINISHING THE JOB

Our life of temporary luxury came to an end and we were ordered back to the Sierra Madres, so that another unit could be pulled out for rest. Company A was assigned the lead, putting it in front of all the other units. At least we did not have to dig new holes as we were taking over another unit's posi-

Japanese Occupation Money

tions. The first night our artillery was firing at random intervals so the Japs could never know when a shell was coming. The rounds going over our heads produced a sort of sucking sound when they hit forty or fifty yards in front of us. As each shell hit, there was a gigantic explosion similar in sound and vibration to a very close lightning strike and its accompanying thunder. Multiply this by forty or fifty times each night.

The air force tried to drop our supplies by parachute but most of the time the supplies landed a mile or two away. Frequently the Japs retrieved them before we did. I later learned that the updrafts in the 100-degree heat caused the parachutes to go off course. Because of this, the army decided to use carabao[50] supply trains to deliver our supplies.

---

[50] The carabao is a type of water buffalo native to the Philippines. They are grey in color with horns that curve backward toward the neck. A male carabao can weigh over 1000 pounds. Source: wikipedia.org

Citizen Soldier or PFC

Carabao supply train

Every unit had a Philippine scout. They were Filipino citizens who had been part of the resistance and who knew the terrain and the people. They were paid the same rate as we were and were considered part of our army. I got acquainted with our scout, Frederico San Diego (pronounced "dee ahg go"), who was about my age. He spoke broken English but with my two years of high school Spanish, we communicated quite well and became very good friends.

One day Frederico was assigned to meet our carabao supply train. Water buffalo were used as beasts of burden and sometimes as many as twenty carabaos were in one train, all driven by native Filipinos. Frederico asked me if I wanted to go along, saying that we could explore a cave along the way. It was one which everyone knew about but that the engineers had not yet blown up. I asked my sergeant if I could go and, as there was practically no danger of any Jap activity during daylight, he gave permission.

Frederico and I stopped at the cave and he declared that he was going in. I could not dissuade him. He had no light except for his cigarette lighter. I took up a position about ten feet in front of the cave and behind a small tree. With the safety off, I had my fifteen-round, semiautomatic carbine aimed at that cave entrance for the Japs that I was certain would come running out. Luckily, the cave was empty and no Japs came out, only Frederico. I told him he was lucky that I had not blown him to pieces as nervous as I was. He said the cave was about twelve feet deep and empty. We then proceeded to the supply train and guided them back to our positions without further delay.

On another occasion as a supply train was approaching our position. A round of artillery fell short, killing one of the carabao drivers and two carabaos. For a time after that we did not get supplied because the carabao drivers refused to deliver to our positions.

Ammunition was never in short supply as it was a priority item. But during that period we were without our C-rations. C-rations consisted of two vacuum-tight cans. One contained the main part of the meal, fifteen ounces of beef stew, frankfurters and beans, pork and beans, or some other high protein food. This entree was usually eaten cold but it was packed with calories and vitamins. The other can held numerous items: hard bread or crackers, cookies, hard candy, an envelope of Nestlé instant coffee, two cigarettes, chewing gum, and the all-important toilet paper. As food supplies ran low, our C-rations were replaced by D-rations for four days. D-rations consisted of high energy chocolate bars three times a day. I got really tired of chocolate. Previously I hated C-rations but after a few days of nothing but chocolate bars, I was happy to have good old, almost home-cooked, C-rations again. Yummy!

In the last week of June 1945, Company A was to be the lead company in the assault on Regimental Objective Hill (ROH). The artillery and our mortars and machine guns pulverized the hill for two hours. Then the navy's planes torched it with napalm just before our riflemen began the attack. Thirty minutes later the weapons platoon of mortar men and machine gunners followed. There was no return fire from ROH. The Japs had withdrawn, probably during our barrages, but they left their dead behind. When the napalm hit ROH, it burned these bodies and caused an indescribable stench.

As we were proceeding up ROH, a jeep carrying three or four officers was driving to the edge of the hill we had just vacated. All of a sudden a huge explosion blew the jeep into the air and flipped it over. It had hit a land mine. These officers were the only casualties we suffered during the initial assault.

As we walked to the top of ROH, the engineers were blowing up Jap caves along the way. They yelled "Fire in the hole!" before they blew each cave. The engineers did not care if there were Japs in the cave or not, and neither did we.

> ### CHOCOLATE FOR THE TROOPS
> "In 1937 the [Hershey] company started to work closely with the US Quartermaster General to develop high-energy chocolate rations that could sustain GIs when they had nothing else to eat. The result was the Field Ration D, a nutrition-packed chocolate bar that contained 600 calories. During World War II the Hershey factory operated around the clock, seven days a week, churning out millions of Ration D bars. By the time the war was over, the company had supplied more than one billion rations to US soldiers—a feat that turned Hershey into a household name."
>
> **-excerpt from an unknown magazine**

When we got to the top of ROH, Sgt. Neukam passed around a jar of Vicks and told us to stuff our noses with it. He said it would lessen the stench if we breathed only through our mouths. We congratulated ourselves on not being fired upon. Most of the old-timers staked claims on the deepest shell holes and the Jap shelters. The rest of us, while waiting for our assignments, took off our packs and weapons. I had been carrying the heavy 60-mm mortar baseplate. We also took off our helmets and wiped away the sweat.

But the Japs had their machine guns zeroed in on ROH from another hill. They knew exactly what we would do once we had achieved our objective. They opened up on us. The instant the firing started, I knew what was happening and dove into the nearest shell hole. I did not have my helmet on and hit rocks at the edge of the hole, putting a three- or four-inch gash in my forehead. Bullets were flying everywhere, slamming into our weapons and equipment, ricocheting off rocks.

Soon D Company's .50-caliber machine guns and 81-mm mortars which had been covering our advance silenced the enemy fire. Our 1st sergeant came around checking for casualties and saw that I had my handkerchief pressed to my bleeding scalp. He

As long as we were receiving no enemy fire, we were told to walk in each other's footsteps to avoid anti-personnel mines.

asked if I was hit. I said "No," that I had hit my head on a rock. He told me where to find battalion aid and to go and get stitched up as soon as possible. Others were not as lucky as I. We found two of our buddies dead and eight or nine more wounded. I knew God was watching over me.

My equipment was shot all to hell. My field pack was riddled. My helmet had a hole in it about where my right ear would have been and my carbine stock was splintered. I retrieved my field pack and unrolled my poncho. It had at least fifty holes. I wanted to keep my poncho and my other bullet-riddled equipment but the only way to get replacements was to give up the originals. That is how the rear echelons got the great souvenirs, which they then sold to the highest bidder.

After the Jap guns were quiet for fifteen or twenty minutes, I took off zigzagging for a hundred yards or so and finally reached the downslope of the hill opposite that exposed to the enemy fire. At the bottom, I found our medics taking care of the wounded. One of our riflemen was weeping over another soldier who had been killed. With his head bowed as if in prayer, he held his friend's hand. They had been best friends, came from the same town, and went to the same high school. Undoubtedly they had pledged to look after each other.

Two riflemen were severely wounded but had been stabilized on makeshift stretchers. At the front we had no real stretchers and they were attempting to use blankets as stretchers with little success. There were seven other walking wounded. The other dead rifleman had been hit in both biceps, the carotid artery, and the torso. He had been bleeding down both arms and the torso but when I saw him the blood was completely dry. When the heart stops, wounds no longer bleed. No medic could have done anything for him before he bled to death.

I asked how far it was to battalion aid and was told about a quarter of a mile. We had to go that much farther to get the wounded and the dead evacuated. I volunteered to carry one dead soldier as he weighed only about 140 pounds. They put him on my shoulder and I carried him in the fireman's carry. The other dead soldier was carried down by his friend. Several times I did not think that I would make it but it helped that it was downhill all the way and that I was able to carry this guy while being thankful that I was not the one to be carried.

When we reached battalion aid all the wounded received care and I got eight or ten stitches in my scalp. I returned to my position and to our immense relief, we received no more Jap machine gun fire. We speculated that the official report to regimental headquarters stated that our casualties were light. To those of us who lived through the Jap counterattack, the casualties were anything but light. Thankfully, none of my mortar squad members were lost.

In another half hour our 1st sergeant came around again. He said that the cooks had brought hot chow for us and that it was in the next hollow just past battalion aid, about a half mile away. We could take turns going to eat. Each man had to decide for himself whether it was worth possibly getting shot for a hot meal. Almost to a man, we all agreed to take the risk as we had not had a hot meal in a couple of weeks. So when it was my turn to go, I again zig-zagged about a hundred yards through the perimeter. At one point, I kicked dirt and rocks in a hole and on top of one of our riflemen. He proceeded to curse a blue streak at me. I cannot say that I blamed him.

I remember that particular hot meal prepared especially for us. It was the standard army meal of chipped beef on toast, creamed potatoes, carrots and peas, honest-to-goodness hot coffee and powdered milk with no taste. Needless to say, everything actually tasted great and I went for seconds. Among the troops, chipped beef on toast was commonly known as "SOS," s___ on a shingle.

Our taking of ROH opened up new avenues for supplies and for bringing in heavier weapons and even flame-throwing tanks, which were used for the first time in the Pacific theater. Company A was held in reserve on the next assault on the hill from which we had received the deadly machine gun fire. We had front row seats and I even felt sorry for the Japanese, especially after the flame-throwing tanks went to work.

Someone in ordnance had decided that our hand grenades made too much noise when thrown. When the pin was pulled on the hand grenade, the handle flew out, making a noise similar to a .22-caliber rifle shot or perhaps a toy cap pistol. After the handle popped, you had five seconds to get rid of the grenade. Ordnance decided that when the enemy heard this sound, they would hit the ground as did all of us. At the end of June we were issued new noiseless grenades.

A new acquaintance of mine was stationed in the next hole. The night after we received the new grenades, at around midnight, a loud explosion was heard close by. Everyone was on full alert the rest of the night. In the morning we found my new friend dead in his hole. The speculation was that he heard a noise and pulled the pin on a grenade. He never saw or heard the handle on the grenade fly out because it was too dark and made no noise. He had it in his hand next to his chest when it exploded. I saw that his head, chest and torso were completely black when I helped lift him from the hole. Speculation was that it was either a horrible accident or a suicide. I think it was an accident.

The last week of July our company commander called all of us who were not on specific duty or on patrol to an assembly. He called for a rifleman, whom I did not know, to come forward. The captain announced that he was going home because he was only sixteen years old. His mother had finally tracked him down.

I do not know how the others felt about this. I was both jealous and resentful. I felt, "Why can't I go home? After all I'm only two years older." We never discussed this but I think everyone in the unit felt the same way.

With nothing better to do one day, I was again

Citizen Soldier or PFC

Photo of Manila by S.Sgt. Fredrick Dale McVay (1916-1989).

cleaning my carbine. With the clip out, I disassembled it into three main parts: the barrel assembly, the stock, and the trigger assembly and as I was oiling the trigger assembly, a tiny spring flew out. I looked and looked for it but it was gone forever in the dirt and muck. That spring pulled the trigger back into position for the next firing. The carbine was still operational, but I had to push the trigger forward manually for the next firing. Sgt. Neukam said he would order a new carbine for me, but I replied that I only needed another trigger housing. (I did not want to clean that d_____ cosmoline from a new carbine.) It took a month but I got a new trigger assembly and once again had a truly semiautomatic carbine.

We were pulled out once more for much needed rest in the first week of August. A friend of mine asked if I would like to go for an airplane ride. His brother was a C-47 transport pilot and regularly flew milk runs[51] all over Luzon. We could get day passes to go into Manila if we wanted them, although Manila was in shambles and there really was nothing to see but ruins. However, there was one huge United Service Organization (USO) club which was always so crowded with military personnel that you could not even turn around in it.

I agreed to the flight and, after we thumbed our way to Clark Field, we met the pilot and copilot, boarded the C-47, found our seats on the floor, and settled down for a nice 300-mile float through the

---

[51] A milk run is a round trip which facilitates both distribution and collection of supplies.

38TH DIVISION, 152ND REGIMENT COMPANY A ROSTER

Chesler, James R., 2305 Englewood Ave., Durham, N. C.
Ebert, Frank M., Philadelphia State Hospital, Philadelphia 14, Pa.
Horrall, Ira M., 514 S. E. 4th St., Washington, Ind.
Keller, Roy W., Route 1, Silverton, Ore.
Laurent, Clyde J., Probasco St., Cincinnati, Ohio
Noelle, Albert T., R. R. 1, Mt. Vernon, Ind.
Pharr, Ralph P., 325 Taylor St., Barnesville, Ga.
Alban, Donald E., Route 1, Nevada, Ohio
Allbritton, Ivey L., Route 3, Oak Grove, La.
Allison, Hector M., 119-22 I71st St., St. Albans, Long Island. N.Y.
Alphin, Roscoe J., Box 153, Dover, N. C.
Alvarado, Johnny S., 1427 Kingman St., San Bernardino, CA
Anderson, Clifford W., 1319 Atapahoe Ave., Salt Lake City, UT
Anderson, Clinton D., 215 Orange St., Fillmore, Calif.
Anderson, Leslie T., Route 6, Decorah, Iowa
Anderton, Garth L., 382 Tod Park, Tooele, Utah.
Andrews, Ortis E., Kanorado, Kan.
Andrews, Roswell H., Gen. Del., Neuville, Tex.
Archer, Donald D., 113 Meeker Rd., El Monte, Calif.
Arnold, Colie B., Route 2, Lexington, S.C.
Arnold, James H., Rotite 1, Petersburg, Ind.
Arnold, James M., Evanston, Ind.
Arnold, Robert G., Bayard, W. Va.
Ashcraft, Fred C., 2701 La Salle Place, Dallas. Tex.
Astran, Albert, Box 776, Seguin, Tex.
Atkinson, Jim T., Route 1, Manila, Ark.
Aust, Roy V., Route 1, Scooba, Miss.
Baczenski, Stanley W., 278 Howard St., Larksville, Pa.
Baehl, Harold A., General Delivery, Armstrong, Ind.
Barker, Esto E., Route 3, Boonville, Ind.
Barnet, Joseph M., 1418 Tuscarawas St., Canton, Ohio
Barranco, Charles P., 3728 N. Kenneth Ave., Chicago, Ill.
Bath, Gilbert W., St. Anthony, Ind.
Bauer, Albert A., 2420 West Franklin St., Evansville, Ind.
Bauer, Elmer A., 2420 West Franklin St., Evansville, Ind.
Bava, Frank A., 1220 Arnold St., Chicago Heights, Ill.
Bavery, Paul E., Route 1, Basco, Ill.
Beason, John E., Route 1, Jamestown, Ala.
Begerman, Ernest, 409 S. E. 6th St., Linton, Ind.
Belcher, Cecil E., Route 3, Vincennes, Ind.
Bellows, Richard L., Fonda, N.Y.
Belk, Jasper, Route 2, Box 984, Louisville, Ky.
Berger, George W., Fairplay, Md.
Berini, Gino J., 83 Smith St., Barre, Vt.
Best, Leland A., R. R. 2, Kingston, Mich.
Bettag, Alvin S., Route 3, Dale, Ind.
Beute, Harold H., 501 Crystal, Grandville, Mich.
Billington, Robert B., 603 East 8th St., Long Beach, Calif.
Blades, Forrest E., Gen. Del., Beaverton, Mich.
Blalock, Charles C., London, Ark.
Bland, William H., 234 Temple Ave., Indianapolis, Ind.
Booth, Frank R., Box 365, Montgomery, W. Va.
Bosler, Ernest M., Route 1, Dale, Ind.
Branch, Charlie B., Jr., 313 Maple Ave., Fayetteville, N. C.
Bright, Walter P., Route 4, Sanford, N. C.
Brinich, George W., Route I, Pottsville, Pa.
Brockriede, Roy W., Route I, Stendal, Ind.
Brooks, Francis A., 16 Walker St., New London, Conn.
Brooks, Orion H., 2126 ½ W. Franklin St.. Evansville, Ind.
Brown, Kenneth W., Route 3, Booneville, Ind.
Brown, Ray M., 1729 E. First St., Bend, Ore.
Burdette, Forest, Route 2, Oakland City, Ind.
Burdulis, Andrew, 69 Covert St., Brooklyn, N.Y.
Burton, Lester M., Hymera, Ind.
Butler, Quinten G., Leola, Ark.
Butler, Ronald C., 11695 Westwood, Detroit 23, Mich.
Cairns, Edward S., 23 Adams Ave., Endicott, N.Y.
Carlson, Glenn R., Sr., 1025 Dakota Ave., South Sioux City, Neb.
Carpenter, Leland W., 140 N. Hester St., Norwalk, Ohio
Castelli, Constantino, 740 E. 225th St., Bronx, N.Y.
Chebunin, Nicholas E., 219 Walnut St., Trenton, N.J.
Christner, John W., Box 703, Dawson, Pa.
Chuk, John, 1327 Summit Ave., Monessen, Pa.
Clark, Harold W., Box 223, Jefferson, Tex.
Clowers, Jake M., Route 1, Joshua, Tex.
Coleman, Benton D • Gen. Del., Leechburg, Pa.
Combs, Titus J., Route 2, Big Spring, Tenn.
Comeaux, John, Route 2, Box 436, Lake Charles, La.
Conrad, Melvin R., Rd. 1, Colora, Md.
Cornacchione, Victorio, 721 Fifth Ave., Pittsburg, Pa.
Cox, Raymon T., Route 2, Amory, Miss.
Cribb, Willie M., Box 706, Andrews, S.C.
Crosby, John D., Shelburn, Ind.
Curran, John P., Jr., 67 Keystone Ave., Upper Darby, Pa.
Danorovich, Alfred T., 299 Quinnipiac St., Wallingford, Conn.
Daugherty, Carl B., 913 S. Harlin Ave., Evansville, Ind.
Davis, Paul H., Kingswood, Ky.
Dawkins, Joseph R., 147 Columbia St., Cohoes, N.Y.
Delaney, Halley L., Jr., LaBelle, Fla.
Del Femine, Dominic, Rd. 1, Route 40, Bedford, N.J.
Dehart, Wavy L., Route 1, Rockport, Ind.
Donaldson, Loyce W., Copperhill, Tenn.
Dotterweich, Ambrose P., St. Meinrad, Ind.
Dowell, James J., Route 2, Hardinsburg, Ky.
Duchi, Angelo A., Box 9~. McCloud, Calif.
Evans, Lowell R., Box 34, New Castle, Ind.
Evrard, Joseph A., Star Route, Gatchel, Ind.
Fairchild, John J., 507 Humphrey St., Monroe, Mich.
Falgoust, Joseph L., Box 222, Vacherie, La.
Fedewa, Harold C., RFD 4, St. John, Mich.
Fisher, Harold, Route 28, Elberfeld, Ind.
Frederick, Charles H., 2116 N. Indiana, Oklahoma City, OK
Friesendorf, Albert L., 982 West Side Ave., Jersey City, N.J.
Garber, Paul R., Route 2, Columbiana, Ohio
Giana, Peter M., 121 Baldwin St., Newark, N.J.
Glass, John S., Route 2, Box 170 A, Yazoo City, Miss.
Gray, Eldon, Route 1, Haubstadt, Ind
Harris, Floyd E., Winslow, Ind.
Hartley, Richard F., 6656 Barton Ave., Detroit, Mich.

continued on page 88

---

heavens. After an hour, halfway to Lingayen Gulf, we hit turbulence. I thought that airplane was coming apart. There was tremendous shaking and rattling. That airplane was going to break up into its very elemental components—and do it with me in it! I had a vision of my mother and father getting another dreaded telegram. The telegram would say I was killed in an airplane crash and they would be puzzled as to why I was even in an airplane.

I prayed harder than I ever did while in a hole at the front. I told God that if He got me out of this safely, I would never fly again. God got me and the plane down safely and, mercifully, we hit no turbulence on the flight back. True to my promise to God, I have never flown in another airplane.

When I was assigned to the 38th Division, I still had revenge in my mind. When the bullets start flying, revenge becomes the farthest thing from the mind. You have no past because it is irrelevant and no future because you may not have one. The only thing that matters is the present and what is happening right now, at that very instant. It did not take long for me to accept the Lord at His word when He said, "The Lord says—vengeance is mine."[52]

These many decades later, I can still remember the names of all my teachers in school and I seem to remember everything that happened in combat. But I cannot remember the names of most of my fellow soldiers and friends. I do remember the names of my mortar squad members and that of our flame-thrower,[53] Ivey L. Albritton from Louisiana, but not the others. They are nameless figures to me.

I have been told that my condition is not that unusual. I am told that the mind shuts down and does not want to remember others' names—in case they are the ones who would never again look up at the Golden Gate Bridge.

---

[52] Romans 12:19

[53] The individual hand-held flame throwers could shoot flames fifteen to twenty feet. The flame-throwing tanks could shoot flames 100 feet or more. We had three flame-thrower men in A Company's weapons platoon.

Citizen Soldier or PFC

38ᵀᴴ DIVISION, 152ᴺᴰ REGIMENT COMPANY A ROSTER

Continued from page 87

Hauser, Walter C., 16th and Franklin St., Tell City, Ind.
Hendrickson, Robert G., 2992 Bruckner Blvd., Bronx, N.Y.
Henry, Robert J., 1026 Eighth, Las Vegas, N.M.
Higgins, Homer L., Route 2, Stroud, Okla.
Higgins, James P., 11 Washington St., Fitchburg, Mass.
Hinojosa, Tony L., 625 20th St., Corpus Christi, Tex.
Holcomb, Carrol, Floresville, Tex.
Holden, Wallace B., RFD 1, Chester, Pa.
Hollander, Albert R., Evansville, Ind.
Hopkins, Donald N., RFD 3, Box 324, North Ogden, Utah
Hornsby, Ace, Route 2, Box 31, Winter Haven, Fla.
Houchens, James E., Route 3, Box 62, Charlottesville, Va.
Huddleston, Archer C., Route I, Farmville, Va.
Ike, Willard L., Rd. 3, E. Stroudsburg, Monroe, Pa.
Ingham, Donald L., 139 Maryland St., Rochester, N.Y.
Ippolito, Anthony J., 98 Pemberwick Rd., East Port Chester, N.Y.
Janota, Frank C., 232 E. 25th St., Chicago Heights, Ill.
Jent, Leander A., St. Meinrad, Ind.
Jew, Richard, 181 7th St., Oakland, Calif.
Jochim, Oliver F., Mariah Hill, Ind.
Johnson, Albert E., Tacoma, Wash.
Johnson, John T., 80,. Redgate Ave., Norfolk, Va.
Jones, Harold F., Railroad Ave., Mahwah, N.J.
Kenney, William H., 106 W. Penn St., Evansville, Ind.
Kincer, Lee W., 1480 W. Spiller St., Wytheville, Va.
Kleban, Joseph, Jr., Excelsior, Pa.
Koenig, Ivan J., Route 3, Schulenburg, Tex.
Kopf, George H., Jr., 1160 Oliver St., North Tonawanda, N.Y.
Koser, Leroy G., Route 1, Columbia, Pa.
Kovarcik, Milan S., 1518 8th St., Muskegon, Mich.
Kruse, Franz A., 1125 Montecito Dr., San Gabriel, Calif.
Kutil, George W., 1809 Douglas Ave., Racine, Wis.
Langsi, Albert M., 3228 B Brokaw St., Honolulu, Oahu, T.H.
Larkin, Thomas J., 828 Greenfield Ave.• Pittsburgh, Pa.
Lawrence, Preston O., Route 3, Sherman, Tex.
Lawson, Charlie L., Route 2, Clinchport, Va.
Lee, Robert E., Gen. Del., Oak Grove, La.
Levy, Jacob, 430 McDonald Ave., Brooklyn, N.Y.
Litherland, Alva, Route 1, Tell City, Ind.
Loehden, Ernest J., Route 1, Box 208, Hillsboro, Ore.
Lynch, Dennis W., Browns Valley, Minn.
MacDonald, Joseph A., Kentville, Nova Scotia, Canada
Macko, Stanley J., 2626 E. Ontario St., Philadelphia, Pa.
Maddox, Robert B., 9427 Ave., "H", Houston, Tex.
Majerowski, Thomas A., 4781 N. 53rd St., Milwaukee, Wis.
Malmstrom, Herbert L., 1381 Searle St., St. Paul (1), Minn.
Markley, Harold I., Rd. 1, Bareville, Pa.
Martin, Walter C., Picayune, Miss.
McAdam, Philip A., 1088 Lombard Ave., St. Paul, Minn.
McCarthy, Robert J., 31 Clark St., Danvers, Mass.
McCorriston, John P., 852 Jack~on St., Apt. 22, San Francisco, Calif.
McIlree, Arthur B., 405 Date St., Apt. 3, San Diego 1, Calif.
Meekman, Robert J., Boothwyn, Pa.
Michina, William J., Box 91, Lilly, Pa.
Miller, Clem F., Route 1, Mt. Vernon, Ind.
Miller, Michael F., 1120 N. Main St., Evansville, Ind.
Miller, Samuel B., 1249 Scott Ave., Kansas City, Kan.
Minko, Stanley, Box 21, Smithmill, Pa.
Moore, George F., Route 2, Dale, Ind.
Morris, Raymond D., Box 247, Exeter, Neb.
Morrow, Lawrence E., 1005 W. New York, Indianapolis, Ind.
Morrow, Marshall R., 1611 W. 261st St., Lomita, Calif.
Mullikin, Lee J., 2116 W. Roosevelt Rd., Chicago, Ill.
Mutryn, Benjamin J., 815 Mason St., Schenectady, N.Y.
Nash, Oral E., 1009 W. Walnut St., Washington, Ind.
Neukam, Oscar C., Dubois, Ind.
Niehaus, Alvin J., Route 2, Ferdinand, Ind.
Nielsen, Herbert R., RFD I, San Pierre, Ind.
Obsharsky, John, Lock 4, North Charleroi, Pa.
Odyniec, Joseph A., 3226 Salmon St., Philadelphia, Pa.
O'Keefe, James D., Box 153, Leona. Tex.
Orander, Roy P., Crumpler. W. Va.
Pascoe, Harry W., 421 Eagle Ave., Hanover, Pa.
Paterson, Robert, 322 West 4th St., South Boston, Mass.
Peach, Donald D., 702 10th St., Huntingburg, Ind.
Peck, Paul R., 616 8th Ave., Altoona, Pa.
Peischl, Edmund W., 11095 Findlay Ave., Detroit, Mich.
Perry, Roy E., RFD 1, Winslow, Ind.
Petti, Fiorentino, P., 451 Maple Ave., Boundbrook, N.J.
Polk, Leonard, 914 Twyckenham Dr., South· Bond, Ind.
Popp, Ernest E., Route 2, Otwell, Ind.
Potts, Michael, 438 Whitridge Ave., Baltimore, Md.
Pursley, James C., 3130 S. 3rd St., Louisville, Ky.
Quinlean, John, 253 Van Buren St., Lockport, N.Y.
Racey, Donald J., Oaktown, Ind
Raines, Clayton M., Route 4, Sylvester, Ga.
Rakes, Junior L., Montcalm, W. Va.
Ramsey, Harlan E., Center St., Corinth, N.Y.
Raney, Robert O., 104 Harden Ave., Washington, Ind.
Rankin. James G., Star Route, Box. 24, Darlove, Miss.
Rath, Lyle D., 917 5th Ave., S. E., Jamestown, N.D.
Reitzner, Edwin A., 227 S. Outagamie St., Appleton, Wis.
Rembacz, Walter L., 1547 W. Walton St., Chicago, Ill.
Rentas, Noel, Bo El Pino, Villalba, Puerto Rico
Reynolds, Charles C., Route 3, Greenup, Ill.
Riccomi, Aldo J., 927 Hampshire St., San Francisco, Calif.
Rickard, Arthur E., Oaktown, Ind.
Robinson, Allen C., Bendville, Ind.
Robinson, Richard B., 510 Manila St., Vincennes, Ind.
Robinson, William .T., R. R. 1, Bruceville, Ind.
Rodgers, Herbert N., Mt. Crawford, Va.
Rogers, Edward L, 4218 Third St., Louisville, Ky.
Runn, Arnold E., R. R. 4, Clay Center, Kan.
Rusnak, Joseph, Bldg., 45, Apt.]., West Run Road, Munhall, Pa.
Russell, Richard N., 203 East Rose, Pittsburg, Kan.
Rutherford, Alvin R., Star Route, Callihan, Tex.
Ryan, Daniel F., 37 South Owl St., Shamokin, Pa.
Sagers, William D., Box 514, Ely, Nev.
Saviri, Frank, 215 East 28th St., New York City, N.Y.
Schrage, Howard, 219 River Ave., Patchogue, Long Island, N.Y.
Schultz, Lloyd O., Fosston, Minn.
Seals, James P., River St., Cannelton, Ind.
Seaton, William A., 1829 Hugher Ave., Owensboro, Ky.
Seger, Oscar F., R. R. 4, Jasper, Ind.
Shearer, Doyle C., Box 32, Bula, Tex.
Shelton, Bonner C.• 279 Vine St., Murray. Utah.
Shipskey, Michael, 21 Jefferson St., Simpson, Pa.
Shores, Earle L., Route 3, Scotteville, Va.
Shuck, Clifford H., 1262 East Division St., Evansville, Ind.
Siano, Albert A., 73 Hackensack, Woodridge, N.J.
Silberberg, Emanuel R., 803 Driggs Ave., Brooklyn, N.Y.
Sivley, Gene M., Route 3, Hartselle, Ala.
Slagle, Leonard P., 116th Queen St., Chestertown, Md.
Slavina, Nicholas, Bentleyville, Pa., Box 237.
Smith, Paul W., 3317 Porter Ave., Ogden, Utah.
Snider, Stanley, Wolfe, W. Va.
Socia, Charles A., 25866 Lawn Ave., Roseville, Mich.
Spengler, Kenneth F., 1723 North Church St.• Portland, OR
Spitzmiller, Charles H., 1201 East Iowa St., Evansville, Ind.
Splater, Rader S., 625 South Meridian St., Washington, Ind.
Spratt, Stephen B., 4128 Joliet, Hazel Park, Mich.
Stahlbusch, Kenneth L., 14209 Faircrest, Detroit, Mich.
Stander, Raymond P., 1539 Lowrie St., N. S., Pittsburg, Pa.
Stanley, Harold E., Route 1, Box 203, Gresham, Ore.
Steckler, Edward A., R. R. 5, Evansville, Ind.
Steinberg, August W., 6734 South Bell Ave., Chicago. Ill.
Stephens, Martin L., Route 1; Painsville, Ohio.
Stimson, Claude L., Bushyhead, Okla.
Strawbridge, Virgil, Route 2, Red Bay, Ala.
Suarez~Agosto, Francisco, Bo Sibuco, Corozal, Puerto Rico.
Szymanski, Stanley W., 3529 Filmore St., Gary, Ind.
Tabor, Thomas L., Prairie Du Sac, Wis.
Taylor, Albert L., 315 Milan, Mitchell, S. Dak.
Teklinsky, Francis J., 17th West 65th St., N.Y.
Thomason, Malcomb A.,. Route 2, Attalla, Ala.
Terrazas, Charles, 4024 Tyler St., Fresno, Calif.
Tillman, Gerald J., 1232 South Kildare, Chicago, Ill.
Tune, Jimmie L. Jr., 3813 Roberts St., Greenville, Tex.
Turpen, Vencie F., Route 2, Lincoln, Mo.
Vaal, Roman, St. Meinrad, Ind.
Vance, Jesse J., Jr., Orkney, Ky.
VanCleve, Edward E., 1225 West Bridge, Blackwell, Okla.
VanDenLangenburg, Wilbert P., Route 6, Green Bay, Wis.
VanTassal, Edward, 609 Sibley St., N. W., Grand Rapids. Mich.
Vargas-Rentas, Julio, Bo Collores, Juana Diaz, Puerto Rico
Vasquez, Pedro C., Box 681, Brawley, Calif.
Visgalio, Frank, 1610 Brighton Place, N., S. Pittsburg, Pa.
Vitelli, Ralph W., 510 Farragut Ave., Trenton, N.J.
Vuylsteke, Paul E. Jr., Route 3, Box 82, Hillsboro, Ore.
Waldrep, William H., Route 1, Dixie, Ga.
Wallace, Sheridan, Stendal, Ind.
Wallaker, Richard T., Frankfort, Benzine, Mich.
Wallensak, Donald J., 3425 North 55th St., Milwaukee, Wis.
Walters, William F., 309 Northeast 1st St., Washington; Ind.
Wanserski, Ralph A., 1500 Center St., Racine, Wis.
Ward, Edward, 1350 Portage, Apt. 4, Kalamazoo, Mich.
Ward, George R., 216 Hatt St., Dundas, Ontario, Canada.
Ward, William S., Route 1, Bladenboro, N. C.
Warner, Clarence L., 1412 Keller St., Evansville, Ind.
Webster, Morris 1., Route 2, Pelican Lake, Wis.
Weigel, Kenneth C.: Route 4, Platteville, Wis.
White, Charles A., Lincoln, Maine
Whitelock, Donald B., 1208 Walnut St., Petersburg, Ind.
Wihl, Robert C., 2129 Sullivant Ave., Columbus, Ohio
Wilhite, Jesse R., 503 Engle St., Evansville, Ind.
Williams, Ovile, R. R. 2, Summer Shade, Ky.
Williams, Thomas E., 295 North Morrison, San Jose, Calif.
Williams, William J.. Reedsville, Ohio
Wiorek, Gerald J., 7142 Arcola, Detroit, Mich.
Winn, Thomas J., 417 Bank St., New Albany, Ind.
Wirth, Melvin F., General Delivery, Kings Valley, Ore.
Wood. Edward 1.. Box 314, De Pue, Ill.
Woodruff, Richard D., 2845 Glenn Ave., Winston Salem, N. C.
Wright, Lawson E., 1419 A. Monroe St., St. Louis, Mo.
Young, George E., RFD 2, Jacksonville, Ala.
Zaiontz, Adrian A., 415 West French St., Cuero, Tex.

Chapter 8
TRANSITION FROM THE 38TH INFANTRY DIVISION TO THE 86TH INFANTRY DIVISION

We were relieved for our ten-day rest during the first week of August 1945. I had my nineteenth birthday, but it was just like any other day. The day after, however, I was called into the company C.O.'s tent. My first thought was "What did I do wrong now?" To my relief and surprise, Lucian Urbanczyk (Uncle Anton's oldest son), who was in the navy, had come to see me. I do not know how Lucian ever found me among hundreds of military units and hundreds of thousands of troops, but here he was in the captain's tent. His ship, the *USS Clearfield*,[54] dropped anchors in Manila Bay and he had liberty so he hitched a ride to our tent city. I was relieved from duty so I could spend time with Lucian.

After we caught up with all the news from home, we entered the mess tent for a meal. Everyone stared at me, wondering what a sailor—a very unusual sight—and I had in common. He said that being a sailor, he had no trouble hitching a ride because wearing navy blues was such a contrast to the khaki and olive drab uniforms in the Philippines. After way too few hours, Lucian headed back to his ship, as it was leaving the next morning. We had shared a great visit.

I had other relatives in the armed services. Alvin Snoga was in an infantry division in the European theater. Victor Hannah was in the navy. Ermit Urbanczyk, Emanuel Gwosdz, and my brother, Claude, entered the services later.

Following a two-day rest, we commenced training for the anticipated assault on the Japanese home islands. We were living in our tent city and went through our basic training all over again—target practice, close order drilling, military tactics, all of that wonderful basic training, again and again. In heavy weapons we were introduced to the new recoilless rifle. Much like a bazooka, it was a shoulder-fired weapon or alternatively supported on a tripod, but actually fired a modified artillery shell down a rifled barrel. This was a very effective weapon, doing as much damage as a large artillery round but used by a couple of infantrymen. Often fired point-blank, it could blow up caves and bunkers.

After eight days intensive training, we again took up combat positions, relieving another company for rest. Our regular routine resumed with daily patrols, with sometimes as many as three patrols out at the same time, setting booby traps every night, and one third of the men awake at all times, every night.

Our only connection to the outside world was *The Cycloner*,[55] our daily division newspaper. Each squad received a copy and each of us read every word. One day *The Cycloner* reported that an atom bomb had been dropped on Hiroshima, Japan. But what did that mean? It was just another part of the war. After all, the bombing of Japan had become an almost daily occurrence. So what was one more bomb? A few days later we learned that another atomic bomb had been dropped on Nagasaki on August 9. Then we read that the Allies were demanding the unconditional surrender of Japan under threat that Japan would otherwise be obliterated. Convinced that we could have had many more such horrendous bombs, the government of Japan—the emperor and his generals—finally decided to comply.

On August 15 Emperor Hirohito addressed the Japanese people and announced the surrender of the Empire of Japan to the Allies. We were ecstatic. Shocked! We could not believe it. The last of our foes was vanquished. World War II was over!

But we were cautioned to be vigilant—to not let down our guard. Japanese forces on Luzon, of which there were still a considerable number, had not yet surrendered. Many enemy units were cut off and desperate. Our location in the Sierra Madre Mountains was still a potentially deadly position.

At the time of the Allied invasion of the Philip-

---

[54] Named after Clearfield County in Pennsylvania, the *USS Clearfield* was a Haskell-class attack transport. Primarily used to transport troops and equipment, she carried twenty-six landing craft.

[55] Sample is attached at the end of this chapter.

Left: Japanese surrendering

Below: The Japanese reactions to surrendering were varied. Here, a vice admiral is bitter, a major happy, a sergeant bewildered, and a private pitiful.

90 Only One Pollack

pine Islands, there were an estimated 500,000 Jap defenders. Long after the official surrender, there were still 50,000 stragglers, some of whom refused to surrender.[56] Many did not know the war was over. We were told not to fire on the enemy unless we were fired upon, in which case we were to eliminate them. We still had quite a few skirmishes with the Japs, especially when our patrols were out. No one wanted to be killed or seriously wounded, especially since the war was officially over.

About this time we were told that the 38th Division, nationalized shortly after the attack on Pearl Harbor, was going home. We were overjoyed, especially the old-timers. A few days later, however, we were told that for a soldier to go home with the division, he had to have sixty points. Points were given for service time and other conditions with one point for each month in the Army, two points for each month overseas and extra points for being married, having children or other dependents, being wounded, or having a Combat Infantry Badge. I had thirty-eight points, not enough to go home.

Roughly half the men in the division did not have enough points to go home with the division. Like me, these were the replacements. My squad leader, Sgt. Neukam, had more than 150 points. I asked him if he would give me some of his. His answer was a definite "No." Actually, no one was allowed to give any of his points to another soldier.

The 38th Division was taken out of combat and replaced by the 86th Division, the Black Hawks. The 86th had recently arrived in the Philippines, having previously seen limited action in the European theater. Everyone in the 86th who had sixty or more points left with the 38th. So we said goodbye to our old comrades heading for home and greeted new ones in the 86th. Those of us left behind filled the military occupation specialty (MOS) that we had previously held. I was again assigned to a mortar squad.

When we joined the 86th, the guys in the 38th were entering their second week of wearing the same, unlaundered clothes while the new arrivals of the 86th had new uniforms and fatigues and looked very fresh indeed. The first night, our newly assigned lieutenant of the weapons platoon wanted to know where he could change into his pajamas. Pajamas! Clean prissy pajamas! We all had a great laugh, easing the tension considerably.

The 86th was not the only division to be redeployed from Europe to the Pacific theater. The war in Europe had ended in May 1945. There were many divisions and other units sent to the Pacific theater in preparation for the final assault on the Japanese homeland.

I am going to editorialize here for a moment. There have been many criticisms of the United States for being the first to use an atomic bomb and for killing so many people. I believe that if our enemies had been the first to develop the atomic bomb, they would not have hesitated in its use. And I believe that if either Japan or Germany had used it first, the free world would not exist today. Furthermore, the Germans were not far behind us in the atomic bomb development process—not far at all.

It has been estimated that in an assault on the Japanese home islands, the Allies would have suffered a half million soldiers dead. Add to these even larger numbers of Japanese casualties, civilian and military. Today's critics would quite possibly not even be able to voice their criticisms because their fathers could have been killed invading Japan proper.

From my experiences the Japanese soldiers were fanatical in carrying out their duties and there is no reason to believe that such fanaticism would not have continued and also been practiced by the Japanese civilians. In all the time that I was in combat, I saw only a single enemy soldier surrender, and he was not a Jap but a Korean. He came up to our perimeter waving a white handkerchief. He was about six feet tall, taller than any Japanese I ever saw. This fellow was grinning from ear to ear but when he was marched through our perimeter, I expected one of our troopers to shoot him. I was happy that such did not happen.

So my buddy Willie Cribb and I were now a part of the 86th Division but in the same combat jobs we had with the 38th. I suddenly found myself one of the most senior members of the mortar squad. And

---

[56] The last Japanese straggler in the Philippines, Lt. Hiroo Onoda, finally surrendered on March 19, 1972.

Willie, who "got shed of the hospital," as he phrased it, was the most senior. I was eligible for promotion from private at least to corporal.

Capt. Arthur Morgan was our new company commander of A Company, 1st Battalion, 343rd regiment, 86th Infantry Division. While Captain Morgan seemed to be a capable leader, we were naturally very skeptical. After all, this was a change to a commander who had never faced Jap fire. But then one of our patrols came back after being ambushed. The sergeant told Captain Morgan that they had to leave behind the body of a rifleman who had been killed. Captain Morgan asked where the soldier had been left. After being told the exact location, he proceeded to go out for the body by himself, returning with it in about fifteen minutes. Everyone in A Company had a newly found respect for Captain Morgan.

Each member of the mortar squad was issued a new and improved carbine. To me it appeared almost the same as my old one except that it had a curved, thirty-round magazine and a selector switch allowing it to be put into fully automatic firing mode. But you know what the problem was? We had to clean off that awful cosmoline, again.

In mid-September 1945, following the signing of the formal surrender documents in Tokyo Harbor, the 86th Division was pulled out of the Sierra Madre Mountains. There was no more training for the final assault on Japan. Everyone speculated as to how long it would be before we went home. My feeling was that every unit in the US Army that had been overseas longer than the 86th would go home first. And there were nowhere near enough ships to take the millions of soldiers home.

In the meantime, the division had to do something to keep us all occupied. Some were assigned guard duty at bridges, buildings, and road check points while others drew the dreaded and dangerous patrols. Some patrols were as long as ten or fifteen miles.

My first assignment was as a bridge guard with Leslie Anderson. Leslie was a rifleman, who like myself did not have enough points to go home with the 38th. When we were dropped off, our orders were to prevent that bridge from being blown up by Jap stragglers and to report any Japanese activity in the area. The bridge was about twenty feet long and of wooden construction, spanning a stream five or six feet wide and some ten feet below the bridge. We were instructed to split the guard time on the bridge every night. Leslie and I decided to split the night into two shifts. First shift was from dusk, about 8 P.M., to 1 A.M. with the second from 1 A.M. to dawn, about 6:30 A.M. We would swap shifts night to night. Every day a truck was to bring our rations, our mail, and other essentials.

After we unloaded our gear, backpacks, and weapons from the truck—which was to become our only link with the outside world—it left the two of us alone. However, we were not lonely very long. Soon a delegation of natives arrived from a village a quarter of a mile away. They were very friendly and a couple of them spoke broken English. Their native language was not pure Spanish but some close derivative. Our communication with them was haphazard at best but progressed by use of gestures and broken English and Spanish. Gradually we began to understand each other. The villagers wore pants and T-shirts. The women wore dresses but all of the clothing was quite primitive.

Our first order of business was to erect our pup tent as it was our only shelter from the almost daily rains. Leslie and I each carried half of the tent in our backpack. When these halves were put together, they made a tent six feet long by four feet high in the center. Each of us also carried a folded tent pole. When these poles were put at each end in the center and the pins driven in the ground to anchor them, the tent was almost finished. Next the sides were staked out with four or five pegs on each side. Last, and of extreme importance, a shallow trench was dug around the tent so rain water could not flow into the tent. We slept on the ground but we had our ponchos and one blanket to sleep on and another for cover.

When the leaders of the village realized what we were doing, they gestured to us to stop. We responded as best as we could that we must have shelter from the rain and a place to sleep. They became more insistent and again told us with body signals to stop. They would build a shelter for us. As we stood aside one of them gave orders and quickly a huge pile of bamboo poles was gathered. Some twenty feet from the bridge a shelter was started with these eight- to ten-foot poles.

Smiling, Leslie and I stood aside and watched in amazement at the efficiency with which the seven or eight Filipinos worked. In two hours we had not a tent but a home away from home. It was six feet high with a floor area five feet by seven feet that was a foot above the ground. The roof was practically water proof with overlapping split bamboo. Our new villa by the stream was built entirely of bamboo except for the native grasses put on the roof and sides and lashed with vines. With our two tent halves as added padding the bamboo floor was fine to sleep upon. By 5 P.M. we were moving in.

Overlapped split bamboo roof.

Just as we were told by our sergeant, a truck came by every day about 10 A.M. It delivered our mail, took the letters that we wrote home, and left rations and the daily division newsletter. The funny thing was that our own supply truck was the only military vehicle to use the bridge. We surmised, probably correctly, that this bridge was not necessarily vital to our military. However, the villagers and other natives used this bridge regularly with lots of foot traffic, carts pulled by carabao, and livestock, including carabao. The bridge was vital to the civilian population, but the village elders advised everyone not to use the bridge at night. I guess they were afraid that we might shoot them.

I suspect that when the war ended suddenly in September 1945, the allies had huge stockpiles of all kinds of materials and rations on hand. Along with our mail, a box of ten-in-one rations was dropped off every day. Ten-in-one rations are enough food to sustain ten men for one day. It contained a pound of dehydrated bacon, dried egg yolks and whites, canned food of all kinds, candy, chewing gum, and lots of Nestle's instant coffee. (Incidentally, my father's shift at the Cudahy Packing Company in Cuero was still dehydrating egg yolks and whites for the war effort.)

Of course, two men could not consume all of these rations in a single day, so we gave our grateful Filipino hosts our excess food. In return they provided us fresh fruit—mangos, papayas, and other fruit we did not recognize—of which they seemed to have a plentiful supply. Our hard candy and chewing gum were given to the children. We had to teach them to chew and not swallow the gum after the sweetness was gone. Leslie and I became very popular, especially around the arrival time of our daily supply truck.

About a week after we took up our post, we found out that the villagers had partially dammed the stream about a quarter mile below the bridge. This made a very adequate bathing pool. Each day men and boys, and later the women and girls, took turns bathing in this pool. Leslie said that he would like to sneak down and watch the women and girls when it was their turn. I told him "No!" because we were on good terms with the villagers. We should not jeopardize that by offending them. I told Leslie that if they became angry, they could "do us in" just as easily as the Japs could. We kept the villagers' trust and they had ours.

Night after night we each performed our duty guarding the bridge by walking back and forth and occasionally looking down at the stream to see if we could detect any movement. Strangely, after an hour or so, I could feel the hair on the back of my neck stand up. I could almost see that Jap straggler sneaking up on me to cut my throat. This had the beneficial effect of bringing me wide awake and fully alert. But the imagined straggler never showed himself. Nothing ever happened to either Leslie or me.

After two weeks, we were notified that we would

be pulled out the next day and to have all our equipment ready to go. When we told our hosts that we would be leaving, they arranged a party that night with Leslie and me as the guests of honor. In the early evening we were taken to the biggest structure in the village. It was sturdily constructed of wooden beams, bamboo, and straw with room for about thirty people on the second floor. We sat on the floor and dined with them, mostly fruit, as they performed many different native dances.

After a couple of hours, we gestured that we had to leave and perform our guard duty at the bridge. It was then about 8:30 P.M. and it was my turn to take the first shift. I told Leslie to turn in and that I would wake him about 2 A.M.

When we left the next morning about 10 A.M., there were quite a number of villagers there to give us a grand send-off. We were not replaced by another guard detail, at least not at the time we left.

We were allowed to lounge around camp for about a week, reading and writing letters, playing poker, cleaning our weapons, and generally enjoying some horse play. But alas, this came to an end when we were informed that most of us would be going on a long patrol: groan, bellyache, feel put upon, moan, wail and whimper, all to no avail. The names were called and sure enough Leslie and I were on the list. A lieutenant and a sergeant would be leading the patrol to villages in the countryside. There would be no mortar squad with this patrol, and therefore no heavy baseplate on my back, but the thirty of us would wield eighteen rifles, six or seven carbines (the new optionally automatic ones), two BARs, a half dozen .45 caliber pistols, two hand grenades each and lots of ammunition. A small fleet of trucks, escorted by jeeps fitted with machine guns, took us out about seven and a half miles. When we left the trucks, we were told to meet them at this same place eight hours later.

After the Japanese surrender, the army utilized a number of former enemy soldiers to accompany all units in the field, including all patrols. Their job was to persuade any of their former comrades we encountered to surrender. Therefore, our thirty-man patrol was accompanied by a former Jap soldier as an interpreter. Now we had been conditioned in basic training, and frequently thereafter, to believe that the Japanese were not really human but subhuman. I think that, to a man, none of us trusted this interpreter. He was not allowed to carry arms of any kind. But deeper than this distrust, a big lesson flowed from his presence: he was, actually, a human being, as were the other Jap soldiers, as were we.

After hiking about three miles on perfectly flat land—the mountains were only visible in the distance—the lieutenant told the sergeant to stop for a fast ten-minute lunch. We pulled our two-can C-ration lunches from our backpacks and, after the usual trading of the can containing the main meal, ate quickly. Some men had their favorites that they would trade for, but to me, all C-rations tasted the same. I really did not care. We forced ourselves to eat quickly because if you did not, you might not get to finish. To this day, I remain a very fast eater.

Our main mission was to locate Jap stragglers who did not know that the war was over or who refused to surrender. If our interpreter could not persuade them to surrender, we were to eliminate them. Our second mission was to make friends with any Filipino natives with which we came in contact.

We came to a village that was heartbreaking. Never had any of us seen such poverty. The Japs had taken everything that the villagers had—all their food and all their livestock. The villagers by the bridge Leslie and I had guarded were poor but nothing like what we saw here. The children were naked. The lieutenant confirmed that the Japs were long gone from the area, then made notes saying he would call Captain Morgan and send a truck with food and pure water.

These poor children had never tasted candy so we gave them ours. They went wild about it and watched our every move, anxiously hoping for more. We could not even go to the bathroom without an audience of children, so we took turns distracting them so the others could have some privacy. Our hearts really went out to the children because they really had nothing in the way of food. We gave them everything we could spare.

While witnessing the hunger in this village, a realization hit me like a pallet of bricks had fallen on me. When we ate in our mess tents back in our tent city, there were always Filipino women around the garbage areas. Suddenly I knew that these women were not freeloaders. They were hungry. They were scavenging to feed themselves and their families, gathering anything edible, regardless of the source.

Even in the field, we always had pure water. Each man carried pills and each pill could purify a full canteen of water, no matter what its source. Within our perimeter we had a Lyster bag[57] as our water supply. This bag was shaped like a huge teardrop and held thirty to forty gallons of water that had already been purified. There were perhaps a half dozen spigots on the bottom so a number of men could fill their canteens at once.

Lyster bag for water resupply.

As we left the village on our return trek, we were accompanied by the villagers for at least a mile. With all of our firepower and our ranks swelled by the local population, it is no wonder that the Japanese stragglers, who were undoubtedly somewhere around and who probably saw us, were reluctant to tangle with us. We were a formidable force ready for any attack.

Another two miles and the lieutenant told the sergeant that we were ahead of schedule and to let the men take a fifteen-minute break. Oh! Welcome relief! How I would have liked to take off my boots! But I knew that if I did, I probably could not get them back on because of the swelling.

We made it back to our rendezvous point in good time, finding three trucks to transport us back to "civilization" just in time for our evening meal. Who cared what it was as long as it was hot and there was plenty of it. Life in the foxholes was in the very recent past but we were well along the path to being spoiled by camp life.

While in camp this time, one of our riflemen became very sick, and was diagnosed with spinal meningitis. To help curtail the spread of this often fatal disease, we were forbidden from having further contact with the civilian population. Then one day, while five or six of us were sitting around, twirling our thumbs, a group of Filipino women arrived and commenced selling souvenirs across the road from our tent city. The bracelets and other items were crafted from the aluminum from some of the 9,000 downed Jap airplanes. We moseyed over to inspect the souvenirs when some colonel caught us and took our names and ranks. No formal action ever came from this; however, my expected promotion to corporal never came to pass and I have wondered about a possible connection.

We settled into an endless number of patrols every two or three days. But none were as long as the one to that unspeakably impoverished village. Around the first of October 1945, the mortar squads were trucked to a real rest camp about sixty or seventy miles south of Manila and on the beach. This was pure joy: no patrols, no KP, no endless de-

---

[57] Maj. (later Col.) William J. L. Lyster developed the method of using a solution of calcium hypochlorite in a linen bag to treat water. For decades, the Lyster bag (also spelled Lister) was the standard method of water purification and distribution for US ground forces in the field and in camps. Source: wikipedia.org

Above: Adrian, on the right, with three soldiers.

Right: Adrian is in the center back. Note the Filipino family (girl with soldiers, others in the background).

tails. What a special treat! The quarantine had been lifted and we made friends with the Filipinos in the area.

Following our week at the beach we returned to find that the buzz around camp was that Congress had passed what was dubbed by the 86th Division as the Red Apple Bill. This bill promised to everyone who reenlisted in the regular army for as little as one year, thirty days at home for each full or partial year of service, to be granted as soon as possible. I had just started my second year as a citizen soldier. So, in my case, it meant sixty days at home for reenlisting for one year and two months, the additional two months covering the sixty days at home.

While in the combat zone each of us always hoped for the Million Dollar Wound. This was a wound that would send you home to recover but one that was not bad enough to make you an invalid for life. I had given up on getting one of these since Japanese activity was severely curtailed by this time. I guessed that I would be in the Philippines or in Japan on occupation duty for at least another year. So what was there to lose by reenlisting for another year? The chance to have two months leave at home might just be worth it. The two other men who joined me in reenlisting and I were subjected to a lot of ridicule. But I took my physical, passed it with flying colors and was to shortly head back to Texas. My reenlistment date was November 21, 1945.

Army of the United States

Honorable Discharge

This is to certify that

ADRIAN A ZAIONTZ
Hq Co 1st Bn, 343rd Infantry

Army of the United States

is hereby Honorably Discharged from the military service of the United States of America. This certificate is awarded as a testimonial of Honest and Faithful Service to this country.

Given at Marikina, Rizal Province, Luzon, P.I.
Date 21 November 1945

JOE A HINTON
Colonel, 343rd Infantry
Commanding

ENLISTED RECORD AND REPORT OF HONORABLE DISCHARGE

1. LAST NAME - FIRST NAME - MIDDLE INITIAL: Zaiontz Adrian A
7. DATE OF SEPARATION: 21 Nov 45
6. ORGANIZATION: Hq Co 1st Bn, 343rd Infantry
9. PERMANENT ADDRESS FOR MAILING PURPOSES: 415 W. French St, Cuero, Texas
18. RACE: White X
19. MARITAL STATUS: Single X
22. DATE OF INDUCTION: 28 Sep 44
23. DATE OF ENLISTMENT:
24. DATE OF ENTRY INTO ACTIVE SERVICE: 28 Sep 44
26. REGISTERED: Yes X
27. LOCAL S.S. BOARD NO.: #1
28. COUNTY AND STATE: Cuero, Texas
30. MILITARY OCCUPATIONAL SPECIALTY AND NO.: Light Machine Gunner 604
32. BATTLES AND CAMPAIGNS: Luzon Campaign
33. DECORATIONS AND CITATIONS: Asiatic Pacific Theater Ribbon
34. WOUNDS RECEIVED IN ACTION: None
35. LATEST IMMUNIZATION DATES: Smallpox 9-30-44; Typhoid 10-25-44; Tetanus 11-25-44; Other: See remarks
SERVICE OUTSIDE CONTINENTAL U.S. AND RETURN: 26 Mar 45 Pacific Thea 25 Apr 45
36. HIGHEST GRADE HELD: Pfc
37. TOTAL LENGTH OF SERVICE: Continental 0 years 5 months 28 days; Foreign 0 years 7 months 26 days
38. PRIOR SERVICE: None
40. REASON AND AUTHORITY FOR SEPARATION: Convenience of Government: AR 615-365, 15 Dec 44 and WD Cir 310, 1945
42. EDUCATION: Grammar 8, High School 4, College 0
41. SERVICE SCHOOLS ATTENDED: None
PAY DATA: 47. TOTAL AMOUNT: $294.80, H.C. RITZE, 1t Col. FD
44. MUSTERING OUT PAY: TOTAL 300, THIS PAYMENT 300
55. REMARKS: Item 35: Typhus 3-11-45; Cholera 8-30-45; Plague 3-11-45
Honorably discharged for Convenience of Government to enlist in the Regular Army, WD Cir 310, 1945.
ASR Score 2 Sep 45 - 21. No time lost under AW 107.
57. PERSONNEL OFFICER: FRANKLIN E MURPHY, 1st Lt, 343rd Inf.

Signature: Adrian A. Zaiontz

The Cycloner

SATURDAY, JUNE 16, 1945

Published by
38th Division I & E Section from United Press Wire Service and ANS

OKINAWA (UP): Desperate Japanese troops today hurled themselves in suicide charges as American Marines and soldiers shattered the last enemy line and compressed the defenders into a 13-square mile death trap. Armed with flame-throwers the Americans smashed the desperate banzai charges and pushed forward steadily in fierce close combat. In one of the largest suicide attacks, 300 Japanese carrying satchels of dynamite charged Marine lines in the western end of the front. They were beaten back and at least 64 of them, including one woman, were killed. (In Guam, it was announced officially that 71,203 Japanese have been killed in the Okinawa campaign thus far.). One of the greatest artillery barrages of the Pacific war shattered Japanese troop concentrations in the summit cliffs of the Yaejudake plateau where three divisions of Marines and Infantrymen were advancing in bitter hand-to-hand fighting. All advances were made against murderous enemy fire. It was a battle to death, with no quarters asked or given. Some of the cliffs were so precipitous that the troops used rope ladders. The ground operation was given close support by American planes which made rocket and bombing attacks through intense Japanese anti-aircraft fire.

SAN FRANCISCO (UP): The Yalta voting formula, including the Big Five's right to veto, was approved by the technical committee today. The Big Five in forcing through their interpretation of the voting formula by a vote of 30 to 2, won a significant victory over the "Little Nations."

LONDON (UP): The Admiralty announced this morning that 4,770 Empire, Allied and neutral merchantships, reaching a total of 21,140,000 tons had been lost to enemy action during the war.

WASHINGTON (UP): President Truman wants a quick Senate ratification of the world security organization treaty in order to strengthen the American position in the coming Big Three meeting, it was reliably reported today. The President's desire to have the treaty approved before his conference with Churchill and Stalin was said to be the major factor in the government's plan to submit the treaty to the Senate as soon as the San Francisco Conference ends. In order to obtain action the Senate may forgo its recess.

TODAY'S BOX SCORE

MOVE IN ON 'EM.....................................AND KILL 'EM

	149 INF	151 INF	152 INF	CAV RCN	TOTAL
Japs Kil today	30	37	25	32	127
Jap PWs today	1	2	0	0	3

DIVISION TOTAL BAG TO DATE: JAPS KIL....19,068   JAP PWs....538

LONDON (UP): Japanese propoganda was taking on the same tone which Nazi Germany used during its last days with Radio Tokyo talking more frequently of "resistance" instead of "winning" the war. Japanese broadcast quoted the Nippon Times as declaring that Japan is "firmly resolved to extort the greatest possible toll from the enemy." This line was practically identical to that taken by Goebbles at the time when Germany was going down to defeat but fighting fanatically to make victory as costly as possible for the Allies in lives. The Nippon Times also was quoted talking of the "actual peril of the enemy landing in force with the existance of the empire at stake," adding: "Japan stand inflexibly and unchangeably resolute in her determination to resist the enemy to the bitter end. There can be no thought of such a thing as unconditional surrender. The German radio was on the same line when it warned the Germans that unconditional surrender to the Allies would result in the final death of the Reich and tried to steel the people to prevent that.

ROME (UP): The six Committees of National Liberation parties were still looking for a political leader whom they could all accept as the new premier of Italy. Holding five meetings yesterday, the parties were unable to reach an agreement. They will meet again today in a furious effort to pick their candidate before Crown Prince Umberto chooses one without the Committee of National Liberation recommendation

WASHINGTON (UP): When the President attends the coming Big Three meeting he will be accompanied by an impressive staff including several who have attended previous Big Three conferences as Roosevelt's aides. They include Harry L. Hopkins, James Byrnes, Admiral William D. Leahy, and Secretary of State Edward R. Stettinius. Joseph Davies possibly would also attend, if his health permits.

WASHINGTON (UP): Philippine business circles universally favor a "20 year period of free trade" rather than Senator Millard Tydings suggested 3 years, Diosdado M. Yap, member of the Philippine Chamber of Commerce, told the Wall Street Journal today. Yap said that Tydings' proposal for a $100,000,000 outright gift to the Philippines is insufficient even to rebuild the houses destroyed by the Japanese.

PARIS (UP): U.S. Navy officials today disclosed that Charles Lindbergh, who is on a "secret technical mission" for the Navy, has left Paris for an unknown destination.

DON'T FORGET THE CYCLONE CENTER OPENING - TONIGHT!

Your new CYCLONE CENTER will be officially presented to the enlisted men of the 38th Division at 7:30 tonight, when Major General William C. Chase opens the special program with the presentation.. A floor show with the Division Cyclone Band will follow the program...Refreshments will be served!

chapter 9
TRANSITION FROM CITIZEN SOLDIER TO REGULAR ARMY

On November 21, 1945, I was discharged from the army as a citizen soldier and a few minutes later sworn into the regular army as a volunteer. "RA" would now be in front of my serial number forever. I was a civilian for about five minutes. Two other men from Company A were sworn in with me, and we were reassigned to Headquarters Company so that we would not be put on long patrols or other assignments that might interfere with our departures for leave in the States.

The three of us were subjected to much ridicule over the next month. How could anyone be so naive as to believe the army? How could we possibly really believe that we were going home for thirty, sixty, or ninety days, as soon as possible, depending on our length of service? As time wore on and as we continued to have endless short patrols and other duties and details, we three began to doubt our choice as well.

Then in mid-December an order came for the three of us, and many others from the other eleven companies and other units of the 86th Division who were now in the regular army, to be ready for transport home from Manila, shortly. "Shortly" turned out to be five days. The tables had turned. On our day of departure many comrades came to see us off and boy, were they jealous! We told them *adios* and were on our way home. And our previous detractors had to stay for how much longer? Nobody knew.

We arrived in Manila and yet another tent city filled with new volunteers in the regular army. Our ranks grew daily as RA volunteers arrived from all over Luzon. The day after Christmas we boarded the *S. S. Marine Jumper*[58] for transport back to civilization.

Six days later 5,000 of us were 300 miles east of

---
[58] A Type C4 class ship. These seventy-five ships were the largest cargo ships built during World War II. Source: wikipedia.org

Authorization to wear ribbons.

S.S. Marine Jumper

the Philippine Islands having an excellent New Year's Day feast courtesy of the US Navy: turkey, dressing, sweet potatoes, all of the trimmings. This was a meal the likes of which most of us had not savored for at least a year. We gorged; tummies filled.

The cyclone struck about five hours later. (In the Atlantic such storms are called hurricanes.) The seas became rough—what the navy called "high." As

> **EXCERPTS TAKEN FROM INSTRUCTIONS FOR GI'S ENTERING THE UNITED STATES**
>
> In compliance with current policies for the indoctrination of troops returning to the States a portion of the course is here included:
>
> **A.** In America there are a number of beautiful girls. These girls have not been liberated. They should not be offered "K" ration chocolate on the street. Now it must be hand dipped chocolates by the box, delivered personally to their front parlors.
>
> **B.** A typical American breakfast consists of many strange foods such as fresh eggs, milk, ham, waffles, etc. These are highly palatable and though strange in appearance, are extremely tasty. Butter made from cream is often served. If you wish some butter, you turn to the person nearest you and say quietly, "Please pass the butter." You do not shout, "Throw me the blasted grease."
>
> **C.** In the event the helmet is retained by the individual he will refrain from using it as a chair, wash bowl, footbath, stew pot, shovel, or bathtub.
>
> **D.** It is not considered good taste to squat Filipino-style in a corner in the event all the chairs are occupied. The host will provide suitable seats.
>
> **E.** American dinners in the most cases consist of several foods served on separate dishes. The common practice of mixing various items such as corned beef and pudding or lima beans and peaches to make it more palatable will be refrained from.
>
> **F.** Upon leaving a friend's home after a visit, one may find that his hat is missing. Frequently it has been placed in a closet. One should turn to one's host and say, "I don't seem to have my hat." Do not say "Don't nobody leave this room. Some S.O.B. stole my hat."
>
> **G.** In America hotels are provided for travelers, where for a small sum one may register and be shown to a room in which to sleep for the night. The practice of entering the nearest house and throwing the occupants into the yard will cease.
>
> **H.** Signs on certain doors will read "Ladies," which when literally translated means: OFF LIMITS TO ALL TROOPS.

passengers, we were not allowed on deck under any circumstances. The ship went up and the ship went down. The ship went sideways then the ship rolled heavily. Then the ship orchestrated random combinations of these primary gyrations. And the turkey, dressing, sweet potatoes, and all those trimmings harmonized with the seas. Onward traveled the 5,000, into the valley of toilets, into the jaws of trash cans, as we defined a new pinnacle of seasickness. The toilets were so full of vomit none could be flushed. The stench alone was enough to cause sickness and always there were the churning seas.

I stayed in my bunk until the next day, and, astonishingly, seasoned soldier of the regular army that I was, I never threw up. Continuously I felt as though I would, but I did not. I was one of the very few who held their dinner. (Recently the news was swamped with stories of horrified vacationers aboard a stricken Carnival Cruise Lines ship who could not flush the toilets due to a power outage. At least they were not confined below deck in a hurricane, following a huge New Year's Day dinner.)

Without further incidents, another three weeks found us sighting land near Seattle, Washington, USA. The good old USA was a very consoling sight indeed. The only drawback was that it was winter and most of us were still in khaki uniforms from tropical Luzon, about the latitude of southern Mexico. Winter, as we know it, is nonexistent in the Philippines because it is 1,000 miles closer to the equator than even Central Texas, let alone Seattle.

But notwithstanding the cold, our welcome home was as warm as Christmas with family. A huge band was playing as if greeting conquering heroes returning from battle. Vivid is my memory of each soldier setting first foot on American soil, personally greeted by a beaming member of some Seattle ladies' organization and handed a pint carton of cold milk. That one gesture made us more at home than anything else they could have done. War over! Homeland! America! It is unimaginable how good that milk tasted. Overseas it had always been reconstituted milk with all the taste of chalk.

We boarded waiting trucks for Fort Lawton.

Right away I noticed that the snow banks along the way were black in many spots, spoiling the view—soot from coal fires used for heating. Upon arrival at Fort Lawton, we were issued wool uniforms, including heavy, dark green wool coats. We were quartered in wooden barracks for a few days while orders were cut for each soldier's transportation home. Heat was provided by a huge wood-burning stove in the center of each floor.

During World War II a popular saying was that every man put his pants on one leg at a time no matter who he was: General MacArthur, the president or even the Pope. During our few days at Fort Lawton—and after a few bottles of PX[59] beer—a new acquaintance of mine announced that he did not put his pants on one leg at a time. So Mr. Nameless—and he will remain so—proceeded to climb onto a top bunk. The theory being that when he jumped off without pants, he would be wearing them by the time he landed on the floor. The practice was that he was still holding both sides of his pants when he hit the floor head first, loosening four front teeth. Needless to say he did not have his pants on when he crashed. But his barracks' mates sure had a good laugh and a new memory to take home. The next day my new acquaintance went on sick call to see a dentist.

After a few days of doing nothing but trying to stay warm, we had our orders. About twenty of us were going to Fort Sam Houston in San Antonio, Texas. We boarded a train during a snowstorm on the 1st of February 1946, crossed Washington state, Idaho, a part of Montana, then turning south into Wyoming. Nearly all the way was white with drifted snow, sometimes as high as six or seven feet. I thought it was beautiful.

Somewhere in Wyoming while bound for Denver, Colorado, the train stopped, halted by too much snow and ice on the tracks. The conductor said that it was forty degrees below zero outside and he cautioned all of us to stay inside the train. He said if we wandered even a few feet from the track we could become lost in the blowing snow. All that snow was going to waste without a single snowball fight. For twenty hours we sat there waiting for the tracks to be cleared. I came to the realization that I did not want to live anywhere with winters that harsh. But that new wool uniform and coat were really comfortable.

The rest of our route was very uneventful, except that as we arrived in Denver I started feeling very sick. Fifty miles south of Denver my fever was 104 degrees. I was taken off the train by stretcher and an ambulance knowing exactly what it was . . . malaria! Everyone posted in the Philippines was suspected of having contracted malaria, but the disease was held in check by taking the several required tablets of atabrine[60] daily and additional salt tablets. Taking atabrine caused our skin to turn a light shade of yellow. Atabrine was developed as an alternative treatment for malaria instead of quinine. Quinine was not available because its source was in Japanese-occupied territory. Upon reaching US territory, we were no longer required to take atabrine so many of us quickly developed malaria.

I was taken to an army air forces (USAAF) hospital in Colorado Springs, probably at Peterson Field. I could see Pike's Peak from the window of my ward.

With this high fever I was really miserable, alternately freezing and burning up. One minute my body was sweltering and I would toss off all covers. The next minute it was as if I were outside that train in Wyoming in a snow drift swaddling myself in all available blankets. This torture lasted for days. Then, after about two weeks, I began to feel a lot better. However, the army air forces doctor assigned to my case would not let me continue my trip to Fort Sam Houston.

I resigned myself to a temporary life of luxury, lounging around, taking advantage of room service.

---

[59] A Post Exchange (PX) on army posts (also a Base Exchange [BX] on air force bases, Navy Exchange [NEX] on navy bases, Marine Corps Exchange [MCX] on marine corps installations and Coast Guard Exchange [CGX] on coast guard installations) is a type of retail store operating on United States military installations worldwide. Source: wikipedia.org

[60] Atabrine was the best substitute available for quinine. Its annual production in the U.S. jumped from two million tablets to 3.5 trillion tablets during the war. Atabrine came in the form of intensely bitter, little yellow pills. Source: wikipedia.org

Travel orders and meal ticket

The hospital meals were fantastic—steaks, chops, soup, all kinds of vegetables, fresh fruit, real coffee, and real milk. I started thinking that I really got myself into the wrong branch of military service. The only bad thing about this stay was that all of my records had continued on down the tracks to Fort Sam Houston—including my pay records. There was an excellent PX in the hospital complex but I did not have any money, could not get paid, and therefore could not buy anything.

After another two weeks without fever, my doctor said I was well enough to travel. Orders were cut to resume my trek to San Antonio; however, I still had no money for incidentals along the way. Someone suggested that the American Red Cross might lend or give me some money. Presenting myself to the Red Cross representative at the hospital and pleading my case embellished my pockets with $10. And I had to sign a loan statement for that! What? Here is this broke, nineteen-year-old soldier traveling a thousand miles to his next assignment, who has taken fire for all of those folks back home and lobbed untold hundreds of $38 mortar shells at the enemy who bombed Pearl Harbor, and this civilian bureaucracy wants him to take out a loan for $10! I signed and took the cash. And there waiting for me when I finally reached home three days later was a letter from the Red Cross stating that I should send back the $10. Never since have I given one penny to the American Red Cross but instead have been a supporter of the Salvation Army.

When I arrived home, Mom greeted me with a warm hug. Dad, never very demonstrative, shook my hand. My brother Claude seemed to have grown about six inches and gained thirty pounds, and even had his driver's license. I had only been gone fourteen months but it seemed like a lifetime. I spent my sixty days at home loving every minute of it. With my parents, Claude and I visited many relatives and friends and attended several wedding parties and dances, driving Dad's 1934 Plymouth. First cousins, Lucian Urbanczyk (navy) and Alvin Snoga (army) were also home on leave and came to visit, hitchhiking from their homes. Being in uniforms no doubt made that easier. After visiting in Cuero the three of us decided to hitchhike to Edna, Texas, about sixty miles away, for a visit with Uncle Leon, Aunt Brigid, and their family. Sometimes it was difficult to hitch a ride even though we were in uniform. Outside of Victoria, Texas, and after a lot of cars passed us by, we decided to let Lucian walk about fifty feet behind Alvin and me. It was surprising that people would stop for a sailor before they would stop for soldiers. When they stopped for Lucian, Alvin and I ran back and piled in the car with Lucian explaining that we were all first cousins.

I spent all of March and most of April at home. But alas, five days before my leave was up, orders came that I was not to report to Fort Sam but rather Fort Hood at Killeen, Texas, to the 2nd Armored "Hell on Wheels" Division. When I reported to Fort Hood headquarters, a captain asked me if I wanted to stay in heavy weapons. I said "Sure" and was assigned to a 155-mm mobile artillery unit. In the army you are always training so the country is ready to go to war in any eventuality. The 155s were the ultimate in heavy weapons. Wow! That beast could throw a better than six-inch diameter explosive charge eleven miles. However, for my first ten days, all we did were dry runs.[61]

Near the end of April 1946, I participated in the Battle of Flowers Parade[62] in San Antonio, commemorating Texas Independence. I did not march, but rode in a detachment of about ten trucks with twelve troops in each truck. This was my first and

Front tank is a 155-mm Howitzer with eight-man crew; other heavy artillery show with their respective crews.

only participation in the Battle of Flowers Parade.

Before we ever actually fired live ammunition at targets, someone at headquarters decided that they could get the most from my regular army enlistment by sending me to clerk's school. I never applied for this but had to follow orders and would be going to Fort Knox where the Army ground forces' clerk's school was located. (Fort Knox, Kentucky, is where the United States gold reserves are cached.)

During WWII government employees and the uniformed services mostly traveled by train. On long trips Pullman sleepers[63] were leased by the government for troop movements. Short trips were carried out by truck convoy. The trip to Fort Knox required two days and a night, so I bunked in a Pullman sleeper upper berth all to myself.

I reported to headquarters at Fort Knox the day before the running of the Kentucky Derby. All the

---

[61] A dry run consists of all the necessary operations required in actual combat except firing live ammunition.

[62] *Fiesta San Antonio* dates to 1891, when local women decorated carriages, baby buggies, and bicycles with live flowers, met in front of the Alamo, and threw the blossoms at one another. That was the first Battle of Flowers Parade. The event was a success and soon became an annual event. Source: wikipedia.org

[63] The man who ultimately made the sleeping car business profitable in the United States was George Pullman, who began by building a luxurious sleeping car in 1865. The Pullman Company, founded as the Pullman Palace Car Company in 1867, owned and operated most sleeping cars in the United States until the mid-20th century, attaching them to passenger trains run by the various railroads. Source: wikipedia.org

```
                                              THE ARMORED SCHOOL
                                              Fort Knox, Kentucky
                      DETAILED SCHEDULE OF INSTRUCTION FOR PERIOD 24 - 29 June 46
                                        ARMY GROUND FORCES CLASS #9
```

Eight week

DATE	HOUR	SUBJECT	TEXT	METHOD	STUDENT EQUIPMENT
Mon	0800-1050	Typewriting & Speed Test	20th Cen Text	PW	NB & P
	1100-1150	Partial Payments	TM 14-502, ARs	C-PW	"
	1310-1400	" "			
	1410-1500	Quiz III			
	1510-1700	Leadership, D			
Tues	0800-1150	Typewriting			
	1310-1600	Typewriting			
	1610-1700	Final Exam, P			
Wed	0800-0950	Orientation,			
	1000-1150	1st Adm Probl			
	1410-1700	2nd Adm Pro			
Thurs	0800-0850	2nd Adm Pro			
	0900-1150	3rd Adm Pro			
	1310-1500	3rd Adm Pro			
	1510-1700	4th Adm Pro			
Friday	0800-1050	4th Adm Pro			
	1100-1150	5th Adm Pro			
	1310-1400	5th Adm Pro			
	1410-1700	6th Adm Pro			

Hq-M-4487-Knox-12-6-

Sample class schedule.

Seventh Week

```
                                   DETAILED SCHEDULE OF I
                                          ARMY GROU
```

DATE	HOUR	SUBJECT
Mon	0800-0950	Typewriting & Speed Test
	1000-1050	Filing
	1100-1150	P/R Prob I, Disc & Crit
	1310-1400	P/R Prob I, Disc & Crit
	1410-1500	Model Remarks II
	1510-1600	Leadership, Drill & Disc
	1610-1700	Orientation
Tues	0800-0850	Typewriting & Speed Test
	0900-1050	Filing
	1100-1150	Filing & General Review
	1310-1400	Model Remarks II
	1410-1500	Quiz II
	1510-1700	P/R Problem II
Wed	0800-0950	Typewriting & Speed Test
	1000-1150	Final Exam, Phase I
"	1310-1700	P/R Problem II
Thurs	0800-1150	Typewriting & Speed Test
	1310-1500	P/R Prob. II; Soldiers Deposits
	1510-1700	Pay Roll Examination
Fri	0800-1150	Typewriting & Speed Test
	1310-1400	Supplemental P/R & Disposition of P/R
	1410-1500	Pay upon Sep from Service
	1510-1600	Review of P/R Exam
	1610-1700	Computation of Pay & Fin Procedure

new arrivals were asked if they wanted to attend, free of charge with bus rides provided. Quite foolishly, I declined. I was tired from the trip and wanted rest to be fresh for my classes on Monday. I had no money for betting on the horses but regret to this day that I did not avail myself of this opportunity, just to experience it.

Amazement! That was the word for our barracks and setting: two stories high of dark red brick construction. We had never seen an army installation built like this. When I say "we" I refer to the forty of us who were there to train as company clerks. These premium barracks lined both sides of a huge parade and sports field, perhaps 500 yards wide and a mile long. The paved parade ground occupied one end while the other end boasted fields for track, baseball, softball, football, and soccer. This grand complex was immediately across the road from our quarters. During my entire army career this was the only time that I was housed in anything but wooden barracks or tents. (Of course, there was that fine little bamboo hut in the Philippines, but as far as the army was concerned we were living in the official military-issued tent.)

So here we were making new acquaintances and friendships. We were all Regular Army and brought in from units all over the world.

Monday found us starting school to become fully qualified company clerks. Courses included everything necessary in any company commander's office: typing, taking dictation, filing (the army way), and a myriad of other skills like completing the all-important morning report. The morning report is sent to the headquarters unit accounting for every soldier and his disposition. I could type sixty words a minute and had two years of Gregg shorthand in high school but we were assured that we would do everything "the army way" and to forget any and everything we had previously learned.

Classes ran from 8 A.M. to 5 P.M. with one hour and twenty minutes for lunch from 11:50 to 1:10. The food in the mess hall was adequate but certainly not the outstanding navy food of my trip back to the States. The greatest thing about school was the absence of detail duty of any kind. No K.P. No patrols. And no guard duty. After our evening meal at 6 P.M. our time was free. I mostly used this time for study and exercise. I loved boxing. It seemed to use or require use of every muscle in my body and I did it just for the exercise and not to hurt anyone.

Weekends were completely free, except that we were confined to the post. No passes were granted to leave the base. All of the athletic facilities were available and some of us played softball, and I soon verified that I still could not judge where the ball would come down when I played in the outfield.

During the second week of June I received a letter from my first cousin, Alvin Snoga, stationed at Fort Campbell in Tennessee. Alvin suggested that we get together for a visit, and we decided to meet at Bowling Green, Kentucky. Neither of us knew anything about Bowling Green except that it was about halfway between us and seemed to be a fairly good-sized town.

I procured a two-day pass for Saturday and Sunday and caught a bus which arrived in Bowling Green about 10 A.M. Alvin arrived about an hour later. After exchanging greetings, we walked down-

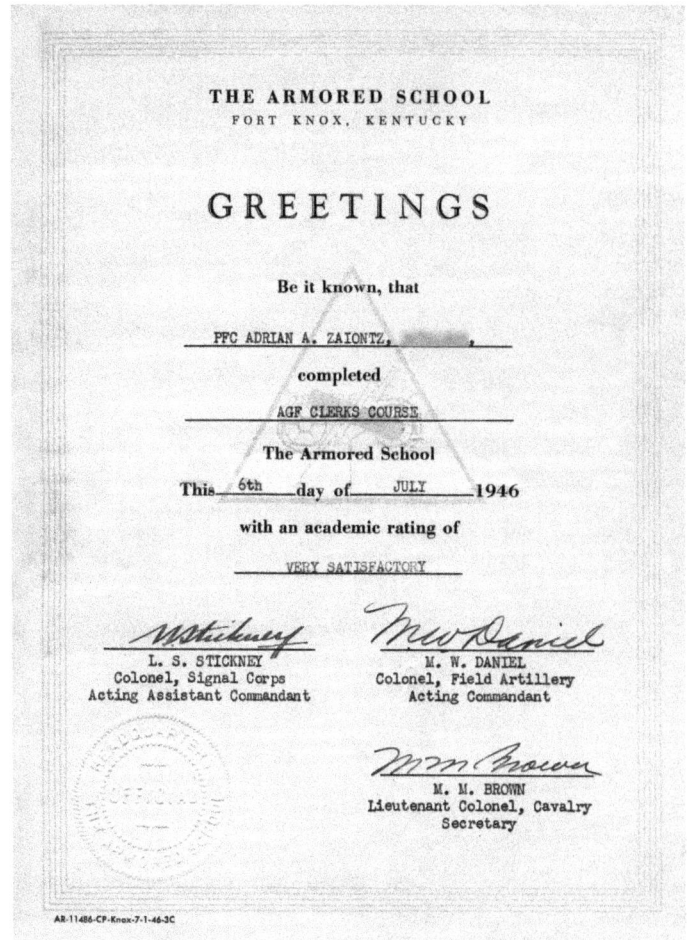

Clerks' School diploma

town and discovered that an American Legion Post was having a dance at a public park that night. We went to that dance and met some friendly people and some nice girls. Alvin danced with one girl all the time. Around midnight, we walked back to the bus station and slept on the hard benches the rest of the night. At least we were there for our early departures Sunday morning. We said our goodbyes and I asked Alvin the name of the girl he had danced so much with. He said he could not remember but it sounded like "Rosie Rusty Bottom."

Almost all of us successfully completed the class. Graduation was the first week of July 1946, whereupon I returned to Fort Hood, the 2nd Armored Division and to my mobile artillery unit. The dry runs with the 155-mm mobile howitzers continued for a few days, then we were transported to Galveston for a recreation leave.

I spent considerable time with Wayne Lorimer from Cincinnati, a new friend of mine, including

Wayne Lorimer and Adrian Zaiontz at Galveston, wearing their Garrison caps.

leave to Galveston.[64] To our surprise the army had several sixty-five-foot fishing boats for recreation. The army has boats? Our excursions were to the "snapper banks" some sixty to seventy miles offshore. Here we dropped very long, weighted lines over the sides of the boats: no rod or reel, just plenty of hand-held line. When you felt a tug on the line, you jerked it and brought up your fish.

Mostly we caught red snappers but occasionally there was a "trigger fish," so called for its two terrible looking front teeth. We were told that these teeth could take off a finger if you got careless. The fish was not edible. With our load of red snappers and a few other fish we returned to the dock and were greeted by a large contingent of indigents who knew the army boat schedule and begged for our fish. We gladly gave away our catch.

Back at Fort Hood this time, I learned that all companies already had clerks. However, a new, very special company was being formed and I was assigned as its clerk. My new outfit was the Fort Hood football company, whose primary function was to train and play games against the football teams of other army units. So every morning I completed the morning report, accounting for every person, and sent it to the post commander. (Everyone was recorded as either present at roll call, on sick call, in the hospital, on K.P., on leave, etc.)

This was my regular job for which I had been highly trained. I made the morning report for the football team, completed a few other office chores, then by a little after noon was free for the rest of the day. I diligently used this time reading, writing letters, and generally goofing off—all in "the army way." I never attended football practice because it was "secret" and closed to everyone but the team.

We did have some interesting soldiers as team members. One man had a normal chest expansion

---

[64] Garrison caps were also referred to as "overseas" caps. The color of the piping (trim) indicated to which branch of the Army you belonged. The infantry cap I previously wore had powder blue trim. In this photo both Wayne and I had dark red piping designating that we were in an artillery unit.

of fifty-six inches. And Lew Jenkins[65] was the lightweight boxing champion of the world. The thing I remember about Lew was his cauliflower ears. I had never seen such huge, misshapen ears. Cauliflower ears result from being hit and otherwise physically abused. With improved medical procedures and modern protective head gear, this condition is seldom seen anymore.

I was not allowed to travel with the team for their weekend games away, so every second weekend, I took the bus home to Cuero for a Friday noon to Monday morning visit. Then every Monday, almost half the team—twenty or more—went on sick call. Most of them had bruises all over their bodies. A few had broken bones and noses. And there were always some cuts. Sometimes one or two of them were left in a hospital on whatever post the team had played. This was real football and the attitude was "win at all costs." Luckily there were never any fatalities. Our record at the end of that first season was six wins, six losses.

What a life it was for a regular army company clerk. But, alas, nothing lasts forever. By Halloween football season was over, the football company was disbanded, and we all went back to our respective units—mobile artillery in my case. Then, a day or two later, I received orders for travel to California and assignment to headquarters, Military Intelligence (the premiere example of an oxymoron) Service Language School at the Presidio of Monterrey. As I endured the three-day train ride, I wondered to what kind of unit I was assigned now.

Upon arrival at Fort Ord, California, I was transported to the Presidio, a few miles away. This part of California is among the most beautiful in the state with scenic Carmel del Mar only a few miles from the Presidio. A mere forty years later, Clint Eastwood was mayor of Carmel del Mar—practically overlapping with my service. The only drawback here was a fish cannery on the coast, just below the mountain which hosted the Presidio. The aroma failed to match the view.

The mission of the Military Intelligence Service Language School (MISLS) was to teach Japanese Americans, known as *Nisei*,[66] to be fluent in their ancestral language in both the spoken and written form. They were to become interpreters for the American units now occupying Japan.

I was initially shocked to learn that there were more than 5,000 Nisei in training at the Presidio. Was the army crazy for sending me to be among 5,000 Japs? I had exchanged deadly fire with their kinfolks for more than six months! Certain to be resentful of them just being in their midst, their hostility toward me would also be evident as soon as it was known that I had been in the infantry in the Pacific. But you know, none of my apprehensions ever came to pass. These guys were not only Americans, they were regulars in the US Army, just as I was. And they had been through the war just as I had been, though most Japanese Americans fought in the European theater.

With so many Nisei in this post, the mess halls had as their main staple rice and other Japanese foods. The rice was served with fish or meat sauce on top. There were thirty or forty Caucasians in the post headquarters and cadre but we ate what the students ate. I personally liked it, though one sure can tire of the same meals day after day, BUT, not as tired as eating C-rations for weeks on end.

I was sent to a small room and told to report to a corporal who informed me that he was being discharged in a few days and that I would be assuming his job: making and delivering coffee to five officers at post headquarters. There was a colonel, a lieutenant colonel, a major, and two captains, each with his own office. Equipment for this job included a rolling cart with a coffee pot, sugar bowl, creamer, cups, saucers, and spoons. For a few days I was in training, following the corporal around, learning how to make coffee and whom to serve first: colonel first then on down the line by rank. I followed and

---

[65] Lew Jenkins served in World War II, serving in the United States Coast Guard, where he participated in troop deployment, and in the thick of several enemy fires during the Allied invasions of North Africa and Europe. He was involved in the D-Day invasion. Jenkins was decorated for gallantry and his actions, including the Silver Star, and saved several men after they were cut off behind enemy lines. When the Korean War broke out he re-enlisted in the infantry. Source: wikipedia.org

[66] Nisei is a Japanese-language term used to refer to children born to Japanese people in their new country. Source: wikipedia.org

Military Intelligence Service Language School, 1946. Adrian is on the top row, third from left.

Military Intelligence Service Language School, Presidio of Monterey, Calif., 16 Nov. 1946

observed. The corporal knocked, then pushed the cart into the office. The officer helped himself to the coffee, sugar, and cream, and if he had visitors, they helped themselves, using the extra cups on the cart. The coffee pot held twelve cups. After about ten or fifteen minutes, we pushed the cart to the next office. Somewhere around 11 A.M., we collected the cups, saucers, and spoons, washed everything, and put it away and we were through for the day. That was it. The coffee, cream, and sugar were replaced as needed by someone else.

I was nervous on my first day alone, but it seemed that all went according to plan. I made my rounds and a little before noon, I was through for the day and, once again, could do anything I wanted. No one ever complained about my coffee.

This duty lasted about six weeks. Then one day, the post commander said he had reviewed my personnel file and saw that I had a Polish background. He asked if I could speak and write Polish, to which I replied that I could understand and speak a little but could not write it. Then he asked if I would be interested in learning Russian. He observed that my I.Q. was 149 and that I should be able to complete the Russian language course with no problems. The Military Intelligence Service Language School for Russian was located at Fort Dix in New Jersey. After two years and after finishing the Russian language course, I would be commissioned an officer in the US Army. What did I think? I asked the colonel if I could have some time to think about this. He gave me two days.

I recognized both pros and cons for my decision. Pro: My career path for life could be decided. I would become an officer and give orders rather than only receive them. Con: I would have to reenlist for two or three years and perhaps longer. My life would be regimented for as long as my enlistment(s) lasted. Once you signed the papers there was no going back. After much soul searching and agonizing I concluded: No! No way! Absolutely not! When my two days were up, I told the colonel that I was but one month away from my discharge and that I really wanted to be a civilian again.

Perhaps there was a repercussion and perhaps not. A few days later, I was relieved from the coffee detail

Cpl. Adrian A. Zaiontz

and reassigned as a file clerk in the main office at post headquarters. There was no end to the papers that had to be filed "the army way." After all, there were 5,000 students plus a large contingent of auxiliary personnel on the post, and every one of them had a file. Also at this time, I received a promotion to T/5, commonly known among the troops as a Model T Corporal. My monthly pay was now the whopping sum of $62. Sixty for the basic pay of a corporal and $2 extra for the award of the Combat Infantry Badge. (I had received this extra $2 a month since May 1945.)

I was sent to Fort Ord to be processed and discharged on January 17, 1947. However, the army kept me there an extra six days "for the convenience of the government." From all indications, it was to give them more time to persuade me to reenlist. But I could not be persuaded and was discharged on January 23, 1947; transportation to Cuero, Texas, and home provided.

In my Army service time of two years, three months, and twenty-six days, I do not think anyone could have had more experiences and adventures than I had. These included:

- learning how to fire all kinds of heavy weapons
- walking farther than any person should ever have to
- cruising all over the Pacific Ocean.
- landing three times from LCI (landing craft infantry), although none were under fire
- fighting the enemy with a front-line infantry division
- meeting several good friends and Freddy, our Filipino scout
- transferring to another front-line infantry division
- meeting and socializing with wonderful Filipino villagers
- reenlisting in the regular army
- returning to the USA to a hero's welcome
- being stranded in Wyoming on a train following a blizzard
- spending a month in Colorado Springs with a view of Pike's Peak from my window while being treated for malaria
- visiting home, with pay, for sixty days
- serving in the 155mm Mobile Artillery Unit of an armored division
- riding in the Battle of Flowers parade
- graduating from the Army Ground Forces Clerks School
- deep-sea fishing from an army boat
- being company clerk for an army football team
- serving with Headquarters Company at the Military Intelligence Service Language School full of Japanese-American soldiers
- learning how to be a coffee jockey
- being offered a commission just for reenlisting and learning the Russian language
- sticking to my "no" and being honorably discharged

From top: Cyclone Company A, 152nd Regiment, 38th Infantry Division April 1945-August 1945; Black Hawk Company A & Headquarters Company 343rd Infantry Division August 1945-February 1946; Hell on Wheels 2nd Armored Division Mobile Artillery Unit Ft. Hood, Texas, February 1946 to August 1946.

During my career in the Army I served in three different divisions. A soldier wears his division patch on his right shoulder. If he is transferred, he wears his new division patch on the right and his former division on his left. When I was assigned to the 2nd Armored Division, I wore the 2nd Armored Division patch on my right and the 86th Division patch on my left.

Transition from Citizen Soldier to Regular Army

Chapter 10
RETURN TO CIVILIAN LIFE

Mother, Father and younger brother Claude were happy to finally see me at home for good. After a lot of visiting with relatives and friends, I commenced settling down to my new non-regimented life. Then the world of civilian life brought the sudden jolt of realization that I had no income, not even my army pay of $62 per month. Flashback to the younger boy who went to war: I had a savings account at the local savings and loan with about $90 in it. That money sat there the entire time I was in the army.

Now when I was in the Sierra Madre Mountains, there was no place to spend money. When we were pulled out for rest, we had a Post Exchange (PX) but I did not smoke or drink beer at the time, so even at $52 dollars a month, I had money left over. Even when we played poker, I always won more than I lost. So I sent $25 a month home by allotment.[67] And without my knowledge, my father dutifully deposited this money into my savings account. Ergo, after my triumphant return home, I walked in to withdraw from my savings account and found that I had not $90, but $653, including $51 in interest. Wow! Oh, boy! Dad had really taken care of me and I had an extra $51 for which I had not even worked. So I learned another new lesson that I have never forgotten: I could earn money by saving money.

Alas, all the clothes I had were either olive drab wool or khaki, even to my underwear. I did have a half dozen pair of white socks purchased from the PX at Fort Ord. Of course there were the clothes I had before I went into the army, but they were now too big for me. Wearing my olive drab underwear was okay with me but not the other stuff. Mother altered some of my old pants to fit my new trim body. She also offered to make some shirts for me if I would drive her and Aunt Pella to the cotton mill in New Braunfels. The mill produced cotton fabric and had a retail outlet.

We journeyed to Aunt Pella's, then on to the mill, a trip of about 100 miles. I drove Dad's 1934 Plymouth, and, as I was not used to driving long distances, this was a horrendous trip full of anxiety, but it was worth it. Mother and Aunt Pella each bought at least fifty yards from ten or more different patterns of gingham and muslin, and soon I had six new shirts. Claude and Father had a few and Mother made herself a couple of dresses. In those days, gingham referred to a cotton fabric dyed in many different patterns of stripes, check, plaids, and solid colors. I had some of my army pants dyed other colors so I would not have to wear olive drab. Many dry cleaners specialized in dying returning veterans' uniforms. The most popular color was brown, obtained by applying a maroon dye to the olive drab cloth.

Some considerable portion of my savings went to other necessities—two pairs of shoes, belts, handkerchiefs, dress shirts and ties, and a new dark blue suit. I also paid for the gasoline and part of the upkeep of Dad's Plymouth, which I drove more than Dad did.

Some kind of job became my next priority. I went to several companies in Cuero: the Coca Cola company; the Guadalupe Valley Creamery; the City of Cuero employment office at City Hall and even the Cudahy Packing Company—my father's employer. No one was hiring and there were 200 to 300 recently discharged veterans looking for work in town. Then there was the lure of Alaska...my dream of Alaska. Let me explain.

When I was hospitalized in Colorado with malaria, a topic of discussion came up about Alaska and what that territory was doing for veterans. (Alaska did not become a state until 1959.) Any veteran wanting to settle there would be allotted an entire section of land (640 acres). If he lived on it for

---

[67] During and after WWII, the government had a system of allotments and allowances. Each soldier was expected to send $22 per month to his wife by allotment. The government would then include a class A allowance of $28. This allowance was a grant provided from federal funds in addition to the serviceman's regular pay. For unmarried soldiers, the allotment could go to the support of parents or siblings. These then included an additional class B allowance of between $15 and $50 per month.

one year, he would be given title to that land.[68] Since I could not find employment in Cuero, I thought long and hard about Alaska and a free 640 acres. But then I had those flashbacks to the time my train was stranded in that blizzard in Wyoming. No! No way! I hated cold weather too much. Alaska? Gone from my system!

Thus my thoughts returned to employment in central Texas. I really did not want to go back to my old employer, Guadalupe Valley Cotton Mills, because the working area was not air conditioned and it was at least eighty degrees Fahrenheit all the time and hotter in the summer, which was nearing. However I soon realized I was out of other options. So reluctantly, I asked to return to work and, true to their word about giving me my old job back after service to my country, they simply asked when I would like to start. My answer was the following Monday, three days hence. When I left to go to war, my pay had been 54¢ per hour. My new rate would be 70¢ per hour or $28 for a forty-hour week. My working hours would be the same as they had been before, 2 P.M. to 10:30 P.M.

I started work and everyone treated me as if I had never left. It is surprising but I fell right into the same routine with no trouble at all. Many employees were still working the same jobs with the same carding machines. Their pay had increased from 40¢ per hour to 55¢, but little else had changed. When the government contracts dried up, a lot of the newer employees were let go. Mother had been one of these, but she was quite glad to go back to being a housewife and a homemaker.

Then, about two weeks after I returned to work, I began feeling very ill. I ran a high fever and my mother was about to call her doctor. (Yes, in those days, doctors still made house calls.) I told her not to as I just had a mild malaria[69] attack. After the fever subsided, I started to feel as if I were freezing. Mother piled blankets on top of me and after twenty-four hours of this, it subsided and I was well enough to go back to work.

I had been working for Guadalupe Valley Cotton Mills for a while when I began to realize that I was getting nowhere and that I would likely have this same job when I retired. But didn't I have the G.I. Bill[70] that I could use to get an education? The thought grew in me that I could get a college education under this law, and I began to dream of where to go to get it. I had heard a lot about Notre Dame in Indiana. In early 1946, I remember listening to the Notre Dame versus Army football game on the radio. They were battling for #1 and #2 in the nation. Glen Davis and Doc Blanchard were in the backfield on the army team. Glen was known as Mr. Outside and Doc as Mr. Inside. The defenses battled to a scoreless tie! Notre Dame was awarded the national championship.

Just from listening to this game, I was all for going to Notre Dame until I realized that it was in

---

[68] One of my wife Mary's brothers, Stanley Lukawitz, settled in Alaska after serving in the military, but we don't know if he went there under this program.

[69] Malaria is transmitted via a bite from an infected female *Anopheles* mosquito, which introduces parasitic protozoans (genus *Plasmodium*) from its saliva into a person's circulatory system. In the blood, the parasites travel to the liver to mature and reproduce. The classic symptom of malaria is paroxysm—a cyclical occurrence of sudden coldness followed by shivering and then fever and sweating, occurring every two or three days. Symptoms of malaria can recur after varying symptom-free periods. This recrudescence is caused by parasites surviving in the blood as a result of inadequate or ineffective treatment. Source: wikipedia.org.

[70] The Servicemen's Readjustment Act of 1944 was known as the G.I. Bill. It provided benefits for returning World War II veterans including low-cost mortgages, low-interest loans to start a business, cash payments of tuition and living expenses to attend college, high school, or vocational education, as well as one year of unemployment compensation. It was available to every veteran who had been on active duty during the war years for at least ninety days and had not been dishonorably discharged. Source: wikipedia.org.

The term G.I. was first used to denote equipment made from galvanized iron, such as metal trash cans. During World War I, American soldiers sardonically referred to incoming German artillery shells as "G.I. cans." Also during that war, "G.I." started being interpreted as "Government Issue" or "General Issue" for the general items of equipment of soldiers and airmen. "G.I." was also used as an adjective for anything having to do with the army or the air force. During World War II, "G.I. Joe" became the general nickname for all American soldiers, no matter what branch of the army or army air forces they were in: infantry, artillery, armor, rangers, paratroopers, logistics, combat support, or the other support wings of the army or the air force. Source: wikipedia.org.

cold country and at least 1,000 miles away. Reoriented once more, I wrote to several schools in San Antonio and Houston. St. Mary's University sent me brochures of their programs, including their law school, in which I had some interest. Their summer session was to start the first week of June 1947, and they stated that they would be happy to have me attend on the G.I. Bill. My mind was made up that quickly. I notified Guadalupe Valley Cotton Mills that I would be leaving my job in two weeks, the last full week in May, to enroll in St. Mary's University in San Antonio.

Upon arrival at the Greyhound bus station in San Antonio, I walked to the YMCA a block away, and registered for a two-night stay at $1 per day for a bed in a barracks-like room. What I remember most about this YMCA was the huge swimming pool in the basement. No swimming trunks were needed as no females were allowed.

Posted in the lobby were various notices for housing. Realizing that I was on my own, I needed to find a place for sleeping and studying. Thus, I answered an ad placed by Frances Levenson and caught a bus to the 200 block of East Craig Street. Mrs. Levenson showed me her second story, which had four or five huge rooms and an outside stairway. She already had six or seven male students staying there for $20 per month. This $20 provided me an army cot, bathroom privileges, and use of a long table with chairs for doing homework. No cooking or eating were permitted at the table.

In about the 1800 block of North Main Street, an elderly Greek gentleman owned a small restaurant and diner called The Red Bird. It had perhaps ten small tables and a counter. From my roommates I learned that if you got there just before closing time, about 7:30 P.M., this kindly old man would give you all you wanted to eat for a dollar. This was a real bargain—really good food and plenty of it. What we did not eat was thrown out. Most days this was my only meal.

Not only did this old gentleman feed us well, he extended credit to all the students a month at a time. Those of us on the G.I. Bill would settle up once we received our subsistence checks. This gentleman, likely in his eighties, ran the restaurant with one cook and one other employee, and never lacked for customers. I regret never quite understanding, and thus recalling, his Greek name.

So I registered at St. Mary's for the summer session in pre-law, handed them my discharge papers and they did all the paper work—out of the army, no more cotton mill, hello college. Under the G.I. Bill my tuition and books were paid for plus $80 a month for sustenance including food and lodging. However, I soon realized that $80 was not enough. I wanted to have enough for occasional bus transportation home, to school, entertainment, movies, athletic events, and maybe even a few dances. That all cost money and eventually I wanted to buy a car which would have gasoline and upkeep costs.

Needing other income, I scanned want ads in the newspaper and spotted one for a helper at the Critchett Piano Company in the 1900 block of West Woodlawn. They hired me to sand and do other preparatory work on pianos so that the refinisher, Mr. Grey, could finish the pianos the next day. Monday through Friday I worked from 2:30 P.M. to 4:30 P.M. for $1 per hour. The pay was meager but every little bit helped.

Thus settling in to college life, I lived at Mrs. Levenson's rooming house for a year or more. But that tropical plague had followed me to San Antonio, and every couple of months I suffered a malaria attack. One day Mrs. Levenson missed seeing me leave for school. Upon investigating, she found me quite disabled and incapable of getting out of bed on my own. I explained that I was having an attack of malaria and for her not to worry. But she did worry. Knowing I was a veteran, she wrapped me in a blanket, helped me downstairs into her car, and drove me to the Veteran's Administration (VA) clinic two blocks south of the Bexar County Courthouse on Main Street. Patiently, Mrs. Levenson sat with me as I waited to see a doctor. With a raging fever of over 104 degrees, I was finally received by a doctor who ran a blood test, gave me medicine, and told me to stay in bed a few days. Mrs. Levenson took me back to my bed where I remained for the rest of the day.

To my complete surprise, two weeks later I received notification that I had a military disability of 50 percent and would be receiving compensation of $90 a month. If not for Mrs. Levenson, and her persistence, I would never have received this. My caring landlady and I became friends and, after she opened a combination antique store and flower shop, I visited her several times in later years.

With my job helping make ends meet, this extra income from the VA would allow the purchase of an automobile. Knowing nothing about buying a car, I strolled onto a used car lot on North Main not far from the Red Bird Café. As testimony to my naivety I confess that this was the first and only place I visited. The salesman assured me that he had the perfect car for me—a 1940, dark blue Mercury convertible V8. I agreed. Boy! This was the car for me! We settled on a price of $900 with $90 down and $810 to be financed for twelve months at $85 per month. I congratulated myself on how easy it was to acquire a car. No more relying on the bus or friends for transportation. I was really independent now! Wow!

The first weekend free from studying, I decided to go home to Cuero, ninety miles away, and show Mom and Dad my Mercury. But as I was cruising along at fifty miles per hour on the way to Cuero, suddenly my sleek, dark blue Mercury convertible started to overheat. In the little town of Sayers, I pulled into a mechanic's shop. He diagnosed the problem as a cracked engine head. Water was contaminating the engine oil. He did not have a replacement head but said he would go to San Antonio to a junk yard and that he could probably find one there. I asked how much that would cost and he said not very much. I had about $45 in my

Frederico San Diego

checking account, so I gave the order to proceed.

The next three hours were spent doing absolutely nothing. All of my books were in San Antonio so I could not even study—just sit and wait, pace and wait, watch the road and wait. After what seemed an eternity, the mechanic returned and in another thirty minutes, had drained my watered-down oil and replaced the engine head. He charged me $25, which I thought was quite reasonable under the circumstances. I resumed my drive to Cuero, arriving without further incident. But I never told my parents about my troubles with my sleek, dark blue, Mercury convertible.

While I was home Mother handed me a letter from my friend Freddy—that same Frederico San Diego, the cave-exploring Philippine scout from my old Company A. The letter was a couple of months old, but I answered it and sent him the addresses he asked for. We corresponded for a while, then I ceased to hear from him. We lost touch.

Once back in San Antonio, I returned to the used car lot and informed the salesman of my breakdown and about trouble I was having with the convertible top. The top was supposed to work using compressed air or a vacuum but the hoses leaked. It was

I remember every one in the company. Especially in our platoon. You know I never heard from Albritton, Anderson, and Newham, the only buddy of mine Meachel Miller is the only one that wrote me of a letter last year, I think I recieved about two letters from him, I answere the letter, but I don't know if he ever got it. For he did never reply me bak.

Zaiontz I want you to send me the address of Mike Best Claim Kowarsick and Ruggerman, for I've lost all the address of of them.

I'm going to close it by two now for it is about twelve oclock p. m. and I am going to be late in draping this letter.

Buddy of yours
Federico San Diego

July 8, 1948

Hello Zaiontz;

I've recieved your reply this day, and I'm so happy to hear your situation back there. You are also asking if I ever get married. I'm still single, now at this very moment, but I am going to be married this coming year. You know, The father of my girl friend died 2 days ago, and I've a hard time, I dint even sleep for a night, untill the body was burried at the Blongaos Cemetery.

Zaiontz; about you? when is suppose to be your wedding? Have you ever have a girl friend since you got discharge in the army? But, I think you is more than one by now. About a picture of your girl friend, are you willing to send me one, and I'm going to send you one picture of my girl friend in my next letter. This time I'm going to send you a picture of mine, taken when I'm about to go swimming to the river. It is not very well taken of course, but I going to give it to just to remind your best buddy of yours.

Your are asking weather I remember Albritton, Anderson, and Newham.

a little trouble but the top could be put in position and lowered manually. The salesman said "sorry" but that the car was sold to me at a "discount" because it was sold "as is," whereupon he produced the paperwork to prove it. I left disgruntled and without being reimbursed for the repair work or the leaky hoses. Another life lesson for the new civilian: Never buy a car without some kind of guarantee or warranty.

About a month later and with my car finally running properly, I decided to go home again. Claude was in basic training at Lackland Air Force Base in San Antonio so I called to ask if he could get a weekend pass to go home with me. He did, so on Saturday morning I picked him up and we were on our way.

Claude commented that he missed driving and asked if he could drive for a while. Why not? At Clark and Rigsby, Highway 87 to Cuero descends a hill. Claude stepped on the accelerator and in a flash a motorcycle policeman was on our tail motioning us to pull over. We were visibly scared as he declared that we were driving over forty in a thirty-miles-per-hour zone. We pleaded that Claude was in basic training at Lackland and that we were brothers going home to visit Mom and Dad in Cuero. With a scolding about watching speed limits, the policemen let Claude off with a warning and wishes for a safe trip and a good visit at home.

Time and college courses passed and I continued working at the Critchett Piano Company until October of 1948, when I answered an ad from a self-service laundry and started work there. This was one of the first self-service laundries in San Antonio and was owned by the San Antonio business man Glen G. Gale. The laundry was in the 100 block of West Avenue in the Los Angeles Heights area of San Antonio. With thirty washing machines and one huge gas-operated drying machine, capable of drying three or four washer loads at one time, my job was to show customers how to operate the machines. They either brought their own detergent or we sold them some. The washing machines were 25¢ and the drying machine was 50¢. A clerk took their money after I told them how much they owed. Still making $1 per hour, and ensuring that my classes did not conflict, I was able to expand my working hours to three or three and a half hours every day and up to eight hours on Saturdays. As a benefit, I did my laundry for free every week.

I left Mrs. Levenson's to move into the upstairs of the home of Dr. Shinn and his family. The price was no better but I had the entire upstairs to myself. Then one day at work, a soldier doing his laundry asked if I wanted a dog. He said they were moving and could not take the dog with them. It was a beautiful Scottish terrier named "Lucky," of which I took charge. When we reached home that night I asked Mrs. Shinn if I could tie the dog in the front yard until I could take him to Cuero. She agreed and allowed her children to play with Lucky; he was such a gentle dog.

The next trip to Cuero I gave Lucky to my Dad, who reluctantly took the dog but declared that he would probably give him away. Lucky was very gentle with children but not so with fowl of any kind. One of Dad's prize roosters escaped the chicken coop and Lucky grabbed him by the neck, then proceeded to make short work of him and killed him. Dad gave Lucky away and later told me that the last he heard, Lucky had killed a whole flock of chickens.

I pressed onward with my studies in the pre-law curriculum, accumulating enough credits to enter law school in the spring semester of 1949. The law school was downtown on St. Mary's Street between Houston and Commerce streets, behind St. Mary's Church. The back of the law school building was on the river. Very nice. But wait. Life was not just study and work. I had a social life as well.

When I had first returned to Cuero after the war, I dated a few local girls. Nothing ever came of these dates and the truth of the matter was: I no longer had anything in common with them. I even dated a few Polish girls from Panna Maria. Same thing. They all seemed shallow to me, and it seemed to me that when they met with their friends, they were always giggling. I never knew whether they were just immature or were perhaps laughing at me. So I started taking my first cousin, Gladys Snoga, to dances—mostly around Panna Maria. At times we would dance with each other, but mostly she would dance with her friends and I would dance with any girl who would dance with me.

By the time I was well along in my pre-law studies, Gladys was in the nursing program at Santa Rosa Hospital in San Antonio. In the spring of 1948, during my third semester at St. Mary's University, and while I was still working at the piano company, Gladys wished for me to meet a classmate of hers. In the lobby of the nurses' residence, she introduced me to Mary Catherine Lukawitz for a blind date. Mary and I, Gladys and her friend—a boy from Pennsylvania—and Jurleen Alblinger, another nursing student and Mary's roommate, went to the movies. We had many choices of which theater to attend as they were all within two blocks of each other and included The Majestic, The Aztec, State, Empire, and Prince. As it was not far and had limited parking, I remember walking to the movie but I do not remember which theater we settled on or what movie we saw. I was mostly watching Mary. Afterwards we all strolled in downtown San Antonio, then back to the nurses' residence three or four blocks away. At the end of the evening I asked Mary if she would go out with me again and, to my surprise and elation, she said "Yes." That date led to another and another and before long we were dating often. Each time I learned a little more about Mary. Both her parents were Polish and she was from New Jersey. She had worked at the Picatinny Arsenal in New Jersey making munitions for the war effort until she herself joined the army.

Now she was an army veteran as was I. Mary had enlisted in the Women's Auxiliary Army Corps (WAAC), later changed to the Women's Army Corps (WAC),[71] on her birthday, in October, 1942. Following basic training at Ft. Des Moines, Iowa, she was deployed to Ft. Sam Houston with the 30th Headquarters Company where she was assigned to

---

[71] The Women's Army Corps (WAC) was a branch of the U.S. Army for women. Originally created as the Women's Army Auxiliary Corps (WAAC) in 1942, it was converted to the full military status Women's Army Corps in 1943. About 150,000 American women served in the WAAC and WAC during World War II. They were the first women other than nurses to serve with the army. Source: wikipedia.org

S.Sgt. Mary Catherine Lukawitz

the ordnance department as a clerk.

While there, retired Sgt. Edward Komorowski introduced himself. He had been called up to serve in the parts department as a civilian employee. Sergeant Komorowski invited Mary to his home to meet his wife, Ida, and enjoy a home-cooked meal with them. The new friendship grew and the Komorowskis seemed to adopt Mary. She even called them "Mom" and "Dad Komorowski" and spent lots of time with them. The Komorowski home was on Marcia Place in Alamo Heights, right across the street from St. Peter's Catholic Church.

The 30th was the first WAC unit to send its women into the field to replace men who were needed on the front lines. Mary was sent to a staging area in California from which she embarked on the long journey across the Pacific. She sailed under the Golden Gate bridge as did I about six months later.

Originally destined for Port Moresby, New Guinea, aboard the SS Lurline, orders were changed to Oro Bay, New Guinea, as they passed the Hawai-

30th Headquarters Company WAAC Post marching past the Alamo on December 17, 1942.

ian Islands. She arrived there in September 1944, just one month after the island was liberated, and her first assignment was as a dental clerk. In April 1945, when Oro Bay was being dismantled, she was flown to Biak, New Guinea, on a C-47 transport plane. Other WACs from her outfit went to Finschhafen, New Guinea, by ship.

In November 1945, after the war ended, the base at Biak was also dismantled. Mary was flown again by C-47 to Manila, Philippines, to await transfer home on the point system. She departed for the good old USA in November 1945 on the same ship that had taken her to New Guinea. On both trips, the entire passenger list was thousands of WACs.

Arriving back at Ft. Sam Houston, Mary was discharged on December 5, 1945, whereupon she reacquainted herself with the Komorowskis and lived with them until, using the G. I. Bill benefits, she applied for nurses' training at Santa Rosa Hospital.

Having served in the South Pacific and the Philippines, Mary and I were familiar with many of the same areas. It was like we spoke some same, higher language. It did not matter that she outranked me in the army or that she was older than I was. I was overjoyed to be with someone who was mature, with whom I could talk, to sit with a fellow soldier who understood where I had been and what I had been through. I count it part of my blessing that her unit had been stationed at Ft. Sam Houston so that she could now be a part of my life.

About one mile out the Austin Highway, off Broadway, was a night club called The Seven Oaks. I now had a car and it was not very far to the club. They had a large dance floor and usually had a live

122 ONLY ONE POLLACK

Graduating class of Santa Rosa Hospital School of Nursing, 1949. Mary is third from the left in the first row; Gladys Snoga is second from right in the second row; Jurleen Alblinger is second from left in the third row.

band. If we had anything to celebrate with others, Mary and I went there. We danced and you could bring your own booze.

Later in the spring of 1948, the nursing class of Santa Rosa was invited to a USO[72] dance at a huge two-story building at the intersection of East Travis and Houston streets. The whole top floor was an immense dance floor. I was invited as an escort. I was infatuated with everything about Mary, especially how she looked in her evening gown, which was accentuating some of her best assets.

That spring of 1949, Mary and I attended a basketball game at St. Mary's gym. After the game we drove for a while then I stopped the car, paused, collected myself, and proposed to this wonderful girl. She said "Yes." I took off for cloud nine and stayed there for about a week. Even today I do not remember who won that game, what the score was, or even who St. Mary's was playing. Mary said "Yes!"

Now we needed to set the date for our wedding. Mary explained that none of her family would be attending as they all lived too far away and trans-

---

[72] The United Service Organizations Inc. (USO) is a nonprofit organization that has provided programs, services and live entertainment to United States troops and their families since 1941. The USO is not part of the US government, but is recognized by the Department of Defense, Congress, and the president of the United States. Although a private organization, it was congressionally chartered. During World War II, the USO began a tradition of entertaining the troops that continues today. Source: wikipedia.org

Adrian with Joe Cherry

portation would be a substantial problem. Her nursing class was to graduate in May of 1949. I was to start my second semester of law school the second week of September. We would set the date in the early fall of 1949 in between my semesters. So Mary and I settled on September 1, 1949. The wedding would take place in Cuero at St. Michael's Church with Father William Jansen performing the sacrament.

In mid-August, we commenced looking for an apartment and eventually settled on one on East Laurel Avenue for $25 per month. Compared to the fox holes I had lived in while in the Philippines, it seemed reasonably big enough for us. It had a very small kitchen and an equally small bathroom. The one bedroom was ten feet by eleven feet and had a Murphy bed. When we had visitors, we pushed the bed up into the wall behind a curtain to use the chairs. Mr. Carr, the apartment building owner, was really nice and he said our rent would not start until September 1. So we paid him the rent for September. In the following days we returned to the apartment several times to give it a thorough cleaning.

Then came the dawn! I should have a real job and not just a part-time one at a public laundry. Through St. Mary's student placement services I found two options: the San Antonio Police Department was recruiting veterans as was the U.S. Post Office. I put in my application at the police station and then I went to the post office at Houston and Alamo Streets. As I talked to an official there he declared that they were giving an entrance exam in about an hour and asked if I would be interested in taking it. I said "Sure." He recorded pertinent information about me and then he escorted me to a room with a large number of applicants waiting to take the exam. With my ten additional points given to veterans with disabilities, I scored in the top 10 percent of the job seekers. I never heard from the San Antonio Police Department, but I received a letter from the post office stating that I would start there on September 28, 1949, exactly five years to the day since entering the army. So began my career with the U.S. Postal Service. I had secured a means to the financial foundation upon which to begin my new life as a married man.

The wedding went flawlessly on Thursday, September 1, 1949, with several nursing classmates, including my cousin Gladys Snoga, attending Mary as bridesmaids. All wore gowns of the same pattern but of different colors. Mary's roommate Jurleen Alblinger was her maid of honor, and my brother Claude was my best man. Joe Cherry, an army buddy from Rock Island, Illinois, was there to give me support to get through the wedding.

The reception with dinner was held at the Cuero Municipal Park Building including the municipal swimming pool for anyone wishing to swim. My parents, Claude, and all of my myriad of aunts, uncles, and first cousins turned out in force for a good old-fashioned Polish gathering. Near 5 P.M. after any who wished had eaten yet again, we caravanned to Panna Maria for the traditional wedding dance. At least twenty vehicles transported all who wished to continue with the festivities.

With an hour before the band was to start playing, Claude became the most popular bachelor as he was giving all the girls rides in my Mercury convertible with the top down. However, there was a problem: For some time I had been having trouble with the hood. The hood latch tended to malfunction and on occasion allowed the wind to force the hood to stand straight up. I had tied the hood down with a length of wire but neglected to warn Claude. So sure enough, while he was giving rides, a gust broke the wire and the hood slammed straight up scaring everyone.

Walter, Adrian, Mary & Lucy Zaiontz.

Claude stopped the car, and, to my great relief, no one was hurt. Giving young Claude a military-style dressing down was wiped from my mind as I realized that the incident was really of my making and not his fault at all.

The dance proceeded at the Panna Maria Hall with the popular Dolph Hofner and His San Antonians[73] providing western swing music. By 7 P.M. a crowd was gathering. All Polish people went to wedding dances whether or not they knew the bride and groom. Dances were always a primary means of entertainment in those years. The wedding party all wore ribbons of a certain color to signify that they were guests and did not have to pay to attend. Others paid at the door. The dance formally commenced with my first cousin, Adeline Urbanczyk Ciomperlik and her husband Frank, leading the wedding march.

Everyone was obviously having a great time and Uncle Felix Snoga danced with Mary so many times that I was becoming jealous. At around 10:30 P.M., as Mary and I were preparing to leave, Uncle Felix called me over to the ticket booth. I panicked. "How much is this going to cost?" But Uncle Felix handed me $115 from the ticket sales. I protested that expenses should be taken from this but he assured me that everything had already been paid including the band, the hall rental, and all of the hall employees. Perhaps there was a tear in the corner of my eye as Uncle Felix handed me the cash and said to use the money on our honeymoon.

Ever vigilant that none of my innumerable cousins were following, Mary and I slipped away to our tiny rented apartment—our honeymoon suite. The next morning, the first day with Mary at my side as my wife, we left for a week's honeymoon in Albuquerque, New Mexico.

---

[73] Adolph John Hofner, of Czech-German heritage, had his first hit in 1940 with "Maria Elena." He formed the Adolph Hofner and His Texans band in 1938. During World War II his group performed under the name of Dolph Hofner and His San Antonians. Some of his hits during this period were "Cotton-Eyed Joe," "Alamo Rag," and "Jessie Polka." Sponsored by Pearl Beer in 1950, Hofner formed the "Pearl Wranglers," performing their musical mix of swing, country, rockabilly, and polka. They recorded a number of Czech-American songs including "Happy Go Lucky Polka," "Prune Waltz," "Barbara Polka," "Green Meadow Polka," and "Farewell to Prague." Source: wikipedia.org

The Zaiontz wedding party with eleven bridesmaids and eleven groomsmen.

Chapter 11
OUR FIRST YEAR OF MARRIED LIFE

We returned from a short honeymoon trip to Albuquerque, New Mexico, in a little less than one week. Surprisingly, my dark blue Mercury convertible—of which my ownership had begun as a lemon—turned out to be quite a reliable automobile.

Upon returning to our apartment on the 400 block of East Laurel Street, I was to register for my third semester at St. Mary's Law School. There was a letter from a Judge Gully, who, as a counselor for the law school, wanted me to make an appointment with him. I did and sat down with him a few days later. He impressed upon me that "C" and "D" with an occasional "B" were not going to make the grade in law school. I told him that I had just been married and was working a lot of hours each week. Obviously I was at a disadvantage. My fellow students were living at home and did not have to work to pay for room and board. A typical class day of four hours required an additional eight hours of study time mostly in the law library. Upon informing the judge that I was to start work full-time at the post office on September 28, he enjoined that I should reconsider my "extracurricular activities" and devote myself to law school full time.

I did reconsider, realizing that there just were not enough hours in the day for law classes, study time, work, and sleep. I would wait at least one or more semesters before trying law school again. As it happened, life got in the way and I never again pursued a law degree, although I did eventually complete a business degree.

Next, I received a letter from the Veteran's Administration informing me that my 50 percent disability benefit was being discontinued. As I had no more malaria flair-ups, I did not dispute their decision.

My work continued at the self-service laundry and I added more hours every day. About the 20th of September, I gave Mr. Gale notice that I would be leaving to start at the post office. By now Mary had graduated from nursing school and was working at Santa Rosa Hospital full-time as a registered nurse.

On September 28 I reported to the main post office at Houston and Alamo Streets with nine others who were starting that day. During the orientation by one of the old timers it was explained that there were two main sections on the ground floor: the Outgoing Section and the City Section. Newt Morris was supervisor in the outgoing section and Fred Matyear managed the city section. The ten of us would be substitute clerks during our trial period. Each day, including Saturday and Sunday, we were to report to the swing room on the second floor at 3 P.M. and work as long as we were needed. We would have no regular hours and would be the extra help needed after all the mail pick-ups were completed.

Almost every day we waited one, two, or sometimes three hours to get "on the clock" and get paid. We all worked in the outgoing section, as new substitute clerks did not work in the city section.

We were called as needed to work at the facing table or in some other area of the outgoing section. As the mail collections arrived, they were dumped on a huge metal table perhaps three feet high and twelve to fourteen feet long. Five or six workers standing along each long side of the table turned all the mail face up, oriented with the postage in the upper right corner. All the letter-sized mail was faced and dropped on a conveyer belt along the outer edge of the table. At the end of the belt another employee loaded the mail into two-foot-long trays to be taken to the cancelling machines. The operators of these machines would pick up a handful of letters at a time to feed through the machines which would cancel the stamps one at a time on each letter. It took about ten seconds to cancel each handful. Most of the time, at least two of the three cancelling machines were working continuously.

In the center of the facing table were slots open to both sides and about one foot above the table surface. These slots were for mail other than letter size such as flats, magazines, small parcels—anything that was not letter size. We tried to face all of this mail in the same direction since periodically another worker would pick up this mail and cancel each piece by hand.

This was tiresome work and necessitated standing on a concrete floor, in one place, for three to four hours until the final mail collection had been cleared from the facing table. After the table was shut down, we were given a short break, then put to work doing other manual labor jobs, such as loading or unloading trucks with sacks of mail and parcels. It seemed a lot like being in the army in that we were used anywhere doing those jobs that no one else wanted to do. But I took this all in stride as I had done worse jobs for a lot less pay. Starting at $1.50 per hour for thirty hours or more per week was okay with me.

Four months later, in January 1950, I was promoted to regular clerk and could count on a regular salary. Then I learned from one of my fellow substitutes that if you worked the night tour, you were paid 10 percent more in salary. The night tour included any hours worked between 6 P.M. and 6 A.M. I asked to join the all-night tour of eleven other clerks and it was granted. My new working hours were 9:30 P.M. to 6 A.M. The worst thing about this tour was trying to get home through the 6:30 to 7 A.M. traffic. But there was surely no problem finding a parking space on the street after 9 P.M.

The mission of the night crew was to get the mail ready for the huge crew coming in at 6 A.M. The incoming mail arrived in large canvas bags, which were then dumped onto a four-foot-wide conveyor belt for separation. Letter mail was tied in bundles of as many as fifty letters—all faced the same way and secured with jute string. Bundles arrived from all over the United States and the world. They were then thrown into carts and taken to the distribution cases where they were stacked two high—all facing one way—and the strings cut. All the incoming mail, parcels, flats, magazines, letter mail, small packages, etc. were made ready for the next day's distribution by the twelve-man night crew. We unbundled, sorted by primary zone or station then began the process of separating it for the individual carriers. The final dispatch to substations started at 8 A.M.

After about a month on the night tour, a window supervisor asked for someone to work the money order window, preferably a new employee who was good with numbers. Forgetting the old army adage "Never volunteer for anything" and believing I was qualified, I volunteered. Though it meant losing my extra 10 percent pay, I thought it would be worth it to work daylight hours.

I was trained as a money order clerk handling a tremendous amount of money each day, sometimes as much as $20,000. The bad thing was that at the end of the day and after completing the accounting, I had to come out even. If I was short a few cents or even a dollar or two, the supervisor would take it out of petty cash. Conversely if I was over, the overage went into petty cash. But, when I was short a larger amount, it came from my salary. In those days, $10 or $20 deducted from my paycheck was just too much, so I returned to the night shift after a year.

Settling in with steady jobs and a family to build, Mary and I started looking for a permanent home. Several subdivisions attracted us and, with all the new veterans also looking at new homes, the competition was fierce. We decided to try to buy a new house in the new Highland Hills subdivision, which had been started by the builder E. J. Burke. This location was on the southeast side of San Antonio and on the way to Cuero and Mom and Dad.

I put another life lesson that I had learned in basic training to good use: If you happen to be hiking in a low area and you look to your right and it is uphill, then you look to your left and it is also uphill, you are more than likely to be in an ancient creek bed. Sooner or later, this area is going to flood. Maybe not in a hundred years but some day it will flood. You do not want to put your tent or shelter there, but instead put it on higher ground especially in inclement weather.

Mary and I decided on a two-bedroom house almost at the top of a hill on McDougal Avenue. Over the years, Clark Avenue, which runs at the bottom of our block of McDougal, has been flooded to a depth of three feet at various times. In more than sixty years, our home has never been threatened with flooding.

My annual salary was a little more than $3,000. But because of that salary, we barely did qualify for an FHA loan of $6,300 and a G. I. loan of $925. Mary and I each had some savings and she decided to make a down payment on the house. The total

Left: House on McDougal.

Below: Adrian watering the runners that Mary had planted.

cost of the house was $8,186. Because of this down payment, our monthly mortgage payment was a lot less than it would have been otherwise. The house was about 750 square feet and had two small bedrooms, a kitchen, bath, and a combination living room and dining area. Our monthly payment on the house was $61 but we still had to furnish it.

My bride and I moved into our new home on McDougal Avenue in May 1950. We furnished our home with bare essentials at first: a refrigerator and a stove for the kitchen, a bed, and a table and chairs for the dining area. All this meant another monthly payment of a little more than $40. Later we added a living room suite with end tables and a lamp. Thank goodness for Mary and her $1,100 savings account.

When we moved into our new home, Mary was almost eight months pregnant with our first child. About two months earlier, I had convinced her to quit working at Santa Rosa because of her pregnancy. No longer working a paying job, Mary took it upon herself to plant our entire lawn from carpet grass runners from my Mom and Dad's lawn in Cuero. The runners were each about a foot long. Mary planted the cut ends, then pinned the rest of the stem to the ground with cheap hair pins so it would take root. With all of this runner-by-runner planting and pinning and frequent watering, we would eventually have a lawn instead of bare dirt and mud. Can you imagine my thoughts running from pride to guilt each day as I returned home from work and found my beautiful wife, eight months pregnant, planting all of those runners?

Highlights of late 1949 and 1950—the first year of family life:

■ We both had steady jobs allowing us to begin growing the roots to sustain our lives together.

■ We committed to purchase our life-long home. The house and even the streets were not finished until the end of April. We moved in May.

■ One hour after midnight on June 20, our first child was born: a beautiful little girl weighing seven and a half pounds and nineteen and a half inches long. We named her Kathryn Ann.

■ In August or September, we bought our first new car—a Ford four-door sedan—from Gillespie Motor Company.

Our First Years of Married Life

chapter 12
MAKING A LIVING AND FAMILY LIVING

A rarity for San Antonio and south Texas, January or February of 1951 bestowed a very heavy ice storm upon us. The early morning news warned that many roads were closed and that all the buses were running partial routes only. Undeterred, I decided to try to get to my job at the post office money order window. I backed the car out of the driveway, then drove and slid my way down McDougal Avenue, miraculously without hitting any of the cars parked in the street. Luckily, when I reached Clark Avenue, there were no cars in sight because I could not stop at the stop sign and slid across the intersection, but without incident.

Realizing that I would not get very far if I drove downtown and might very well wreck my car, I abandoned the car and carefully walked about a mile to the intersection of Steves Avenue and Clark Avenue, which was as far as the buses were running on that route. I caught the bus and arrived at work only about a half hour late. Perhaps only half of the work force made it to work at all that day.

Not surprisingly, there were very few money order customers that day. About an hour before the scheduled closing of my window at 5 P.M., an outgoing section supervisor, Mr. Elley, spotted me and ordered me to report to the outgoing section when my time at the window was up. Most of the outgoing section employees were absent and that section was very short-handed. I pleaded that I could not as I had abandoned my car in the street and caught a bus to work. The bus would be my only transportation to near where I left my car.

So having no practical choice, I disobeyed and did not report to the outgoing section as ordered. Rather, I caught the bus and retrieved my car. This precipitated a Letter of Reprimand for disobeying a direct order and a summons to Postmaster Dan J. Quill's office. I pleaded my case, explaining all the circumstances about the weather, leaving the car, walking a treacherous mile to catch the bus, and finally reporting for work when so many other employees did not even make the effort. The letter was eventually removed from my record.

Thankfully the rest of 1951 was pretty much uneventful, allowing Mary and me to settle into our new family life. In May I gave up my daytime window job and went back to my all-night job of 9:30 P.M. to 6 A.M. I could not afford the additional expense from my paycheck when I accidentally gave the customer too much change. (Although I do remember one occasion when a customer came back and said I had given him too much in change, an act for which I thanked him profusely.) In my defense, there were no electronic machines to calculate charges and specify the amount of change to give. There was only a hand-operated adding machine at each window.

On October 13, 1951, Mary called me at work and said the time was near. Another beautiful baby girl was born. We named her Patricia Lee.

In late fall I surmised that if I were to ever complete my education and get a college degree, I had to return to St. Mary's University, and do it right away. Sure enough, the spring of 1952 found me back on campus part-time on Mondays, Wednesdays, and Fridays. Working all night, attending classes, and studying during the day was really rough, but with the few credits I had received from my law school subjects plus my two years prior to law school, I finally graduated in May 1954. I could never have graduated without the support of a great family. Mary maintained a muted household while I was sleeping, allowing me to go back to work each night.

After graduation I envisioned leaving my postal job and applying my newly earned credentials in the private sector. I applied at Allied Stores Inc., which was the parent company of the department store Joskes. During my initial interview, I was told my starting salary as a trainee would be $3,000 annually. I was making more than $4,500 at the post office, and that did not include overtime pay. Up went that pipe dream in smoke. I retired from the postal service on December 30, 1981, but that leaves out a few details.

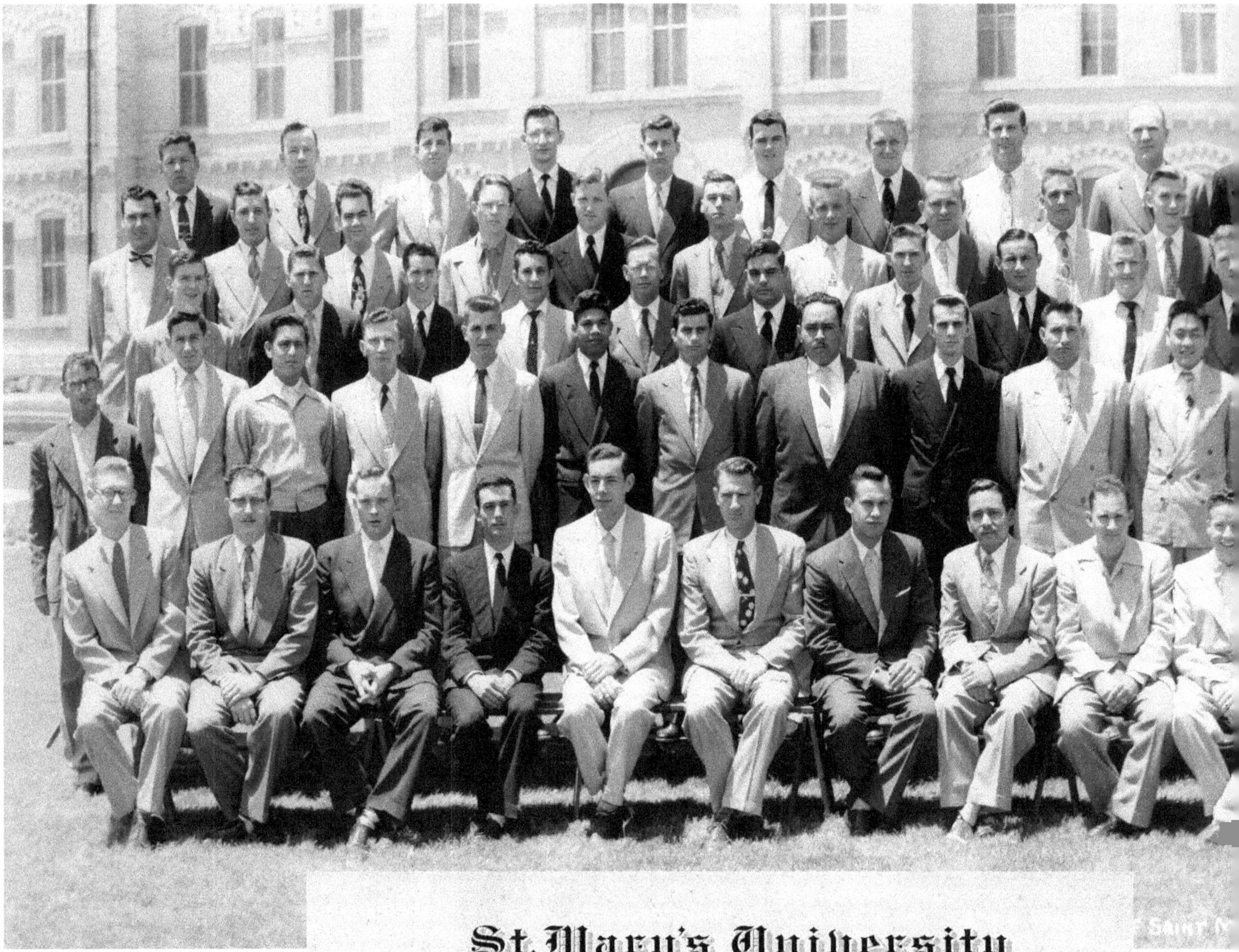

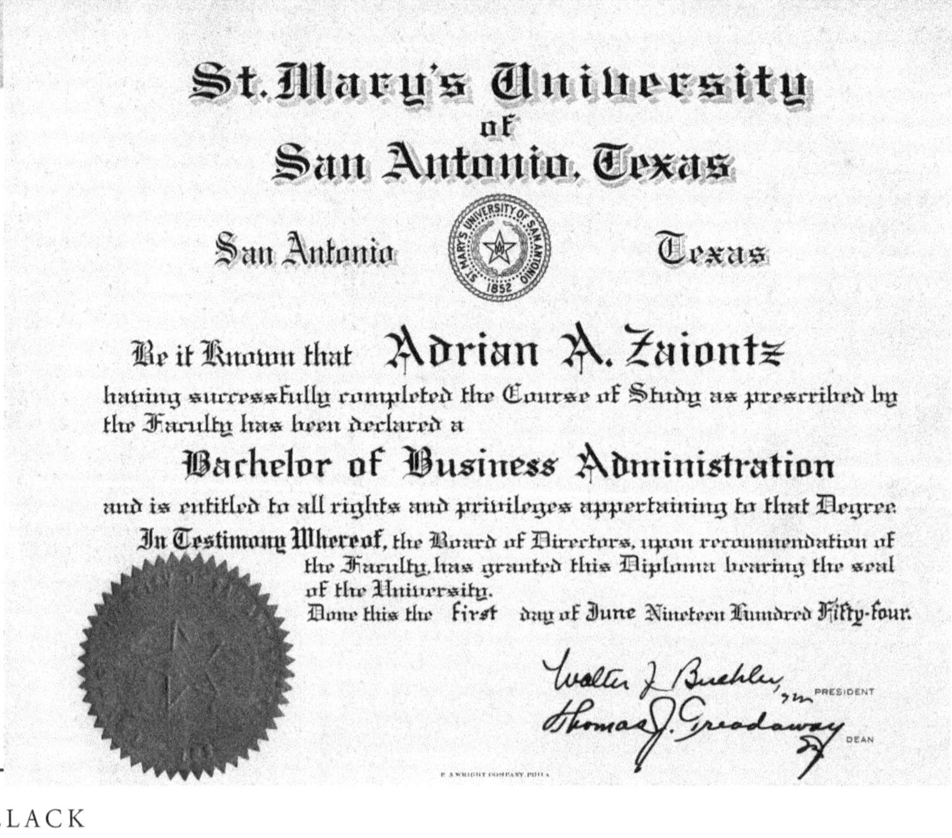

St. Mary's University
of
San Antonio, Texas

San Antonio Texas

Be it Known that **Adrian A. Zaiontz**
having successfully completed the Course of Study as prescribed by the Faculty has been declared a

Bachelor of Business Administration

and is entitled to all rights and privileges appertaining to that Degree.

In Testimony Whereof, the Board of Directors, upon recommendation of the Faculty, has granted this Diploma bearing the seal of the University.
Done this the first day of June Nineteen Hundred Fifty-four.

Walter J. Buehler, S.M. PRESIDENT
Thomas J. Treadaway, S.M. DEAN

F. A. WRIGHT COMPANY PHILA.

Above: 1954 graduating class of St. Mary's University. Adrian Zaiontz is the second from the left in the front row.

Right: Bachelor's degree in business administration from St. Mary's University, 1954.

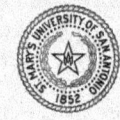

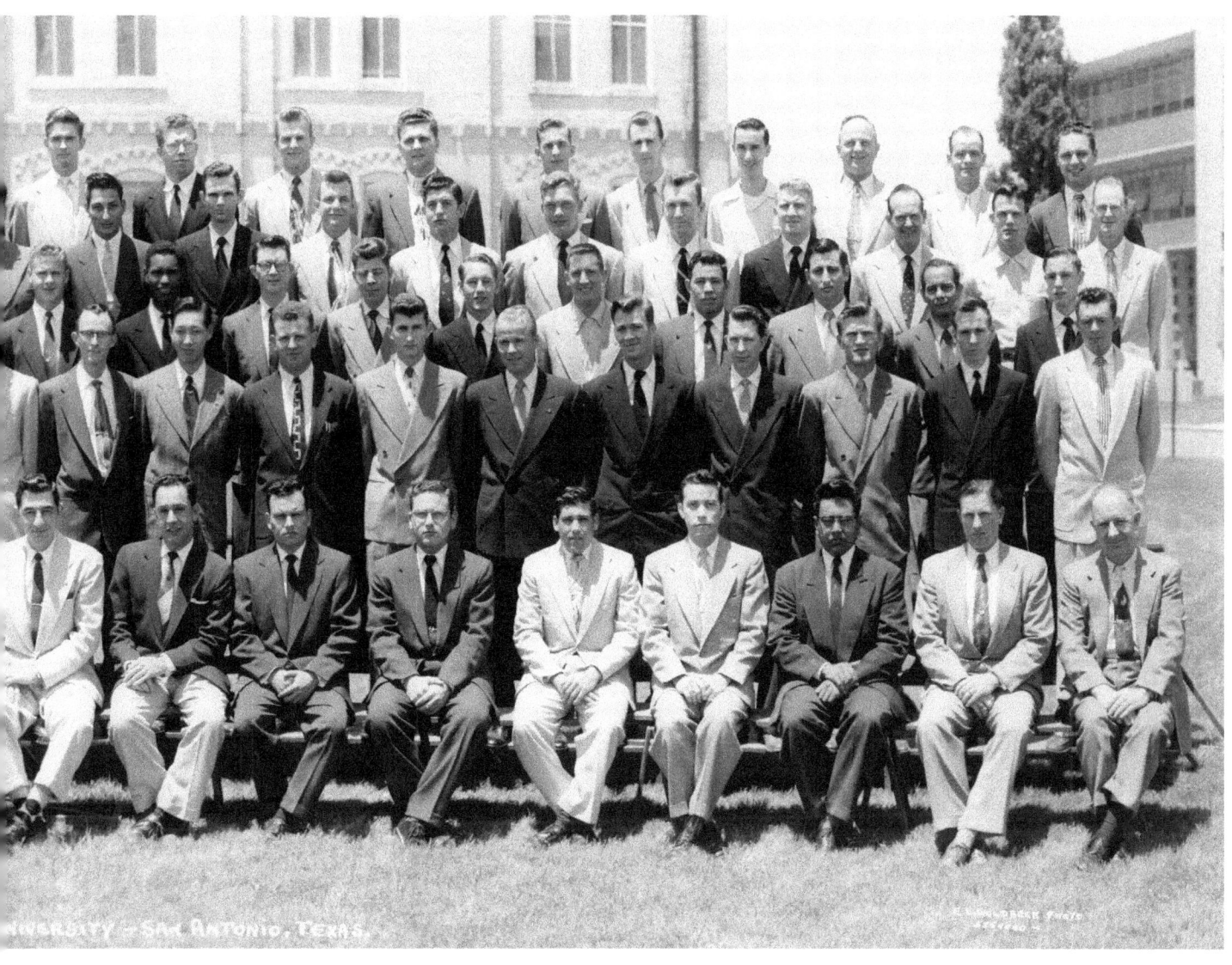

My first promotion came on November 16, 1967, to special distribution clerk, level 5. All the other regular clerks were level 4. In this position, I was responsible for the resolution of all mail that failed to be delivered on the first try, regardless of the reason. This level 5 position was raised to a level 6 position after I had worked in it a few months.

On June 20, 1968, I was promoted to foreman, mails, a level 7 position, and assigned to the registry section as a working supervisor. While the work that a regular supervisor could do was limited by the Postal Clerks Union,[74] as a *working* supervisor, I could do everything that any regular clerk could do unrestricted by the union.

The registry section was physically located in an 800- to 900-square-foot area, completely enclosed by a floor-to-ceiling chain-link fence. There was a huge walk-in safe for storage of high-value registered mail, such as bags of money or jewels. Entrance required a key, although a simple latch provided easy exit. Several windows above stainless steel counters allowed authorized postal employees to sign for and receive registered mail. At 8 A.M., the normal time for dispatching mail to the outlying stations, each clerk who was delivering regular mail to outlying stations was required to sign for and pick up a sack of registered mail for that station.

---

[74] The Postal Clerks Union defined what work must be done only by clerks who were required to be members of the union. This effectively restricted what acts supervisors and other management could perform.

Making a Living and Family Living

POST OFFICE DEPARTMENT
REQUEST FOR RANKING OF POSITION

INSTRUCTION: *Forward original and 2 copies to Reviewing Office.*

1. NAME OF OFFICE OR ORGANIZATION	(FOR DEPARTMENTAL USE ONLY)	
Main Post Office San Antonio, Texas 78205	APPROVED TITLE SPECIAL DISTRIBUTION CLERK	
2. SUGGESTED TITLE OF POSITION Special Distribution Clerk	POSITION IDENTIFICATION SP 2-41	APPROVED PFS LEVEL PFS– 5
3. RECOMMENDED SALARY LEVEL *(From item 6D below)* PFS– 5	KEY POSITION USED FOR RANKING Distribution Clerk RPO/NPO	KEY POSITION NO. 16
4A. DATE OF SUBMISSION 9-28-67	4B. REASON FOR THIS REQUEST New Position	SIGNATURE OF APPROVING OFFICER Daniel J. Quill, Postmaster	DATE OF APPROVAL 9-28-67

5. POSITION DESCRIPTION *(Attach continuation sheet if additional space is needed)*

A. BASIC FUNCTION

Reviews incoming and outgoing mail removed from normal distribution channels because of apparently illegible, incomplete, or incorrect address, or for other reasons; disposes of it on the basis of broad knowledge and special skill in mails distribution methods and problems.

BASIC HOURS: Relief of Special Distribution Clerk on Tours 1, 2 and 3.

B. DUTIES AND RESPONSIBILITIES

(A) Examines incoming mail with illegible, incomplete, or incorrect address, routing to proper destination, where possible, in accordance with detailed knowledge of city distribution, business firms, organizations, prominent personages, etc.
(B) Examines outgoing mail items which cannot be normally distributed because of apparently illegible, incomplete, or incorrect address, routing to proper destination, where possible, or routing to sender.
(C) Inspects outgoing mail items addressed to foreign countries which do not meet the mailing requirements of such countries; returns to sender with explanation.
(D) Refers mail matter which requires directory service to inquiry clerks.
(E) May perform any type of mail distribution.

C. ORGANIZATIONAL RELATIONSHIPS

Reports to a foreman or other designated supervisor.

POD FORM 820
MAR. 1965

Description of a special distribution clerk's duties.

I had one regular clerk working for me and the two of us ran the registry section from 9:30 P.M. until 6 A.M. The registry section cares for all mail of high value or needing assurance of relatively timely delivery. Sometimes extra help was needed in the registry section because of unusually high mail volume. In this case a clerk was recruited from the all-night tour until the mail volume was under control. I had worked the night shift for many years and I was familiar with the work in the registry section as I, too, had worked there on occasions when that section needed extra help.

Timely delivery and secure handling were achieved by mandatory signature of every employee who handled a piece of registered mail. The employee did not necessarily sign for each individual piece but generally for a sack of as many as a hundred pieces. A lock with a counter in it was attached to each sack and the counter advanced the number by one every time it was opened. Every postal employee who handled the sack was required to sign for it regardless of whether he or she was a truck driver, clerk, mail handler, or supervisor.

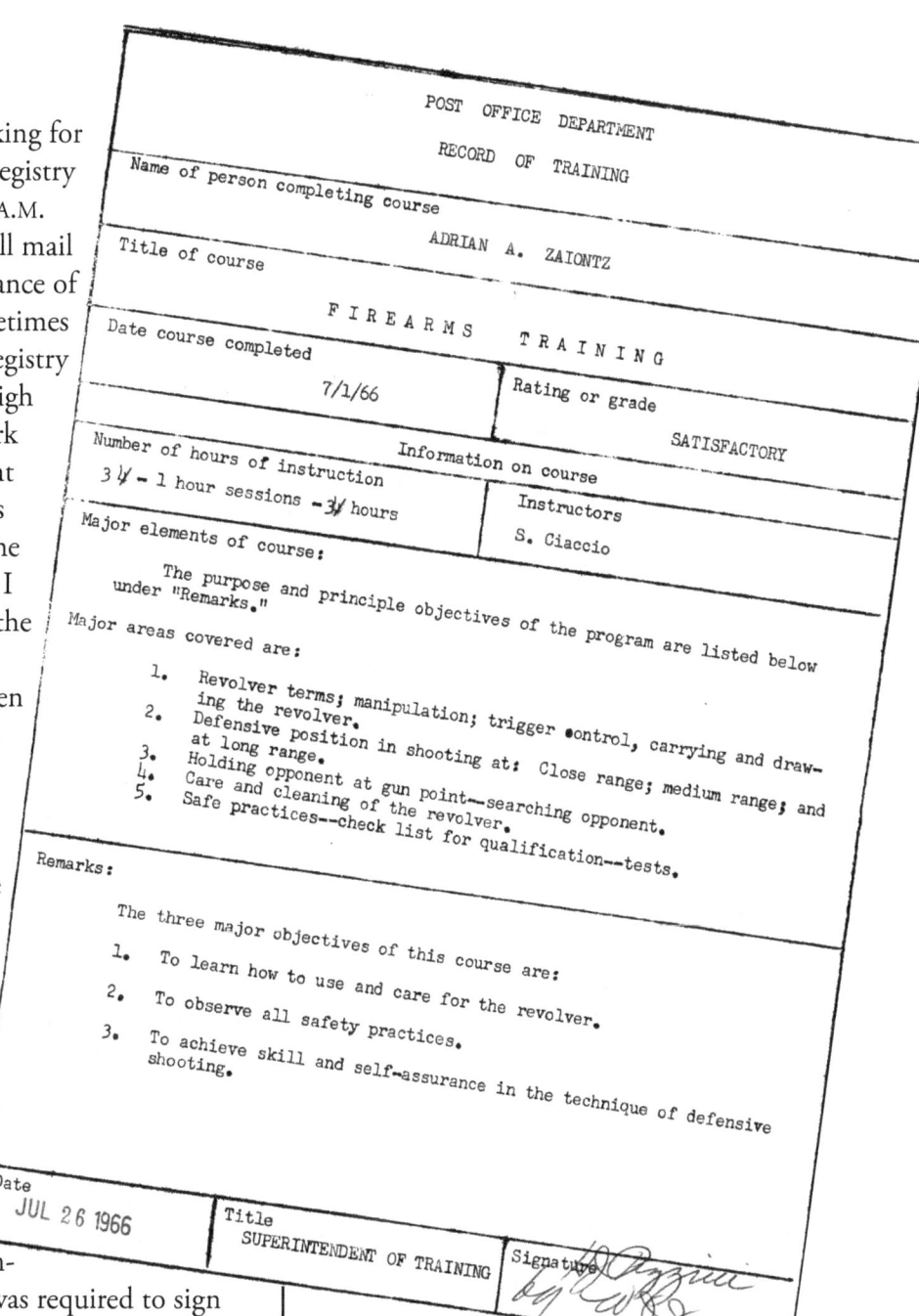

Firearms training certificate.

Holding this position required me to be familiar with firearms to protect valuable mail. All of my military training and combat experience with a myriad of different firearms notwithstanding, I was required to qualify with a pistol. Mr. Ciaccio, who taught the course, was an infantry veteran of the European theater. While I was not required to wear a pistol while on duty, the firearms had to be within my easy reach at all times.

The registry section was not my only experience with firearms while in the Postal Service. On several occasions while on temporary detail to the city section daytime tour, I was asked to accompany a finance section supervisor while making large deposits at Alamo National Bank. I had to sign for and carry a sawed-off shotgun! Thank goodness I never had to use that thing.

In early 1972 I was detailed to the city section as a supervisor-in-training. The hours were from 5:30 A.M. to 2 P.M. and I hated to lose the 10 percent extra pay for working night shifts, but in my new position, I had a substantial increase in pay. Follow-

Making a Living and Family Living 135

ing a six-month trial and training period, I was promoted to a level 15 permanent supervisor position and assigned to the secondary sorting section, putting me in charge of clerks who were separating mail to the carrier level at six or eight workstations. My job was to make sure each workstation had adequate personnel so that all the mail was separated to as many as twenty to thirty carriers by the 8 A.M. dispatch time. Clerks were expected to maintain their proficiency in sorting to handle forty to fifty letters a minute. They had to pass a test by the scheme examiner every six months. After 8 A.M. all of these clerks moved back to primary sorting. About two hours before quitting time, all the clerks returned to the secondary sorting section to again separate the mail for the next day's dispatch. A new crew came in at 3 P.M.

So went the job, with its changes, which supported our lives. But during this time Mary and I experienced many other changes. We were blessed with three more children. My only son, Edwin Joseph, was born on our fourth wedding anniversary in 1953. He was named for the doctor who delivered him and my lost brother Joseph. Barbara Lucille, whose middle name was for my mother Lucy, came along September 23, 1954. And finally, on August 12, 1957, Sharon Jean arrived. Sharon will forever remain the baby in the family.

When our oldest child Kathy started school at St. Margaret Mary Catholic School in 1956, she commenced bringing home all the usual childhood diseases. Measles, mumps, chicken pox, and others were passed among all her siblings. A hidden benefit of this exposure was that the four younger children got these diseases behind them before starting school. No doubt this contributed to Patricia and Eddie having perfect attendance records all the way from the first grade through high school, though neither one was officially recognized for this accomplishment.

When Kathy, our first child, was born, Mary and I knew nothing about parenting. But by the time Sharon arrived, we had somehow managed to survive and become reasonably competent at it. We kept them fed, clothed, healthy, and had started their educations at St. Margaret Mary Catholic School. While I was working nights and sleeping days, Mary was not only trying to keep them quiet but made great strides in teaching them how to take care of themselves and each other. To me it is mind-boggling how busy Mary was caring for this family. Most of the credit goes to her for turning the Zaiontz children into outstanding citizens. When Sharon started school in the early 1960s, Mary commenced filling her new brief periods of free time by becoming the vice-president of the St. Margaret Mary PTA.

We had the five greatest children that any parent could have. They understood our financial situation and understood that when Christmas came they would not receive a lot of toys. Many times they made up their own games and toys. They drew names at Christmas and each bought a Christmas present for that person from their meager allowances. Santa always brought practical gifts like clothing (socks and underwear) and other essentials, and they understood and accepted them with joy.

Daddy was seldom at home during the Christmas holidays except to sleep. During the month of December, postal clerks could work as much overtime as they wanted. I used the Christmas season to catch up on the bills and make a little extra money. I usually worked twelve to seventeen hours a day. But after one such seventeen-hour day, I remember being so tired and confused that I could not remember where I had parked my car. After searching for fifteen minutes or so, I concluded that it had been stolen. Finally I came to my senses, found it, and drove home, exhausted but relieved. Some people can lose their Christmas spirit when working long hours and I certainly did.

All five of my children attended and graduated from the University of Texas at Austin. They understood that Mary and I could not pay for all their education and necessities. We provided some of their financial assistance, they each took out student loans, and they worked their way through college. And I am one proud parent knowing that each one promptly repaid that loan after graduation.

Patricia, Kathryn, Edwin, Sharon and Barbara in 1958.

As our family grew from only two to seven, it became evermore apparent that our small, two-bedroom home was not large enough and had no more room for a growing family. We added onto the house twice. In 1954 we extended the living room eastward by seven feet and added a large, third bedroom to the southeast corner. Then in 1960, we added a twelve-foot-by-fifteen-foot den and a patio on the southwest side. Our 750-square-foot house for newlyweds had become a more comfortable 1250 square foot house for a family. These additions gave our only son Eddie a separate room while the four girls shared the large bedroom.

In 1964 my ten-year old son Eddie and I replaced the leaky roof. We purchased the shingles and tar paper through our neighbor, Fred Koelzer, who acquired them for us at a discount while replacing his own roof. Taking this opportunity to impart some sage, fatherly advice to Eddie, I tried to impress upon him that if he did not want to do this type of work for the rest of his life, he must pursue a good education. Apparently he took my words to heart. Mary and I sought and succeeded in instilling this philosophy in all our children.

Finally, also in 1964, we started digging out dirt from under the girls' bedroom for a basement. This was a family project with everyone helping. The basement was to be six feet deep with a seven-by-nine-foot concrete floor. There would ultimately be a work area and a large space for storage. All the dirt from the excavation was spread over the whole lawn. That phase was completed but the final concrete work remained to be done at the time we left for a vacation that year. But upon returning, we found that the west side had caved in. Fortunately, the damage was manageable with a little extra concrete. Archie Franklin and another one of my good friends from the post office installed all of the rebar and poured and finished the concrete. Archie was the leader for this major project. The walls were twelve inches thick and a water-proofing compound was used with the concrete. This basement is still in use as my workshop more than fifty years later.

With a growing and maturing family came increasing demands for transportation. Our second new car was a 1958 Chevrolet four-door sedan. It was easily identified by the gull-like wings on the rear fenders. My personal philosophy was that if a car started giving me trouble after six or eight years it was time to get rid of it and let it become someone else's headache. The 1958 Chevrolet was traded at a good price for a 1964 metallic-tan Chevrolet Malibu station wagon. With children ranging in age from eleven to four, 1961 found us with increasing schedule conflicts. Mary was shuffling children where they needed to go while I was commuting to and from work at the post office and my part-time jobs. I rode the bus for a while but that always seemed to take too long. Becoming a two-car, suburban family seemed to be the solution. Enter a used 1958 Ford Fairlane, which we bought really cheap. Hmm, there was a reason for that "bargain." Within a month it struck home that I had thrown caution to the wind and purchased someone else's headache. The transmission failed, but fortunately, a fellow postal employee, Emelio Uregas, had previously been an auto mechanic and helped me replace the transmission with a used one, allowing this car to become my conveyance to and from the post office and my part-time jobs. Mary used the more reliable station wagon for domestic needs and especially to transport the children hither and yon to their various activities.

After we divested ourselves of the '58 Ford, a green four-door 1972 Buick Skylark was the next vehicle to share duties with the 1964 station wagon. Childhood memories swayed me to try owning a Buick. My father had once owned a 1932 Buick, which served him well. That thing looked like a hearse but it proved reliable transportation for a number of years. Dad never could afford a new car so he always bought used ones. That old Buick was stolen once while we lived in Beeville. As we were departing a church picnic, we discovered that the car was missing. It was recovered some thirty miles from Beeville, where it had been abandoned after running out of gas.

So, judgment tainted by childhood memories of a forty-year-old vehicle, I purchased this new Skylark. And I confess here that new 1972 Buick was actually the worst car we ever owned. As soon as the warranty expired, the routine began of repairing or replacing parts on it. The windshield wiper motor died, the hood hinges on both sides failed, and so on and on and on. Of course there was no "lemon" law in Texas at this time.

It seemed that we never had quite enough money to make ends meet and this made it necessary for me to find part-time work. My first such job was to set up TV sets and collect TV rental fees at Santa Rosa Hospital. (This was the same Santa Rosa where Mary had been a nursing student, had graduated as an RN, and had worked for a short time.) My job was to deliver TVs to rooms that requested them and go to all rooms where sets had already been rented and collect the money that was owed. The sets were on five-foot-tall rolling stands and cost $1 per day to rent. In the mid- to late-1950s, TVs were still in their infancy and frequently broke down. They had remote controls but these were not very reliable. The rental inventory at Santa Rosa was fifteen to twenty TVs and if any did not work properly I left notes for the repairman. He came in once or twice a week as needed. At the end of my shift I reported to Sister Mary Clare in the office and gave her the money I had collected that day. My pay was $1.50 per hour and I usually worked three hours per day, five days per week. Leaving Santa Rosa, I reported for my all-night tour at the post office at 9:30 P.M. This lasted a few years before I decided to try something else.

I briefly tried working for the Retail Credit Company, whose job was to assess the financial condition of applicants for businesses providing consumer financing or insurance. Retail Credit Company would send an employee to visit the applicant's neighborhood, talk to neighbors, and observe the applicant's home, making an assessment of the home, upkeep of the premises, type and condition of any automobiles, and so forth. After returning to the office, a report was then prepared estimating the character and net worth of the applicant.

At the end of my unpaid, two-week orientation with an instructor, I decided that this job just was not for me. One of the hardest determinations was to independently estimate the net worth of an applicant. I realized that it was almost impossible to do this only by observation. As a business student, I had been taught to deal with facts and figures. This job required me to use my observations to guess at someone's net worth and character. I did not want someone to be denied insurance, or perhaps something more serious, because of a report I wrote. My business degree was from a Catholic university where all of the instructors were either priests or brothers. Time and again, in all the classes, personal ethics were stressed in our lives as well as in business. Elements within me just could not accept this type of job.

Fortunately, my brother Claude was just starting his aircraft accessories business, the Zee Company, and he hired me part-time to get the office up and running. I did his payroll and all other routine office jobs. Initially, he only had two full-time employees, Bob Hay and Red Harlos, with me working three hours a day, two days per week. Claude, on the other hand, was working fourteen to sixteen hours a day, including weekends. I worked for Claude for about two years.

Next, I decided to become a substitute teacher for the San Antonio Independent School District. During my interview they suggested that since my degree was not in education, it would be beneficial to take several courses in child psychology and education. So I enrolled at San Antonio Junior College, located between Main Street and San Pedro Avenue, not very far at all from my first San Antonio address on West Craig Street. I could only manage one subject per semester in the evening just before work at the post office. Arriving home about 6:30 in the morning, I would take a short nap, then arrive at my assigned school by 8 A.M. I substituted for all grade levels in the elementary schools. When I first started as a substitute teacher, I went to any school that needed help. But after a few months, I narrowed down to only two schools: King Elementary on the west side of town and P.F. Stewart Elementary on the east side closer to home. Both principals knew that I had to get home for some sleep and forgave me all after-school duties. Each day of substitute teaching earned me $15.

Even with all the work, part-time jobs, classes, raising a family, and children in school, there was still time for family outings. Some weekends we

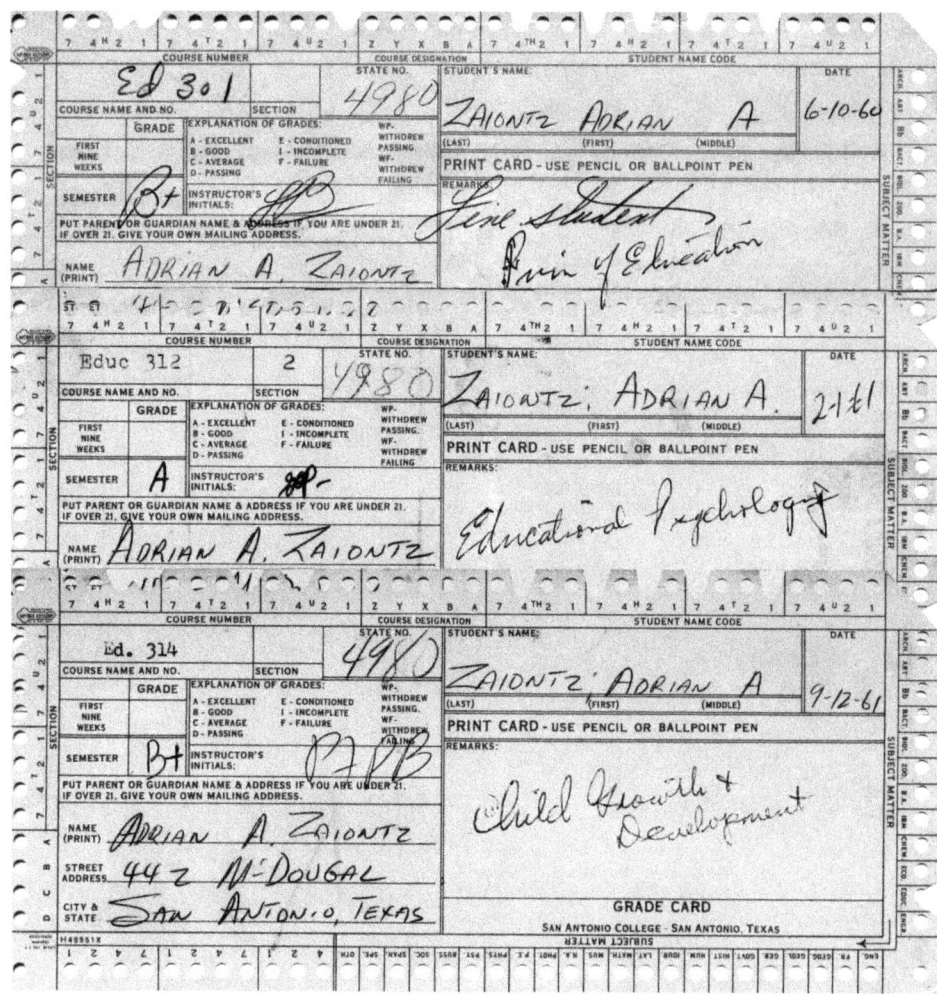

Grades from education classes.

drove to Cuero, Texas, to visit my mother and father. The longer days of summer permitted more far-ranging vacations. Postal Service employment was quite generous with vacation time with fifteen days annual leave per year until fifteen years of service had been reached, after which twenty-six days were available annually. I was also allotted thirteen days of sick leave for every year of service and I did not have to use it, but could accumulate it for emergencies.

Our first long vacation trip was during the summer of 1956 to New Jersey to see Mary's numerous relatives and friends. We stayed with Mary's friend Lena Vinci and her mother in their home. Lena was Mary's good friend from the years that they worked side-by-side at the Picatinny Arsenal. Kathy and Pat slept in the room in the attic because there were not enough beds on the ground floor. Lena had a large family and all of her brothers and sisters treated us like family. One of her brothers owned a bar and treated Mary and me to drinks on the house. On

Making a Living and Family Living

June 20, Kathy's birthday, Lena's sister Lillian hosted a party for Kathy complete with many children and presents. In the midst of the party little Barbara, our toddler, tripped and fell against the edge of a coffee table, producing a terrible laceration on her eyebrow. We rushed her to an emergency room. Astonishingly, the ER doctor never administered any anesthetic of any kind, ever, nothing for pain. Barbara screamed and screamed while her wound was being sewn up. Still no anesthetic! I was coming unglued and almost went in to waylay that doctor before he finally finished. Lillian was distraught that Barbara was injured in her home.

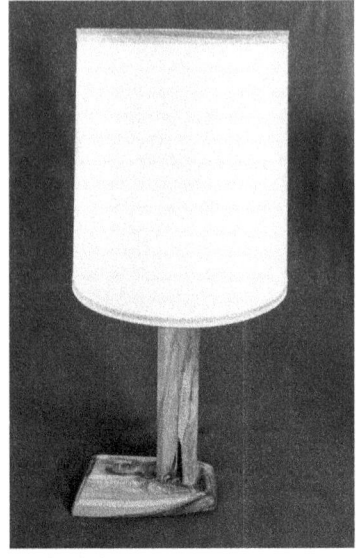

Adrian's lamp.

When the visit came to an end, we decided to take the southern route through Washington, D.C., North and South Carolina, and Georgia rather than a more direct route. But not long after we left New Jersey, Eddie caught a cold. He coughed and ran a fever for several days but eventually recovered. I have to say that all of our children were marvelous travelers. They invented a game in which whenever one of them spotted a license plate from a new state, they accumulated a certain number of points. Not being certain that the rules were not changing, I could never understand their system, but they were entertained. These little troopers kept themselves occupied and entertained with other games as well—what good travelers on a very long trip.

The next major vacation was to Anaheim, California, in 1961 to every six-year-old child's dream world—Disneyland! All seven of us crowded into our gull-wing 1958 Chevrolet sedan. As always, funds were tight in the Zaiontz family. I remember carrying Sharon at Disneyland so we did not have to pay an admittance fee for her. Next, heaping on the childhood wonders, we visited nearby Knott's Berry Farm. We economized by eating bologna sandwiches at rest stops and taking hot dogs we had already prepared into the parks. Lodging for two days in California, tickets to the parks, and rides plus gas and upkeep for the car cost a little more than $100.

Our new 1964 Chevrolet station wagon allowed us to spread out a little as it bore us on another trip to New Jersey and the east coast. With two adults and five children, all of whom were larger by now and still growing, we really needed the extra space in the station wagon. Once more we stayed with Mary's long-time friend Lena Vinci and her mother. The highlight of this trip was to be among the 51 million people who attended the 1964-65 New York World's Fair. Eddie and I—ever the baseball fans—took the catwalk from the World's Fair to see the just-opened Shea Stadium, brand new home of the two-year-old New York Mets.

In April of 1965 we made a trip to the Astrodome[75] in Houston, Texas—the home field of the Houston Astros. Mom Komorowski, Mary's good friend and surrogate mom, was a huge Astros fan. She never missed listening to a game on the radio. We asked her if she wanted to go with us, and she accepted as she really wanted to see at least one game and some of her favorite players in person. As it happened, we saw the third game ever played in the Astrodome. The Astros played the New York Yankees in an exhibition game. Mickey Mantle and Roger Maris were among the Yankee players. Needless to say, Mom Komorowski enjoyed this trip immensely, getting to see her favorite Astros players, especially the third baseman Bob Aspromonte, in action.

By 1976 the nest was empty. Our oldest daughter Kathy and her husband Patrick Uhr were living in Ruidoso, New Mexico, and Kathy invited the whole extended family—spouses included—to gather there for Thanksgiving. Patrick, who had a communications degree from the University of Texas at Austin,

---

[75] The name of the Harris County Domed Stadium was quickly changed to the Astrodome. It was the first indoor baseball stadium and was completely air conditioned. It had been designed to accommodate multiple sports and featured a display screen to show rockets and fireworks, cowboys and steers, and the Texas and US flags, all accompanied by a soundtrack. We now take indoor sports arenas with their many amenities for granted.

Highlands High School state champion American Legion baseball team. Front: Salvadore Calvo, Richard Guerra, Andy Dominquez, Craig Wolfenbarger, Edwin Zaiontz 2nd from right, Larry Causey; Middle: Dennis Bendele, Frank Romero, Ever Hermes, Michael Arranbide, Jessie Alderete, Richard Petri; Back: William Powell (Coach), Wayne Cordaway, Terry Peel, Jessie Causey, Mitchel Villereal, Walter Glenney (Manager)

was working as a disc jockey at the local radio station. Mary and I drove the 600-plus miles alone—the first extended trip for just the two of us since our honeymoon. So the clan gathered for a joyous family Thanksgiving celebration. But then came a weather forecast predicting below-freezing temperatures with a major snow storm for the next day, Friday. We all decided that it would be prudent to leave that Thursday afternoon to ensure that everyone would be safely back at school or work on Monday. Mary and I made it a few hours down the road to Carlsbad, New Mexico, before stopping for the evening. The gathering had been cut short, but we loved it just the same.

Through the years with a large family living at home, Mary and I were forced to economize on furnishings. I built some furniture myself, including book cases and shoe racks for the closets. I even made a lamp from a cedar log. It is a good thing I was young enough to be able to hold a full-time job, part-time jobs, and still be household odd-job handyman on weekends.

As if I was not busy enough, I got roped into and agreed to be the manager and coach for my son's Little League baseball team. We played two games a week and practiced another two days, including Saturday mornings. Our sponsor was High Slope Ice. Eddie was the catcher and Steve Calderon was my ace pitcher. The first year, 1963, we won the league championship. The second year, 1964, we ended up in the league cellar. The third year, 1965, after a good draft, we again won the league championship. During the off-season, Eddie played Pop Warner[76] football, mostly as a linebacker or running back. After completing the eighth grade at St. Margaret Mary Catholic School, Eddie went to Rogers Junior High for one year, where he won the Davidson Trophy for the most promising athlete for 1968. Later he received a Ward's Award[77] for being a star athlete with a sterling academic record.

Eddie played catcher in both the American Legion Pony League and Senior League. His first year at Highlands High School, he was the back-up catcher to Bubba Hermes, when the Highlands boys won both the UIL (University Interscholastic League) Class 4A state championship and the American Legion State Championship (summer league). I like to take some credit, having coached some of these boys when they were in Little League baseball.

---

[76] Pop Warner Little Scholars (also known as Pop Warner, Pop Warner Football) is a non-profit organization that provides youth football, cheerleading, and dance programs for participants in forty-three US states and several countries around the world. It is headquartered in Langhorne, Pennsylvania. Consisting of 425,000+ young people ranging from ages five to sixteen years old, Pop Warner is the largest and oldest national youth football, cheer, and dance organization in the United States. Source: wikipedia.org

[77] The retailer Montgomery Ward awarded students with outstanding achievements a plaque and an article in the local paper.

Eddie was a freshman and not on that varsity squad but my daughter Kathy was a senior. She and I drove to Austin to watch that game. With Kathy in high school and both of us working, our time together was limited. But we got to spend that whole day together, just the two of us. That was a memorable day with Dad and his eldest daughter watching her classmates win the state 4A championship.

Barbara and Sharon were the female athletes of the family. In high school they both lettered in varsity tennis under the coaching of Mr. Mangold at Highlands High School and each won several tournaments. In 1972 Barbara and her doubles partner won the San Antonio city-wide high school championship.

All of my children were excellent students. Kathy was one of only twenty-five students from a class of 819 recognized as an honor graduate. And she managed this while working twenty hours a week for the telephone company. Patricia was in the National Honor Society, the Future Teachers of America, and the Science Club. She helped win the donation of a telescope to Highlands High School. Eddie graduated sixteenth in a class of over 850 students. Barbara was tied for salutatorian and Sharon was valedictorian of her high school class.

The spring of 1971 began a dark time for me. In April I was suffering flu-like symptoms and went to see Dr. Dolph T. Wells, our long-time family physician. Unrelated to the flu, during his examination Dr. Wells found a large melanoma—the size of a half-dollar coin—on the left side of my back, just above the shoulder blade, and very close to my spine. He insisted that it had to be removed as soon as possible. The operation was scheduled for July 22, 1971, with Dr. Nathaniel Tippett as the primary surgeon and Dr. Wells assisting him. Although Mohs surgery[78] existed, the physicians did not use it in my case.

As I regained consciousness, I felt someone sticking a pin in my left foot. From the gist of the conversation of which I was becoming aware, I surmised that they were trying to find out if I was paralyzed from the operation so close to my spine. Without a doubt I was feeling that pin, so they quickly gained an answer to that question. When I reacted to the prick of the pin, a cheer erupted from the doctors and nurses. My first thought was that they were cheering because I was in pain.

There was no paralysis but I did have a general numbness on the entire left side of my body. My left arm was taped to my chest so that I could not move it. I remained thus restricted—with my left arm immobilized—for about ten days. When a specialist came to free my left arm from my chest, my lungs collapsed. I was fully conscious and heard the specialist call for help. After some very anxious moments, my breathing was normalized by forcing air into my lungs. Being unable to breathe was the scariest part of my melanoma operation.

Even though my father was very sick at this time, he and my mother came to see me in the Baptist Memorial Hospital in downtown San Antonio. Dad was seventy-seven years old and Cuero, Texas, where they lived, was ninety miles away.

It took me thirty days at home to recuperate before I could go back to work at the post office as an MPLSM-ZMT supervisor (Multiple Position Letter Sorting Machine-Zip Mail Translator). I had to wear a neck collar for another six weeks, and that was excruciating.

In the early fall my father was diagnosed with cancer. His physician in Cuero decided that his best chance was to go to M. D. Anderson Hospital in Houston, where they specialized in cancer treatment. But Dad did not survive and succumbed on January 29, 1972. Walter Zaiontz served in the 7th Division in France during World War I. His machine gun unit suffered a mustard gas attack. I have always wondered if that attack might have contributed to his development of cancer.

---

[78] Mohs surgery was developed in 1938 by a general surgeon, Frederic E. Mohs. It is microscopically controlled surgery used to treat common types of skin cancer. During the surgery, after each removal of tissue, while the patient waits, the tissue is examined for cancer cells, and that examination controls the decision for whether or not additional tissue removal is necessary. Mohs surgery is one of the many methods of obtaining complete margin control during removal of a skin cancer. Mohs surgery allows for the removal of a skin cancer with very narrow surgical margin and a high cure rate. Source: wikipedia.org

chapter 13
FAMILY OBLIGATIONS

My father, Walter Adolph Zaiontz, died on January 29, 1972. He never used his middle name, especially during and after World War II, for he wanted no name association with Germany's Adolph Hitler. The funeral Mass was held on February 1 at St. Mary's Church in Panna Maria and he was interred in the parish cemetery. He was still considered a parishioner even though he had been living elsewhere for almost fifty years. Three priests officiated at his Mass. During, and for a while following his funeral, innumerable, treasured memories poured through me.

Dad's education was only through the sixth grade as his father needed him to help work the family farm. He did learn all the essentials at the Polish Catholic School, like reading, writing, and arithmetic. Later he taught himself penmanship. No one in the family had as good handwriting as did my father.

He could converse in three languages, English, Polish and Tex-Mex, an impure version of Spanish. He never met a stranger, as anyone who was not his friend upon introduction was one by the time they parted.

Dad loved to laugh. He would listen to comedy on the radio and be laughing and chuckling to himself well afterward. When Claude or I would tell him a joke we heard at school, he would always laugh, even if it was not very funny. Once I remember prompting his chuckle with this one:

> A mother was watching her son riding his bike while saying "Look, Ma, only one hand." He came around again and said "Look, Ma, no hands." It took a little longer but the third time he came around, he said "Look, Ma, no teeth."

Dad always ensured that there was food on our table. It may not have satisfied a gourmet, but our tummies were always filled. Providing was especially hard during the depression years of 1929 through 1939 when our staple was corn bread and pinto beans with an occasional bit of ham bacon[79] sold to us by a butcher for 15¢ a pound with a soup bone given free.

During my entire childhood, Dad spanked me but once—the time I went to the river with my friend Lucian Mika without permission. (Much later I realized that I really deserved that one.) As far as I know, he never spanked Claude. Of course, when Claude did something wrong, it was usually I who had led him astray. I remember Joe once being on the receiving end of such punishment, but I never knew why.

During my youth, our family would visit various aunts and uncles at least once a year or they would visit us, usually overnight and one or two days. When we visited Uncle Ignatz, one of Dad's brothers, in San Antonio, or Uncle Anton, one of Mother's brothers, in the country, the men would sit on the porch and talk until well past midnight. Uncle Ignatz was in the army in France at the same time Dad was. I was fascinated by stories of their war experiences. Once my uncles started talking, the beer came out, Dad would make his single beer last as long as the conversation lasted. I never saw my father drink excessively or ever become inebriated. I, myself, do not like to drink much. I drank too much a time or two while in the service and really paid for it the next day with a hangover that incapacitated me for a whole day. It did not take long to learn it was just not worth it.

Not long after Dad was gone, Mother decided that she wanted to move back to Panna Maria, where she would be closer to old friends, relatives, other Polish people, and Dad's grave. The problem was that the house she owned in Panna Maria was rented, as it had been since 1948 when Father rebuilt it.

It fell to me, as the oldest surviving son, to inform the renters that they had to move. It took them a whole year to find another place to live. The

---
[79] Ham bacon is what is now known as Canadian bacon.

rent they had been paying was only $15 to $25 a month. It was usual when renters vacated for my father and mother to spend an entire week cleaning and repairing the house to make it suitable for the next occupants. After these renters finally moved, Mary and I spent a whole week cleaning and painting to get the house ready for Mother.

The house was finally suitable for the move in May 1973. Uncle Felix lent me his huge, ancient, Ford flatbed truck with three-foot-high side boards. (This was his truck for hauling hay for his cattle.) Even though this was a large, tall truck, I was amazed that a lifetime of accumulated mementoes, furniture, and necessities, could fill only one eight-foot-by-fourteen-foot flatbed truck plus a pickup truck. I was concerned that I did not have the required commercial driver's license for operating such a large truck. Luckily Panna Maria was less than fifty miles from Cuero and I decided I would be driving little-traveled roads all the way. If I got a ticket, so be it.

My son Eddie and Claude's oldest son Kevin used Claude's pickup and with these two vehicles stacked quite high we managed to transport all of my mother's possessions to her new home in one trip. The trip was without incident, except for the wind force breaking the mirror on Mom's dresser. It was in a myriad of pieces on the bed of the pickup. Fearing seven years of bad luck, she was quite upset. I promised to replace it, which I did within a month. Uncle Felix was very happy to have his older sister back as a neighbor in Panna Maria.

Aunt Ella and Uncle Felix invited us all to the evening meal on the day of the move. After unloading Mom's furniture and packed boxes, we were more than ready for a good meal. It was quite a feast with a huge platter of Polish sausage as the main course. Eddie and Kevin ate as if they had not eaten in a week. They exhausted Uncle Felix's supply of Polish sausage and the rest of Aunt Ella's good home cooking. The older generation had apparently forgotten how much young men could put away at one sitting.

It also fell to me to make several trips to Cuero to consult with a real estate agent about selling her former home. After several months, the house was sold and Mom finally settled into her new home in Panna Maria. She was seventy-two and it was undoubtedly very hard to leave her old friends in Cuero: Mrs. Schmidt who lived in the same block; Mrs. Hirsch, who lived across the street; and Mr. & Mrs. Blakesly, who lived across the alley and had taken her to church every Sunday. But in Panna Maria, she had new neighbors and made friends quickly, receiving a lot of help unpacking and setting up housekeeping. Mrs. Felix Mika, Mother's Aunt Mary Pilarczyk, and Mrs. Edmund Pawelek were all nearby residents. Mrs. Pawelek eventually moved in with Mom to help care for her for several years. Another comfort was that St. Mary's Church was only about a half block away.

As Mother settled into her new home, I felt obligated to visit her at least every other week, sometimes sooner if she had a problem or a doctor's appointment. Her new doctor, Dr. Stubbs, was in Karnes City, only four miles away, but I had usually worked all night and then had to drive an hour to Panna Maria. By the time I drove there, took her to the appointment, and drove home, it could be three, four, five hours or more, so I did not hesitate to doze in the busy waiting room.

I went to Panna Maria every other weekend and I did all Mom needed me to do: filling her numerous prescriptions, paying her bills, balancing her check book, grocery shopping, and doing yard work. Sometimes I bought many of her groceries in San Antonio before driving to Panna Maria. I assumed responsibility for most of these types of things as Claude had his aircraft accessory company to run and a large family to care for. It was the right thing for me to do.

In 1976 Mother decided her nine-foot-by-twelve-foot garden beside the house was too small. She wanted a larger one. I built a new one, beyond the fenced-in back yard. The new garden was 70 feet wide by 110 feet long. Mr. Robert (Rap) Katzmarek, a long-time friend to my father and me, helped me erect a fence around the new garden to keep out the critters. (This was the same Rap Katzmarek who was on the Panna Maria baseball team at the same time as my brother Joseph. Rap was now in his seventies.) I actually learned a lot from working with Rap. He also helped me build a sixteen-foot-by-twenty-foot shed on a concrete slab for all my tools, lawn mower, and riding mower, which I left at Mother's. I knew she would be unable to work such a large garden but I was committed to help, taking on the extra work during my frequent visits.

I spent many hours cutting grass and kept an area of about two acres across from the church and around the house free of Johnson grass and weeds. I did everything that was necessary for my mother. Claude and his family helped whenever they could.

Chapter 14
AT LAST, RETIREMENT!

Before I get to the subject of this chapter, let me digress. After my melanoma operation in 1971, I continued to go to our family physician, Dr. Dolph T. Wells, three or four times each year. Every time he found new, suspicious areas on my face and upper torso and burned these areas off with some kind of electrocautery pen. I remember the smell of burning flesh. It reminded me of napalm-burned Japanese bodies littering a newly captured hill. If these dead bodies had started decaying, the smell was even worse—indescribable. We felt that this smell got into our hair and clothes, and we could never get rid of it. Even worse was that before zero hour came to advance, we usually ate our C-ration meal, as we never knew when we would have time for our next meal. Most of the time we had Vicks to stuff in our noses, but at times even the strong scent of that ointment was not enough. We usually had to do a lot of work before we could effectively occupy the newly taken hill. Sometimes I lost my meal, but I was not alone. There was a lot of work at these times—burying the Japanese dead, digging new fox holes, making new fortifications, and zeroing in all small arms on targets on all sides of our new perimeter because we expected a counterattack soon. Haunting memories, years and years later.

Continuing with the dermatological issues, when Dr. Wells retired in 1991, he sent me to Dr. Gregory W. Thompson, a dermatologist just starting his medical practice. I have stayed with Dr. Thompson these past twenty-five years. I have had thirty to thirty-five in-office surgeries on basal cell or squamous cell carcinomas and a few more melanomas. During each visit, Dr. Thompson does the necessary surgery and, in addition, destroys fifteen to twenty-five pre-malignant skin lesions. Since 1992, this has probably amounted to several thousand skin lesions removed. All of these procedures are on my face, ears, neck, and upper torso, and I attribute them to excessive exposure to the sun during my army days in the Philippines. I have never had any skin cancer below the waist.

As noted earlier, I retired on December 30, 1981, from the Postal Service. Oh, boy! I could hardly wait to start on all the activities that I had put off since the early 1970s: visits to places that were encumbered by job and family obligations, fishing when and wherever I pleased, treasure hunting in the western United States with my metal detector and with my conglomeration of treasure maps and directions that I had accumulated over the years. (Many years ago my children collaborated and gave me that metal detector as a Christmas present.) Hunting was deliberately omitted from my wish list of activities. Though many hunts with various relatives had spotted my childhood and juvenile days, after the war there was an aversion to stalking and killing defenseless animals.

I have news for all of you who think that you will catch up with everything very shortly upon retirement. As of this writing I have been retired longer than the time I served in the military and Postal Service combined. I have used my metal detector only twice and that was at the old picnic grounds at Panna Maria where I found a few old coins. I am still trying to accomplish all that I hoped for in retirement. As the old saying goes, "The harder and faster I try, the further behind I get."

Gardening is the exception to dreams unfulfilled. My fascination with vegetable gardening dates to my early years in Cuero, Texas, where I had a garden of sorts. This little plot, on the widow Schmidt's previous small horse farm, gave me some basic knowledge of gardening and fertilizing and instilled a longing to work the earth, plant, cultivate, and grow. Now in retirement, I had Mother's place in Panna Maria to fulfill that desire. Mom could no longer work outside but she had plenty of space. Thus, I assumed another task in Panna Maria

After fencing the 110-foot-by-70-foot garden, I prepared the soil by tilling it. The garden was only slightly smaller than my lot where my house is located in San Antonio. I planted cauliflower, onions, red and russet potatoes, hot peppers, sweet peppers, four or five varieties of tomatoes, New Zealand spinach, Swiss chard, cabbage, carrots, string beans, okra, sweet potatoes, lettuce, eggplant, and broccoli. I even tried corn and popcorn. One year I had an incredible crop of 1015[80] variety onions. Conditions must have been just right, because thirty onions filled a wheel barrow. The largest one weighed in at two pound three ounces. The 1015 onions always produced better than white onions, and red potatoes produced better than white russets.

The New Zealand spinach is a vine-growing spinach only planted once, as it returns year after year. Once I tried cantaloupes and watermelons but for some reason they never produced—I suspect that they needed more watering than my biweekly visits could provide. If it did not rain, then the plants suffered. For the tomatoes and peppers, I dug a two-foot-wide moat with an island in the middle for the plant. I filled the holes with water each time before I left and this seemed to provide enough moisture for those plants. Nowadays, this produce would be considered organic because I used natural fertilizers and avoided chemicals.

At the time of my retirement our five children were all graduates of the University of Texas at Austin. They all had good jobs and their student loans were virtually paid off thanks to them having part-time jobs while they were getting educated. Kathy and Barbara were married. Kathy and her husband Patrick Uhr were living in El Paso, Texas. Patricia was teaching high school math in Austin. Barbara and her husband Mike Lawson were living in Clear Lake City, Texas, where he was an engineer for NASA. Eddie was not married yet but would be in two weeks. His bride-to-be was Mary Louise Wiley, who was a fellow teacher at the school where Eddie taught. Sharon was not married yet, but worked for Datapoint in San Antonio.

Reality awakened me to the fact that retirement did not absolve me of commitments and exigencies. While I no longer had crises at work, there were still many other commitments and family emergencies. Just because my five children were either married or on their own with jobs, we still had to be ready to help when problems arose. And as the oldest surviving son, it fell to me to see that my mother had everything she needed to live a normal, happy life. I was committed to the garden, so Mother always had fresh vegetables. Of course, most of the vegetables we consumed in San Antonio also came from the garden in Panna Maria.

In 1982 Mother decided living alone at home was too challenging and she wanted to move into a nursing home. Her brother Pete lived in the nursing home in Karnes City, four miles from Panna Maria, so that is the place she chose. I made the arrangements for her and after a few months an opening occurred, and she moved into the Karnes City nursing home. About a year later she learned of the Catholic nursing home in Kenedy, John Paul II Nursing Home. It was full but after a few months an opening occurred there. The monthly rate of $600 was about the same as in Karnes City. Mother stayed at John Paul until she passed away on December 8, 1985, just five days after her eighty-fifth birthday, one day after the Pearl Harbor anniversary, and on the Catholic Feast Day of the Immaculate Conception.

Working nights for the Postal Service had denied me another long-desired activity: joining the St. Margaret Mary's Men's Club. This organization exists to assist and serve the parish and to provide a social environment for its laymen. The Men's Club helps keep the church grounds, contributes to the financial needs of other parish organizations, and performs other similar activities. At 7 P.M., on the third Thursday of each month, the club members gather for a meal, formally conduct business, then play games such as dominoes and dealer's choice penny-ante poker. Most of my good friends were already members and I was delighted to finally join their ranks. These men were mostly founding members of St. Margaret Mary's Parish in 1950, including yours truly. (A few years after the founding, the new parish came under the direction of its first priest, Rev. Edward Dworaczyk, who had been the pastor of St. Mary's Church in Panna Maria for many years and who authored the book *The First Polish Texans*. Rev. Dworaczyk was a good friend of

---

[80] The yellow 1015Y onions should be planted on October 15th for best results. A variety of super sweet onion, they get sweeter as the bulb gets larger.

my father's and he was as elated as we were when he was assigned as pastor of our parish in San Antonio.)

One particularly fine member of the St. Margaret Mary's Men's Club was Walter Langehennig. Wally was in charge of the St. Vincent de Paul Society, with a mission to feed the hungry and give others in need temporary assistance, even cash to pay utility bills. Towards this goal, the St. Vincent de Paul Society managed a thrift store where donated used clothes were sold for as little as 25¢. The income from this store was used to purchase grocery items for distribution to the needy.

As if he was not busy enough, Wally was also responsible for the Meals on Wheels program. Once the house in Panna Maria was sold in 2002, I had more free time, so I joined Wally and his Meals on Wheels group. Every Tuesday, I drove one of four routes in the St. Margaret Mary's area delivering twelve to fifteen ready-made meals. These meals were brought to our office, as well as other offices throughout the city, from a central location. Each driver then delivered his meals to the elderly and housebound people on his route. This usually required one and a half to two and a half hours one day each week. The volunteer drivers gave their time, used their own vehicles, and absorbed the fuel costs, the satisfaction derived from helping others being their only compensation. I felt very well paid each time I witnessed the joy of a brief visit on a shut-in's face and brightened the day for them. The people to whom I delivered meals did not want me to leave. I suspect that I was the only person they had a chance to talk with all day.

Another organization seeking volunteers was the San Antonio Food Bank. I tried it out for a day, was impressed with my experience, told Mary about the work, and we both joined the volunteers. We worked at the food bank two days a week from 8 A.M. until noon unpacking donated boxes of food, stocking the shelves, and packing banana boxes with different groceries that organizations picked up to distribute to needy families. We both made a number of new friends and got plenty of exercise bending and lifting. This involvement lasted from 1984 to 1992 when the food bank moved from near downtown to the northeast side. That was a much longer drive and a major reason we decided to give up this service.

After we left the food bank, I started volunteering at a recycling center started by David Schott, a teacher at St. Margaret Mary's School. This center accepted almost everything including clear, brown, and green glass, cans, metal, all types of paper including cardboard, and plastics. The glass had to be separated by color and broken, then placed in strong cardboard containers that were approximately five-foot cubes, which were transported to Waco, Texas, by semi-trailer. The glass was remanufactured into new glass containers.

Cardboard was bundled into huge bales. Firms in Asia were paying $40 per ton for cardboard. Income from selling these items supported the full-time employees. The volunteers, like me, mostly worked on Saturdays. Cars and pickups were unloaded by the two employees during the week. David established a route for picking up recyclables from people who had no means of bringing them to the center. Once a week, I drove the route for David.

During my youth in Panna Maria and on many occasions afterwards, I heard complaints about how in 1854 the first Polish immigrants settled in the "poorest" part of Texas. The soil was poor for growing crops and living off the land was very harsh. The people doing the grumbling seemed to think that the immigrants had a choice of where in Texas to settle. In reality, they had no choice at all and were in fact quite grateful that they had a place to go to escape the oppression in Europe.

Today, no one in Panna Maria or anywhere else in Karnes County disparages the land settled by the Polish immigrants. Horizontal drilling through ancient petroleum-bearing shale strata has placed Panna Maria near the heart of the twenty-six-county Eagle Ford Shale oil and gas field with over 18,000 wells. This has resulted in quite a few newly wealthy Polacks. Now the only ones complaining are the county maintenance staff that must repair the roads and a few people that cannot sleep at night because of the constant noise of the oil field trucks.

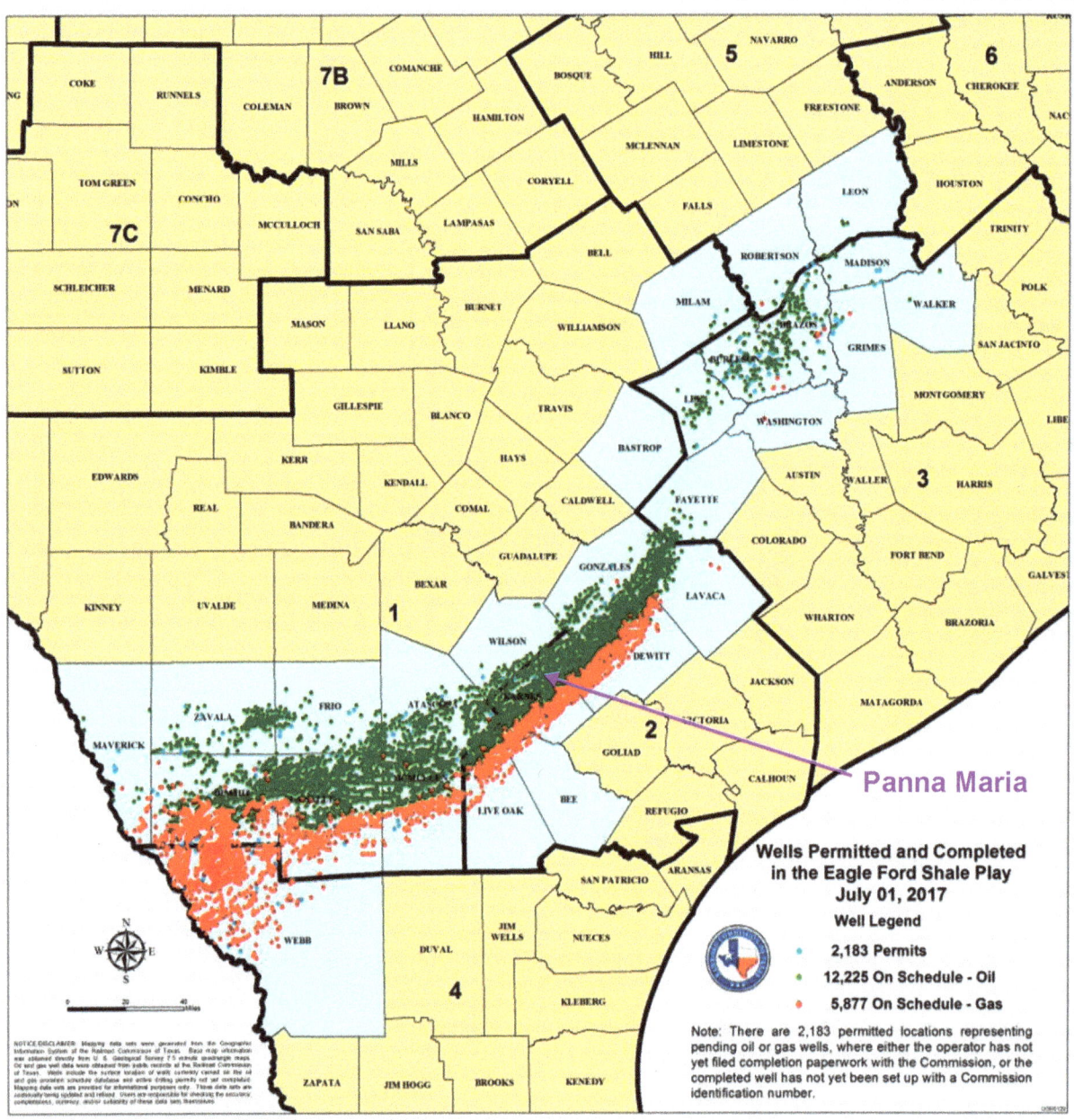

From the September 18, 2016, San Antonio Express-News paper:

The University of Texas at Austin's Bureau of Economic Geology released new, unpublished research on the Eagle Ford Shale that indicated at least 80,000 more wells will be drilled and companies could recover 10 billion barrels of oil at today's prices. The research was released at Hart Energy's DUG Eagle Ford conference in San Antonio.

A NOTE FROM ADRIAN'S FAMILY

No, Adrian is not one of the newly wealthy Polacks, though he is quite rich in many other ways.

Born into a simple, hardworking American family, he started school speaking only Polish and along the way learned charity, loyalty, sorrow, love, and the rewards of hard work. He defended his country, was the first in the family to graduate college, served the community, and married the love of his life with whom he raised, provided for, and mentored five exceptional children, a tradition which continues.

The lives of his children, grandchildren, and their children are a testimony to the character of this ninety-one-year-old American Polack.

PHOTOGRAPH CREDITS

Peyton Hoge, *38th Infantry Division, Avengers of Bataan*, Albert Love Enterprises, 1947: 75, 77, 80, 84, 90

Bob Keller: 41

Nick Kenny: 63

Barbara Lawson: 24, 140

Darryl Pearson: 7

Robert Smith, *HyperWar: US Army in WWII: Triumph in the Philippines*. Washington: Office of the Chief of Military History, Dept. of the Army, 1963: 73

Patrick Uhr: Back cover

Adrian Zaiontz: Front cover photo, 11, 15, 28, 29, 30, 34, 37, 61, 62, 69, 81, 96, 108, 110-111, 112, 118, 121, 122, 123, 124, 125, 126, 129, 132-133, 137, 141

All other non-copyrighted photographs were taken from public websites.

www.ingramcontent.com/pod-product-compliance
Lightning Source LLC
Chambersburg PA
CBHW061812290426
44110CB00026B/2856